ETTERHEAD + LOGO DESIGN 5

ROCKPORT

First published in the United States of America by:
Rockport Publishers, Inc.
33 Commercial Street
Gloucester, Massachusetts 01930-5089
Telephone: (978) 282-9590
Facsimile: (978) 283-2742
www.rockpub.com

ISBN 1-56496-878-2

10 9 8 7 6 5 4 3 2

Designer: Argus Visual Communication, Boston
Front Cover Images: left to right from top, p. 14, 19, 121, 122, 34, 28
Back Cover Images: p. 42, 136, 74
Manufactured in China.

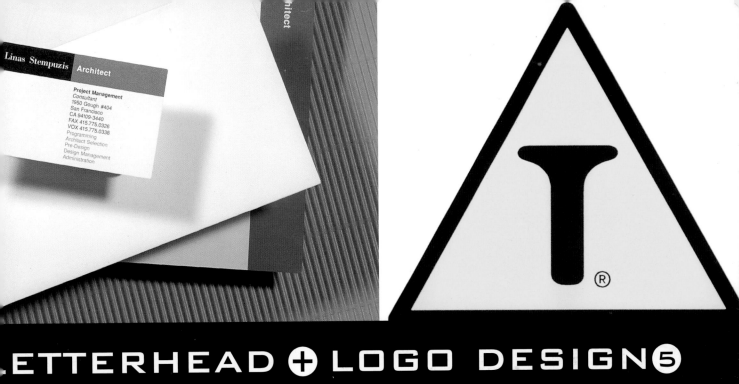

Linas Stempuzis | Architect

Project Management
Consultant
1950 Gough #404
San Francisco
CA 94109-3440
FAX 415.775.0326
VOX 415.775.0338
Programming
Architect Selection
Pre-Design
Design Management
Administration

ETTERHEAD + LOGO DESIGN 5

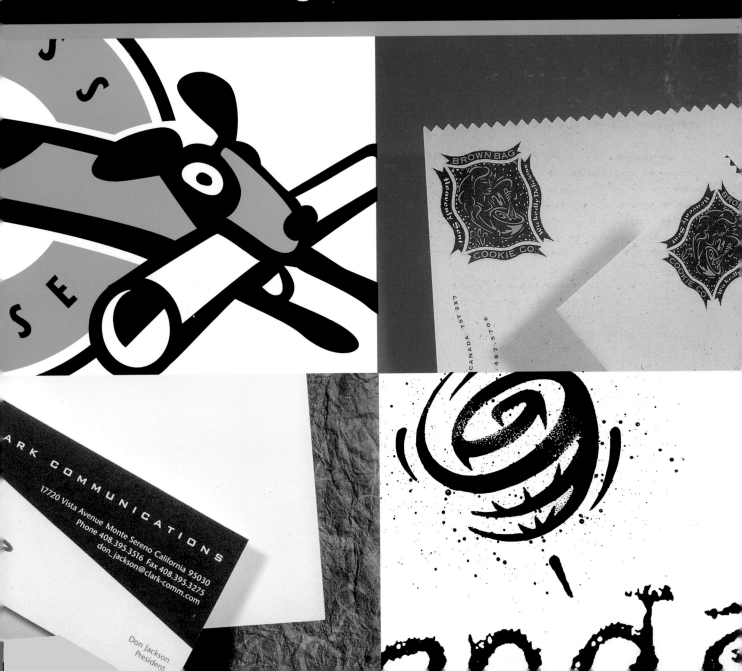

BROWN BAG
Heavenly Sent
Wickedly Delicious
COOKIE CO

CANADA T5T 2X7

487.5706

ARK COMMUNICATIONS
17720 Vista Avenue Monte Sereno California 95030
Phone 408.395.3516 Fax 408.395.3275
don_jackson@clark-comm.com

Don Jackson
President

CONTENTS

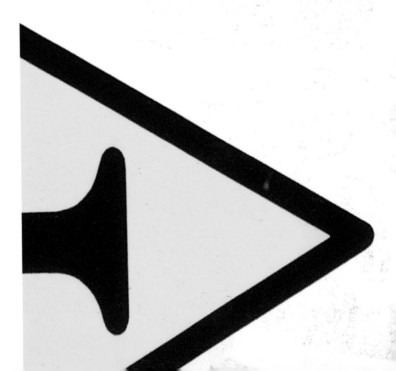

DESIGN FIRM | TRACY SABIN GRAPHIC DESIGN
ART DIRECTOR | ANDRÉ DUGGIN
ILLUSTRATOR | TRACY SABIN
CLIENT | YOU CAN SOAR, INC.
TOOLS | ADOBE ILLUSTRATOR

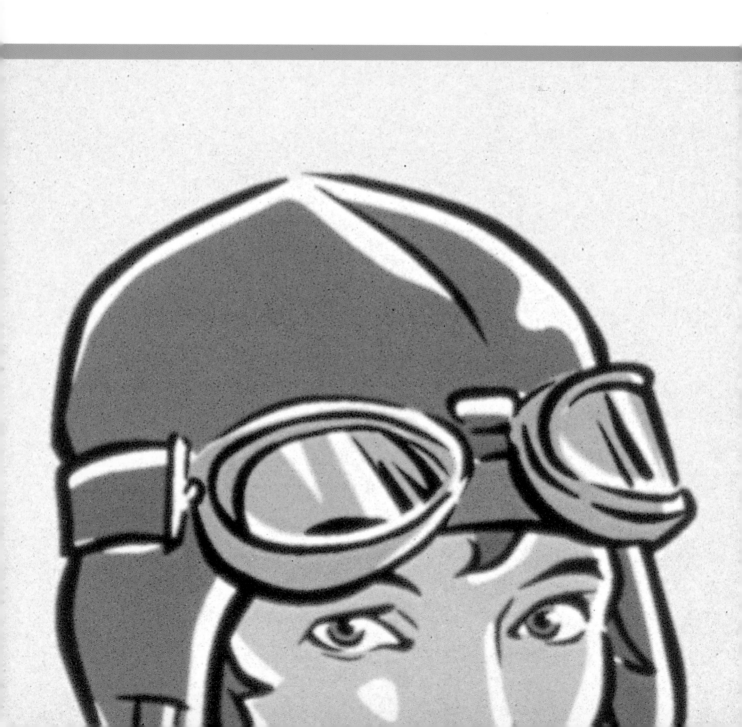

INTRODUCTION

WHO CAN DENY THE IMPORTANCE OF A LOGO? A GOOD
BRAND IDENTITY WILL SELL A PRODUCT OR CONFIRM THE
LEGITIMACY OF ANY PROJECT. IN DESIGNING THIS GRAPHIC
ELEMENT TO BE SUCCESSFUL IN THE GLOBAL MARKETPLACE,
FLEXIBILITY IS KEY. A LOGO MUST TRANSLATE ON PAPER,
OVER A FAX, OVER THE INTERNET, AND BE EASILY RECOGNIZ-
ABLE IN EVERY LANGUAGE. COLORS AND SHAPES MUST
CAREFULLY BE CONSIDERED IN ORDER TO EFFECTIVELY CROSS
ALL CULTURAL BARRIERS. IT MUST BE TIMELESS IN ITS STYLE
AND NOT BE CAUGHT IN CURRENT TRENDS.

THE LOGOS PRESENTED IN THIS BOOK ARE EXCITING, NEW,
AND VARIED. MOST HAVE SUCCESSFULLY MET THE REQUIRE-
MENTS OF A SUCCESSFUL GLOBAL DESIGN, OTHERS ARE ON
THE WAY. WHILE THIS BOOK SHOWS THE LOGOS PRESENTED
ON LETTERHEAD, IT IS CLEAR THAT THE BUSINESS WORLD IS
MOVING AWAY FROM PAPER TO ELECTRONIC MEDIA.

ASSUREDLY, THE NEXT VOLUME IN THIS COLLECTION WILL
SHOW MORE ELECTRONIC EXAMPLES OF INTERACTIVE LOGOS,
PLUS FANTASTIC ASPECTS THAT ONLY THE CREATIVE GENIUS
OF THE GRAPHIC DESIGN WORLD COULD IMAGINE.

ROY ALDEN, DESIGNER

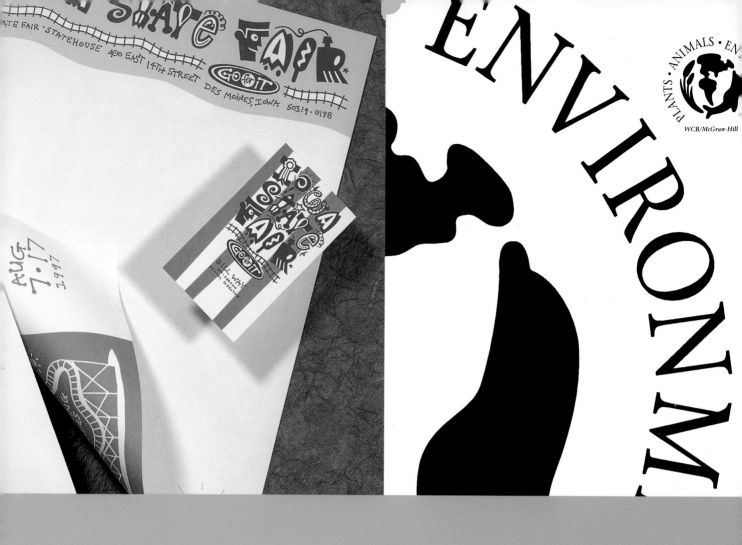

STATE FAIR
STATEHOUSE 400 EAST 14TH STREET
DES MOINES, IOWA 50319·0198

GO.F.IT

AUG 7·17 1997

BILL WAY
ART DIRECTOR

ENVIRONM

PLANTS · ANIMALS · EN

WCB/McGraw-Hill

SPO
SATEL

SPOT
SATELLITE

CLARK COMMUNICATIONS

17720 Vista Avenue Monte Sereno California 95030
Phone 408.395.3516 Fax 408.395.3275
don_jackson@clark-comm.com

Don Jackson
President

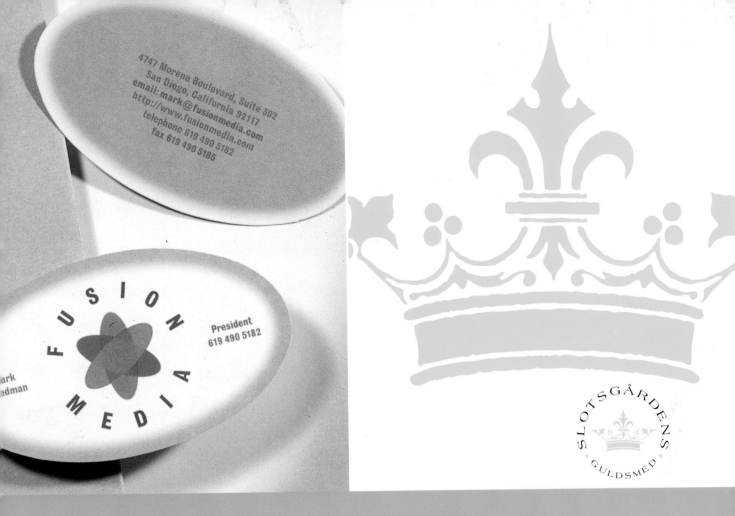

4747 Morena Boulevard, Suite 302
San Diego, California 92117
email: mark@fusionmedia.com
http://www.fusionmedia.com
telephone 619 490 5182
fax 619 490 5185

FUSION
MEDIA

President
619 490 5182

Mark
Redman

SLOTSGÅRDENS
GULDSMED

PROFESSIONAL SERVICES

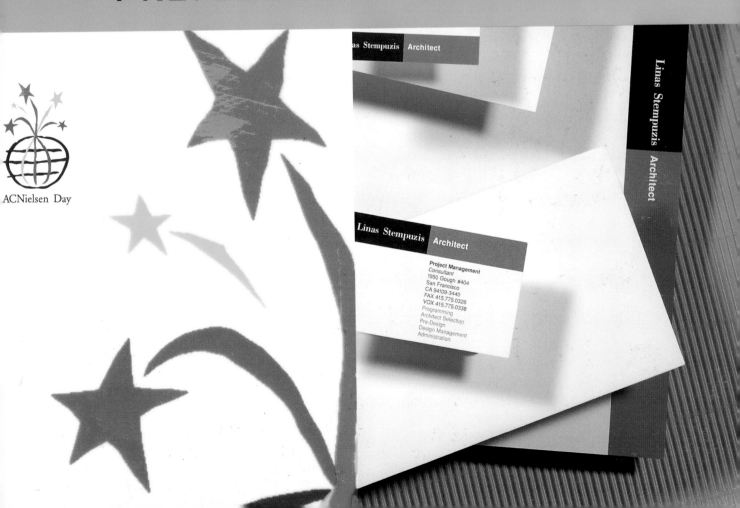

ACNielsen Day

Linas Stempuzis Architect

Linas Stempuzis Architect

Linas Stempuzis Architect

Project Management
Consultant
1950 Gough #404
San Francisco
CA 94109-3440
FAX 415.775.0326
VOX 415.775.0338
Programming
Architect Selection
Pre-Design
Design Management
Administration

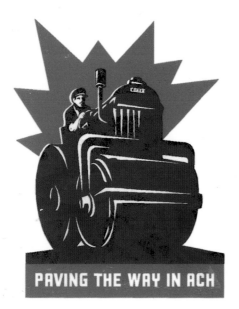

DESIGN FIRM | WEBSTER DESIGN ASSOCIATES
ART DIRECTOR | DAVE WEBSTER
DESIGNER/ILLUSTRATOR | ANDREY NAGORNY
CLIENT | ACH, INC.
TOOLS | MACROMEDIA FREEHAND

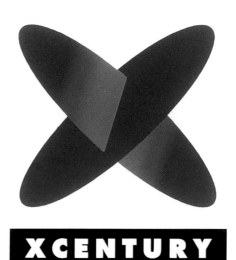

DESIGN FIRM | SHIMOKOCHI/REEVES
ART DIRECTORS | MAMORU SHIMOKOCHI, ANNE REEVES
DESIGNER | MAMORU SHIMOKOCHI
CLIENT | X-CENTURY STUDIOS
TOOLS | ADOBE ILLUSTRATOR

DESIGN FIRM | LSL INDUSTRIES
DESIGNER | ELISABETH SPITALNY
CLIENT | JP DAVIS & COMPANY, INTERNET PRESS
TOOLS | ADOBE ILLUSTRATOR

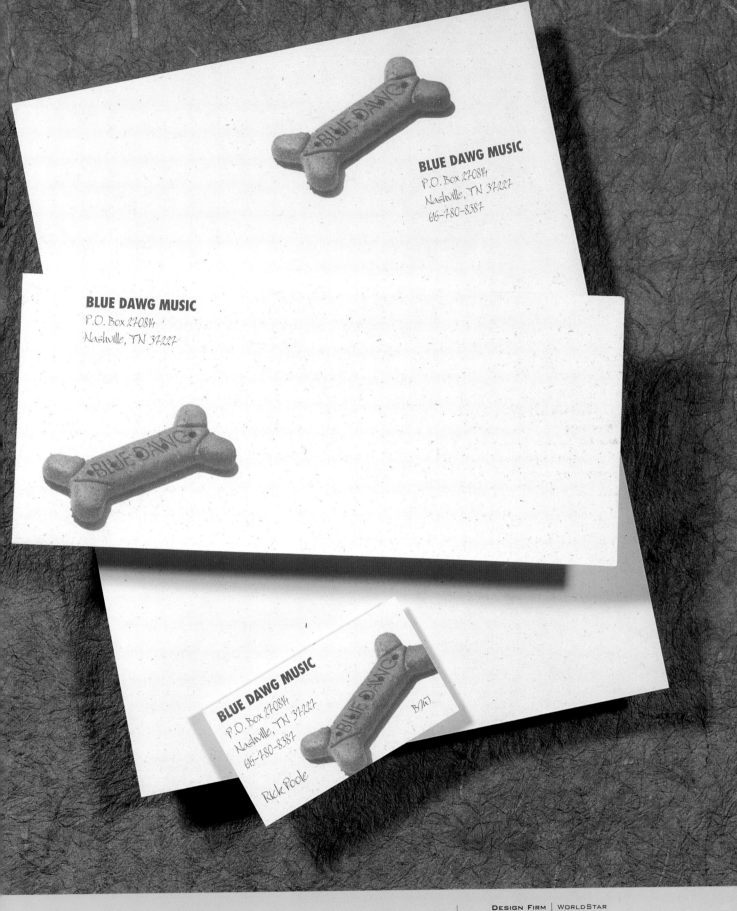

BLUE DAWG MUSIC
P.O. Box 27084
Nashville, TN 37227
615-780-8387

BLUE DAWG MUSIC
P.O. Box 27084
Nashville, TN 37227

BLUE DAWG MUSIC
P.O. Box 27084
Nashville, TN 37227
615-780-8387

BDM

Rick Poole

DESIGN FIRM | WorldStar
ALL DESIGN | Greg Guhl
CLIENT | Blue Dawg Music
TOOLS | Adobe Photoshop, Adobe Illustrator

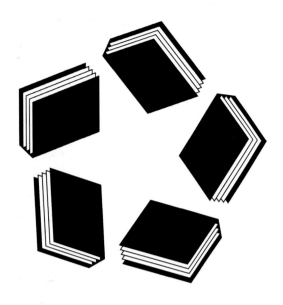

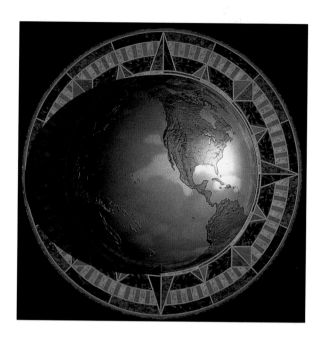

DESIGN FIRM | SULLIVAN PERKINS
ALL DESIGN | BRETT BARIDON
CLIENT | DALLAS PUBLIC LIBRARY

DESIGN FIRM | DESIGN GROUP WEST
ART DIRECTOR | JOAN MALONEY
ILLUSTRATOR | TRACY SABIN
CLIENT | HAHN/TRIZEC
TOOLS | STRATA STUDIO PRO

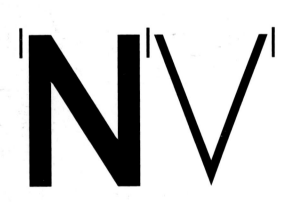

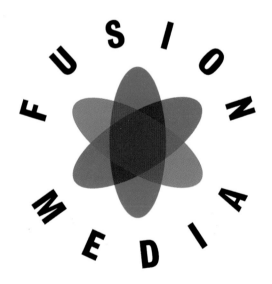

DESIGN FIRM | TANGRAM STRATEGIC DESIGN
ART DIRECTOR/DESIGNER/CREATIVE DIRECTOR | ENRICO SEMPI
CLIENT | ORDINE DEGLI ARCHITETTI DI NOVARA

DESIGN FIRM | MIRES DESIGN
ART DIRECTOR | JOHN BALL
DESIGNERS | JOHN BALL, DEBORAH HORN
CLIENT | FUSION MEDIA

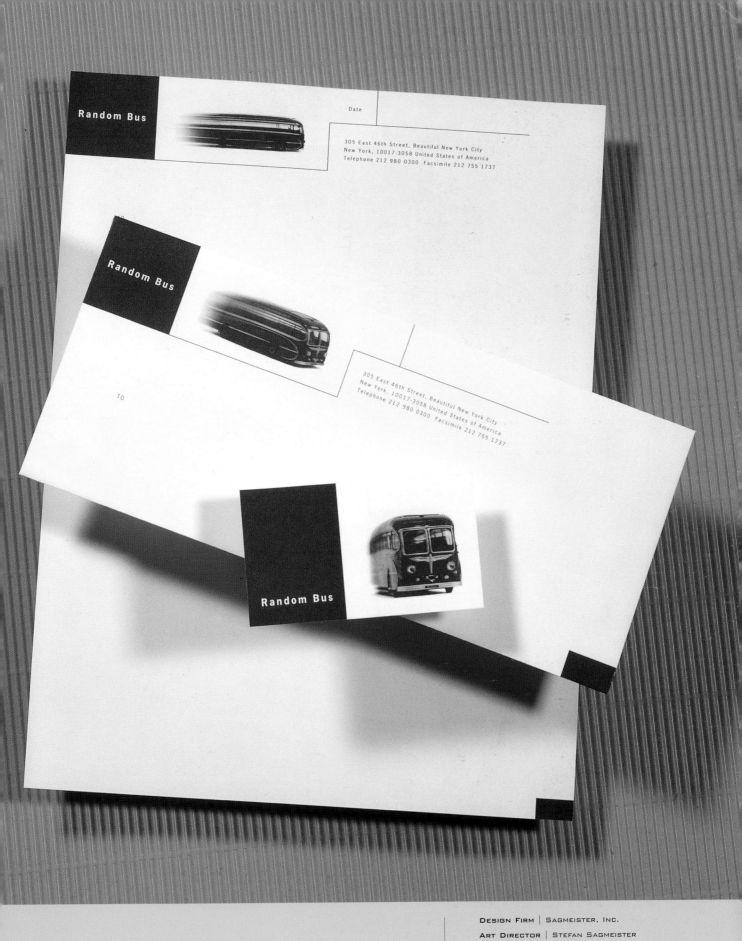

DESIGN FIRM | SAGMEISTER, INC.

ART DIRECTOR | STEFAN SAGMEISTER

DESIGNER | ERIC ZIM

PHOTOGRAPHY | TOM SCHIERLITZ

CLIENT | RANDOM BUS

TOOLS | MACINTOSH, 4 X 5 CAMERA

PAPER/PRINTING | STRATHMORE WRITING 25% COTTON

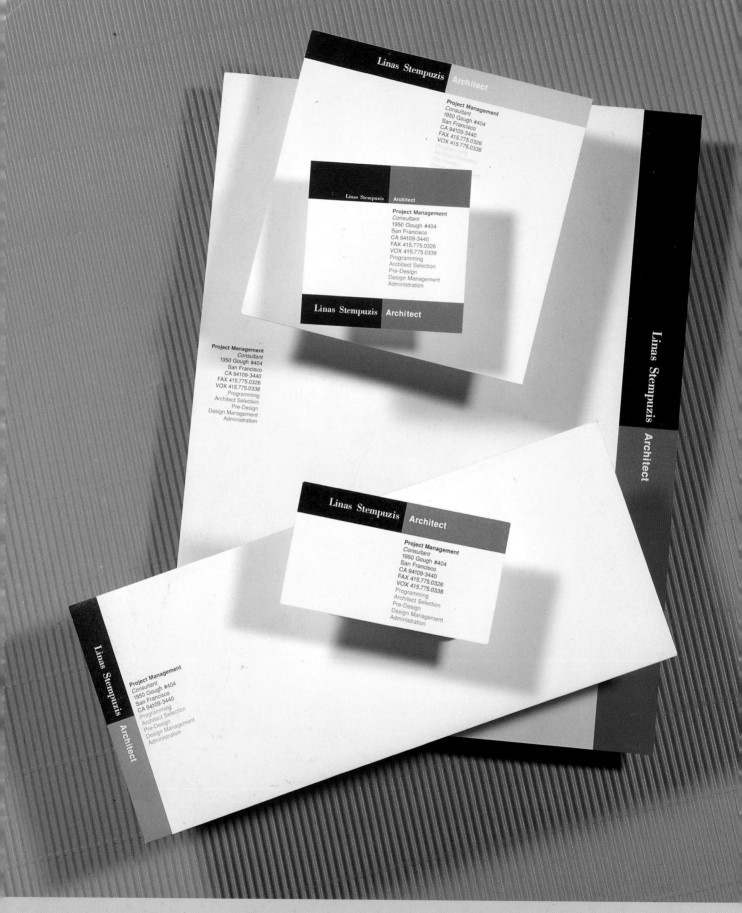

DESIGN FIRM | MELISSA PASSEHL DESIGN

ART DIRECTOR | MELISSA PASSEHL

DESIGNERS | MELISSA PASSEHL, JILL STEINFELD

CLIENT | LINAS STEMPUZIS

PP = MG²

PRINTELLIGENT PEOPLE

CORPORATE COMMUNICATION & PRINT PROJECT MANAGEMENT
ACN 007 074 393   A DIVISION OF PRINTELLIGENCE PTY LTD

Mick Mercieca

SUITE ONE, 20 COMMERCIAL RD MELBOURNE 3004
PH: 03) 9866 4966 FAX: 03) 9866 4164 MOBILE 018 352 827

Garry Furzer

Establishing the Theory of Reliability
Re-Inventing the Laws of Quality

DESIGN FIRM | STORM DESIGN & ADVERTISING CONSULTANCY
ART DIRECTORS/DESIGNERS | DAVID ANSETT, DEAN BUTLER
ILLUSTRATOR | DEAN BUTLER
CLIENT | PRINTELLIGENT PEOPLE
TOOLS | ADOBE PHOTOSHOP
PAPER/PRINTING | SAXTON SMOOTHE/THREE PMS COLORS,
SPECIAL VARNISH, EMBOSSING

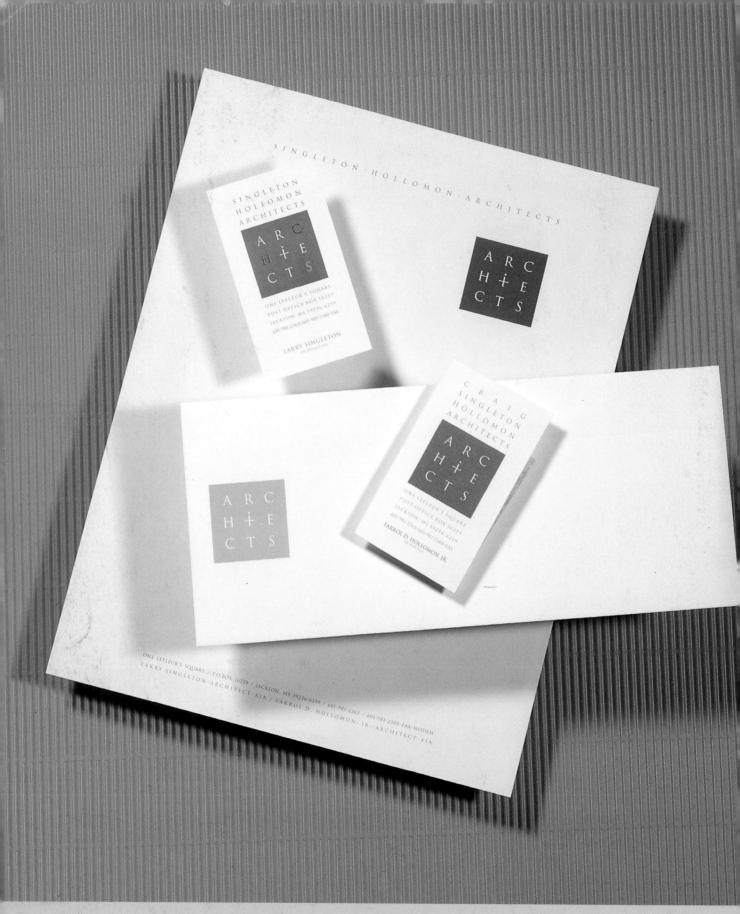

DESIGN FIRM | COMMUNICATION ARTS COMPANY

ART DIRECTOR/DESIGNER | HILDA STAUSS OWEN

CLIENT | SINGLETON-HOLLOMON-ARCHITECTS

TOOLS | MACINTOSH

PAPER/PRINTING | STRATHMORE WRITING/OFFSET LITHO

DESIGN FIRM | IMAGINE THAT, INC.

ALL DESIGN | SUE MANIAN

CLIENT | JIM McGOWAN, AIA

TOOLS | MACROMEDIA FREEHAND

PAPER/PRINTING | CLASSIC CREST/CLARKS LITHO

DESIGN FIRM | SHIMOKOCHI/REEVES

ART DIRECTORS | MAMORU SHIMOKOCHI, ANNE REEVES

DESIGNER | MAMORU SHIMOKOCHI

CLIENT | IZEN

TOOLS | ADOBE ILLUSTRATOR

PAPER/PRINTING | GRAPHIKA LINEAL

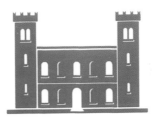

CENTRO INTERCULTURALE TAVOLINO ROVESCIATO

DESIGN FIRM | TANGRAM STRATEGIC DESIGN
ART DIRECTOR/DESIGNER/CREATIVE DIRECTOR | ENRICO SEMPI
CLIENT | COMPACT
TOOLS | POWER MACINTOSH

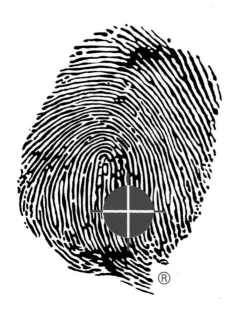

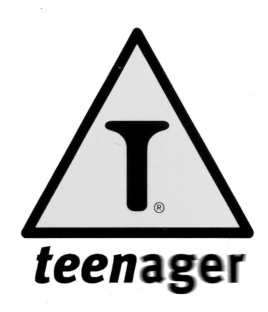

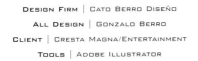

DESIGN FIRM | CATO BERRO DISEÑO
ALL DESIGN | GONZALO BERRO
CLIENT | CRESTA MAGNA/ENTERTAINMENT
TOOLS | ADOBE ILLUSTRATOR

ALL DESIGN | JOSÉ TORRES
CLIENT | TEENAGER BOUTIQUE
TOOLS | ADOBE PHOTOSHOP, MACROMEDIA FREEHAND

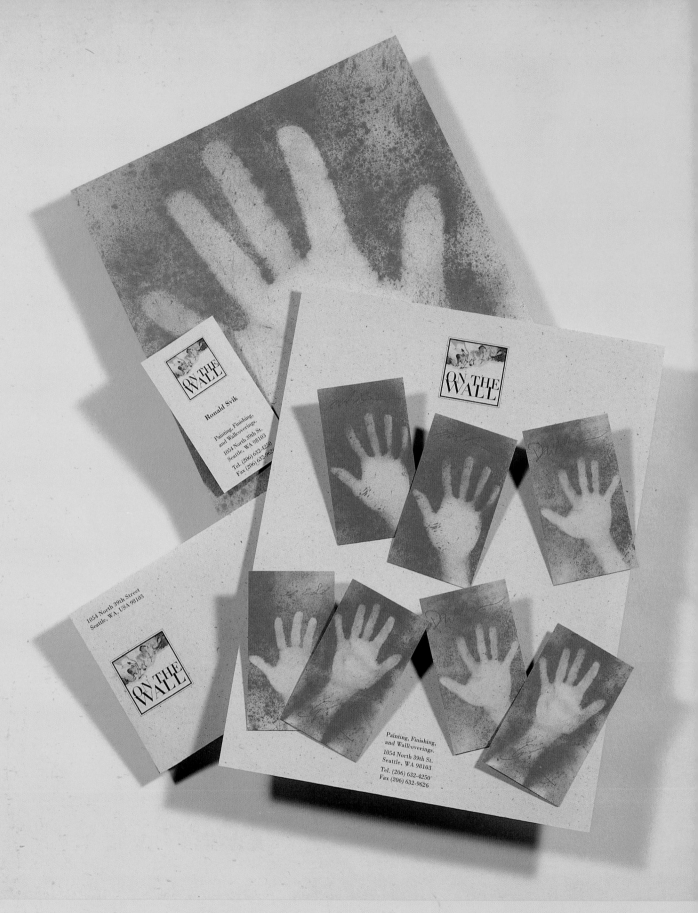

DESIGN FIRM | RICK EIBER DESIGN (RED)

ART DIRECTOR/DESIGNER | RICK EIBER

ILLUSTRATORS | DAVE D. WELLER (LOGO), GARY VOLK (HANDS)

CLIENT | ON THE WALL

PAPER/PRINTING | SPECKLETONE TWO COLOR (ONE METALLIC)
OVER ONE COLOR

DESIGN, CONSTRUCTION & MAINTENANCE OF FINE TURF SURFACES – 19 DERMOT STREET SOUTH OAKLEIGH 3167 PH 9570 1809 FAX 9570 1809

DESIGN FIRM | WATTS GRAPHIC DESIGN
ART DIRECTORS/DESIGNERS | HELEN WATTS,
    PETER WATTS
CLIENT | GREEN CONCEPTS
TOOLS | MACINTOSH
PAPER/PRINTING | THREE COLOR

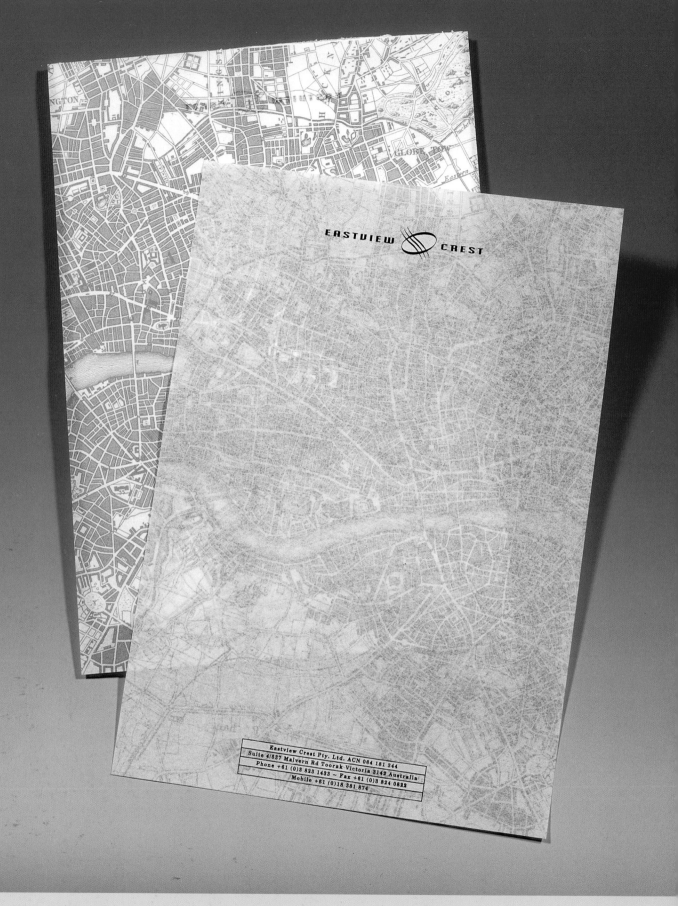

EASTVIEW CREST

Eastview Crest Pty. Ltd. ACN 064 181 344
Suite 4/537 Malvern Rd Toorak Victoria 3142 Australia
Phone +61 (0)3 823 1433 ~ Fax +61 (0)3 824 0822
Mobile +61 (0)18 381 874

DESIGN FIRM | WATTS GRAPHIC DESIGN

ART DIRECTORS/DESIGNERS | HELEN WATTS, PETER WATTS

CLIENT | EASTVIEW CREST

TOOLS | MACINTOSH

PAPER/PRINTING | PARCHMENT/ONE SIDE ONE COLOR,
    ONE SIDE TWO COLOR

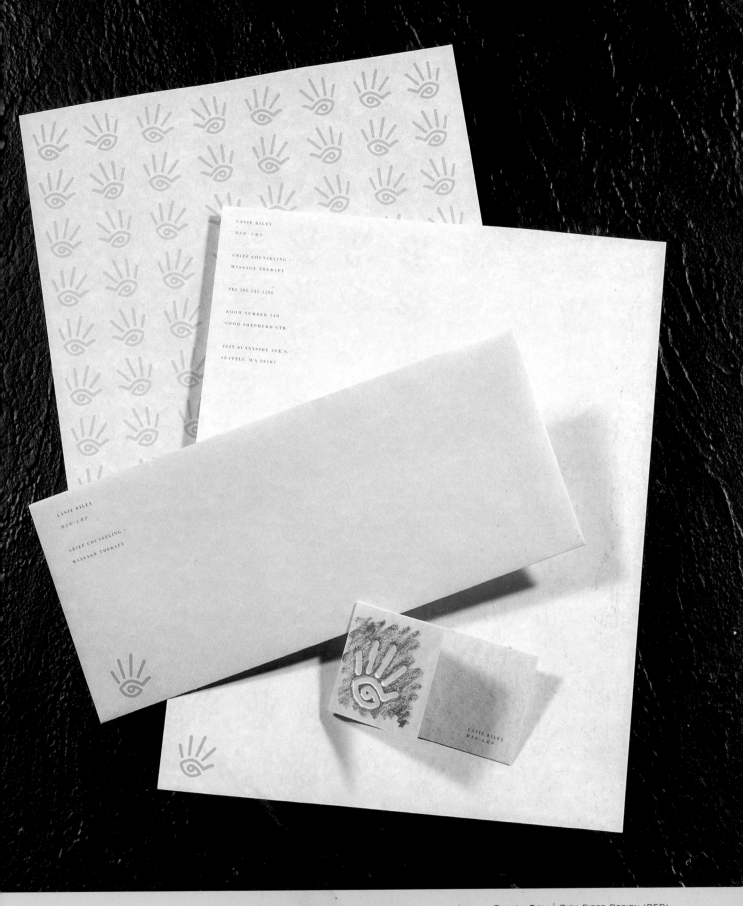

DESIGN FIRM | RICK EIBER DESIGN (RED)

ART DIRECTOR/DESIGNER | RICK EIBER

CLIENT | LANIE RILEY

PAPER/PRINTING | PARCHTONE

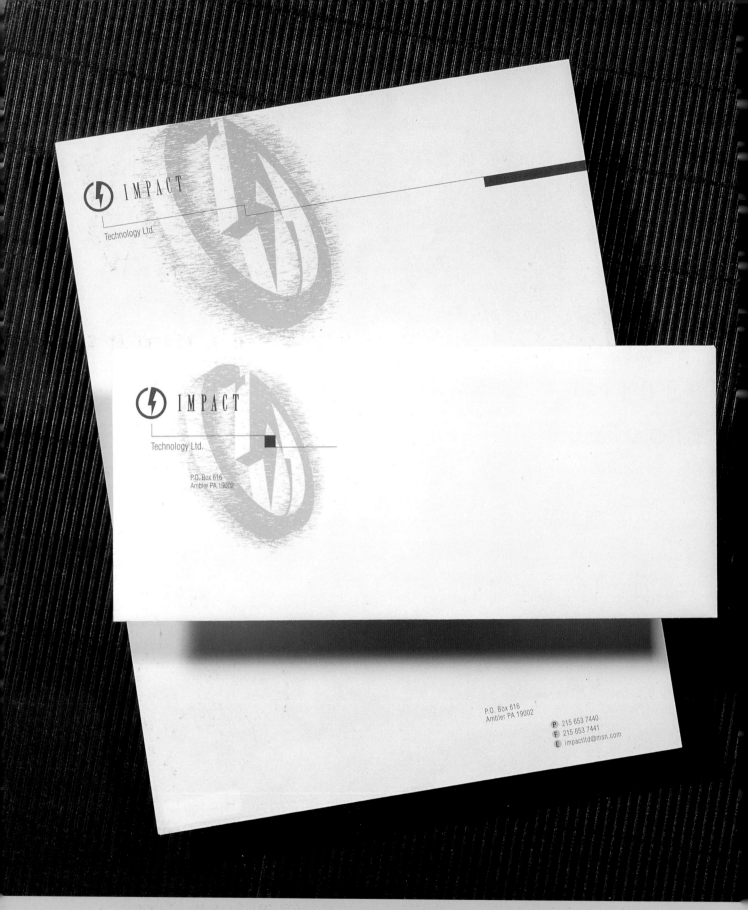

IMPACT
Technology Ltd.

IMPACT
Technology Ltd.

P.O. Box 616
Ambler PA 19002

P.O. Box 616
Ambler PA 19002

P 215 653 7440
F 215 653 7441
E impactltd@msn.com

DESIGN FIRM | MUSSER DESIGN
ART DIRECTOR/DESIGNER | JERRY KING MUSSER
CLIENT | E W AND A
TOOLS | MACINTOSH QUADRA, ADOBE ILLUSTRATOR

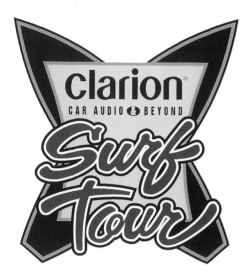

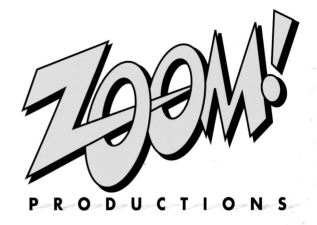

DESIGN FIRM | GILLIS & SMILER
ART DIRECTOR/DESIGNER | CHERYL GILLIS
CLIENT | CLARION SURF TOUR
TOOLS | ADOBE ILLUSTRATOR

DESIGN FIRM | PENCIL NECK PRODUCTIONS
ART DIRECTOR | GARY HAWTHORNE
CLIENT | ZOOM! PRODUCTIONS
TOOLS | ADOBE ILLUSTRATOR

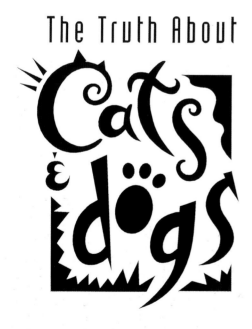

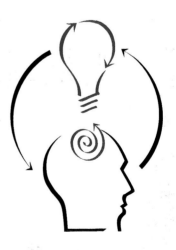

DESIGN FIRM | GILLIS & SMILER
ART DIRECTOR/DESIGNER | CHERYL GILLIS
CLIENT | NEW LINE CINEMA
TOOLS | ADOBE ILLUSTRATOR

DESIGN FIRM | ROBERT BAILEY INCORPORATED
ALL DESIGN | CONNIE LIGHTNER
CLIENT | IDEA CATALYSTS, INC.
TOOLS | ADOBE ILLUSTRATOR

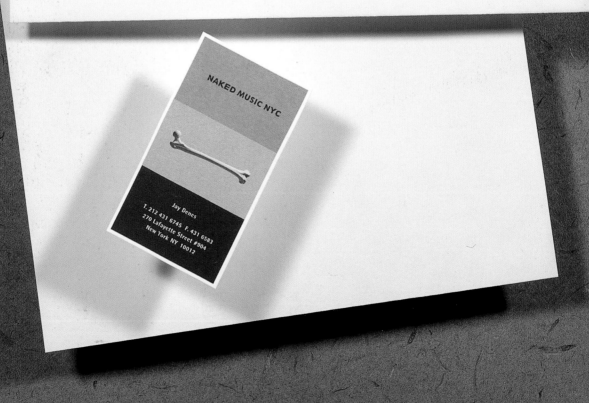

DESIGN FIRM | SAGMEISTER, INC.

ART DIRECTOR | STEFAN SAGMEISTER

DESIGNERS | STEFAN SAGMEISTER, VERONICA OH

PHOTOGRAPHY | TOM SCHIERLITZ

CLIENT | NAKED MUSIC NYC

TOOLS | MACINTOSH, 4 x 5 CAMERA

PAPER/PRINTING | STRATHMORE WRITING 25% COTTON

430 Oak Grove Street • Suite 311
Minneapolis, MN 55403
Tel (612) 872-8418 • Fax 872-8467

430 Oak Grove Street • Suite 311 • Minneapolis, MN 55403

DESTINATI●N✈MSP

DESTINATI●N✈MSP

DESIGN FIRM | DESIGN CENTER
ART DIRECTOR | JOHN REGER
DESIGNER | SHERWIN SWARTZROCK
CLIENT | DESTINATION MSP
TOOLS | MACINTOSH
PAPER/PRINTING | CLASSIC CREST/PRINTCRAFT

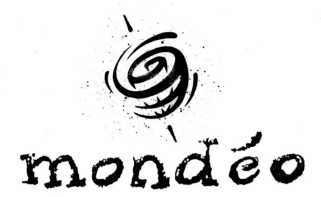

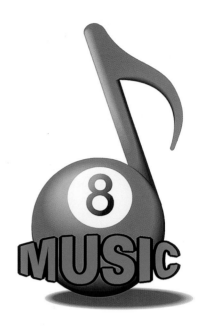

DESIGN FIRM | HORNALL ANDERSON DESIGN WORKS, INC.
ART DIRECTOR | JACK ANDERSON
DESIGNER | JACK ANDERSON, DAVID BATES
ILLUSTRATOR | DAVID BATES
CLIENT | CW GOURMET

DESIGN FIRM | XSNRG ILLUSTRATION AND DESIGN
ALL DESIGN | KEVIN BALL
CLIENT | 8 BALL MUSIC
TOOLS | CORELDRAW

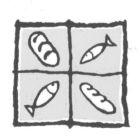

LOAVES+FISHES

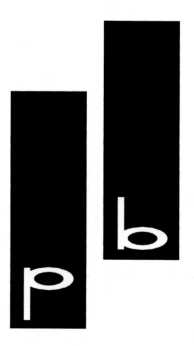

DESIGN FIRM | CREATIVE COMPANY
ALL DESIGN | RICK YURK
CLIENT | LOAVES & FISHES
TOOLS | MACINTOSH

DESIGN FIRM | A1 DESIGN
DESIGNER | AMY GREGG
CLIENT | PETER BELANGER PHOTOGRAPHY
TOOLS | MACINTOSH QUADRA, ADOBE ILLUSTRATOR

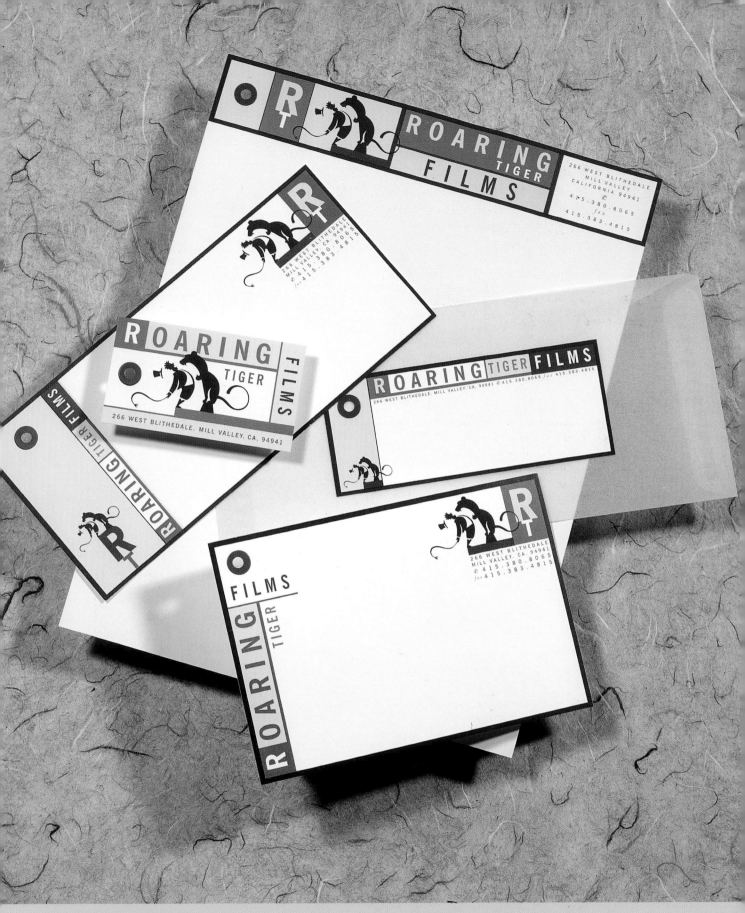

DESIGN FIRM | DOGSTAR

ART DIRECTOR | JENNIFER MARTIN

DESIGNER/ILLUSTRATOR | RODNEY DAVIDSON

CLIENT | ROARING TIGER FILMS

TOOLS | ADOBE ILLUSTRATOR, STREAMLINE,

MACROMEDIA FREEHAND

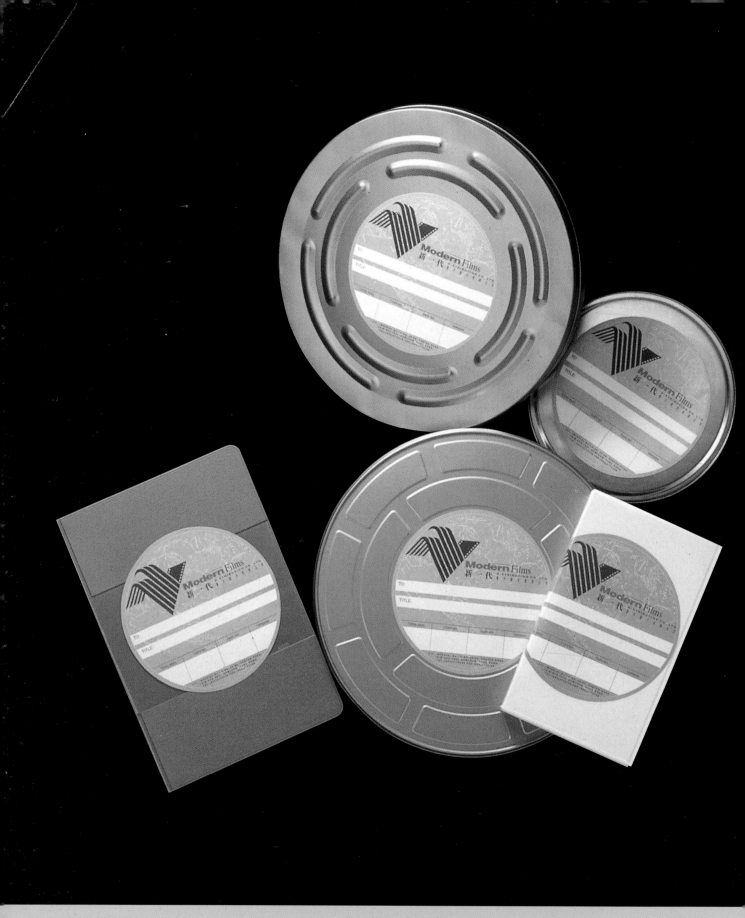

DESIGN FIRM | GRAND DESIGN COMPANY

ART DIRECTOR | GRAND SO

DESIGNER | GRAND SO, KWONG ETTI MAN

ILLUSTRATOR | KWONG ETTI MAN

CLIENT | MODERN FILMS

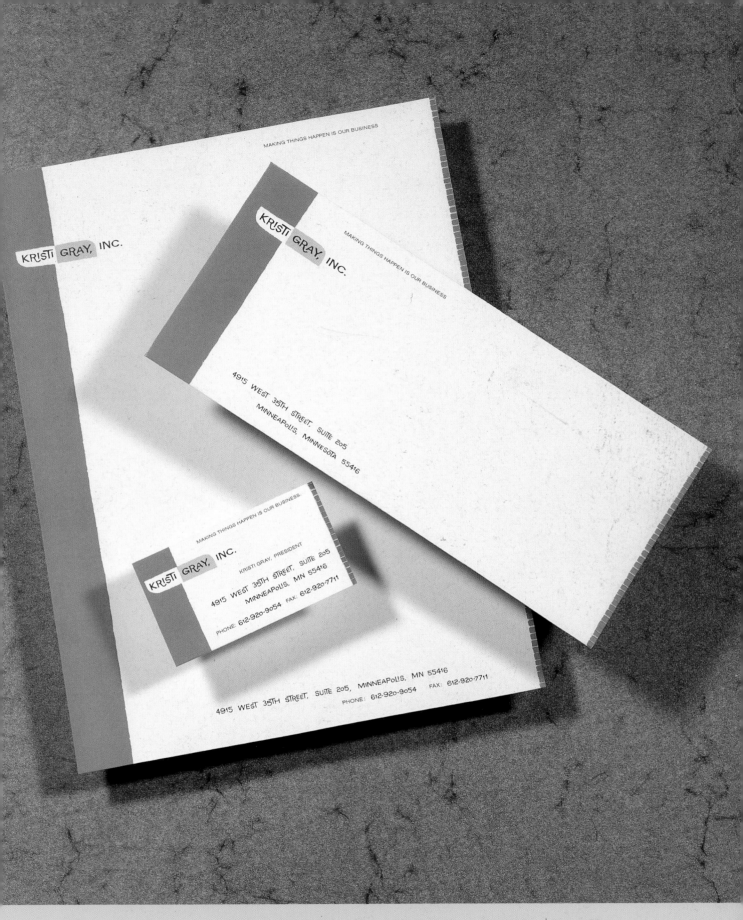

KRISTI GRAY, INC.

KRISTI GRAY, INC.

MAKING THINGS HAPPEN IS OUR BUSINESS

4915 WEST 35TH STREET, SUITE 205
MINNEAPOLIS, MINNESOTA 55416

MAKING THINGS HAPPEN IS OUR BUSINESS

KRISTI GRAY, INC.

KRISTI GRAY, PRESIDENT

4915 WEST 35TH STREET, SUITE 205
MINNEAPOLIS, MN 55416
PHONE: 612-920-9054   FAX: 612-920-7711

4915 WEST 35TH STREET, SUITE 205, MINNEAPOLIS, MN 55416   PHONE: 612-920-9054   FAX: 612-920-7711

DESIGN FIRM | ZAUHAR DESIGN

ALL DESIGN | DAVID ZAUHAR

CLIENT | KRISTI GRAY, INC.

4016 Farm Hill Blvd #103
Redwood City, California
94061-1017

Amy Jo Kim
Creative Director

4016 Farm Hill Blvd #103
Redwood City, California
94061-1017

Tel 415.369.0313
Fax 415.369.0939

amyjo@naima.com
http://www.naima.com

Strategic Design for Online Environments

Amy Jo Kim
Creative Director

4016 Farm Hill Blvd #103
Redwood City, California
94061-1017

Tel 415.369.0313
Fax 415.369.0939

amyjo@naima.com
http://www.naima.com

Strategic Design for Online Environments

Strategic Design
for Online Environments

4016 Farm Hill Blvd #103
Redwood City, California
94061-1017

Tel 415.369.0313
Fax 415.369.0939

amyjo@naima.com
http://www.naima.com

DESIGN FIRM | AERIAL
ART DIRECTOR/DESIGNER | TRACY MOON
CLIENT | AMY JO KIM/NAIMA PRODUCTIONS
TOOLS | ADOBE PHOTOSHOP, QUARKXPRESS
PAPER/PRINTING | CLASSIC CREST SOLAR WHITE 80 LB.

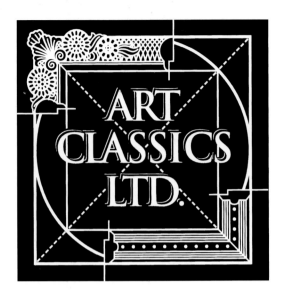

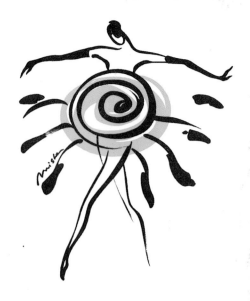

DESIGN FIRM | PHOENIX CREATIVE, ST. LOUIS
ALL DESIGN | ED MANTELS-SEEKER
CLIENT | ART CLASSICS LTD.
TOOLS | MACROMEDIA FREEHAND

DESIGN FIRM | MISHA DESIGN STUDIO
ART DIRECTOR | MICHAEL LENN
DESIGNER | MICHAEL LENN
CLIENT | BOSTON BALLET
TOOLS | HAND BRUSH STROKES

THIS CAPTION WAS PRINTED INCORRECTLY IN A PRIOR PRINTING

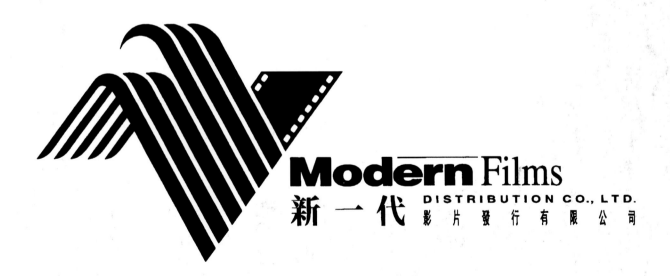

DESIGN FIRM | GRAND DESIGN COMPANY
ART DIRECTOR | GRAND SO
DESIGNER | GRAND SO, KWONG ETTI MAN
ILLUSTRATOR | KWONG ETTI MAN
CLIENT | MODERN FILMS

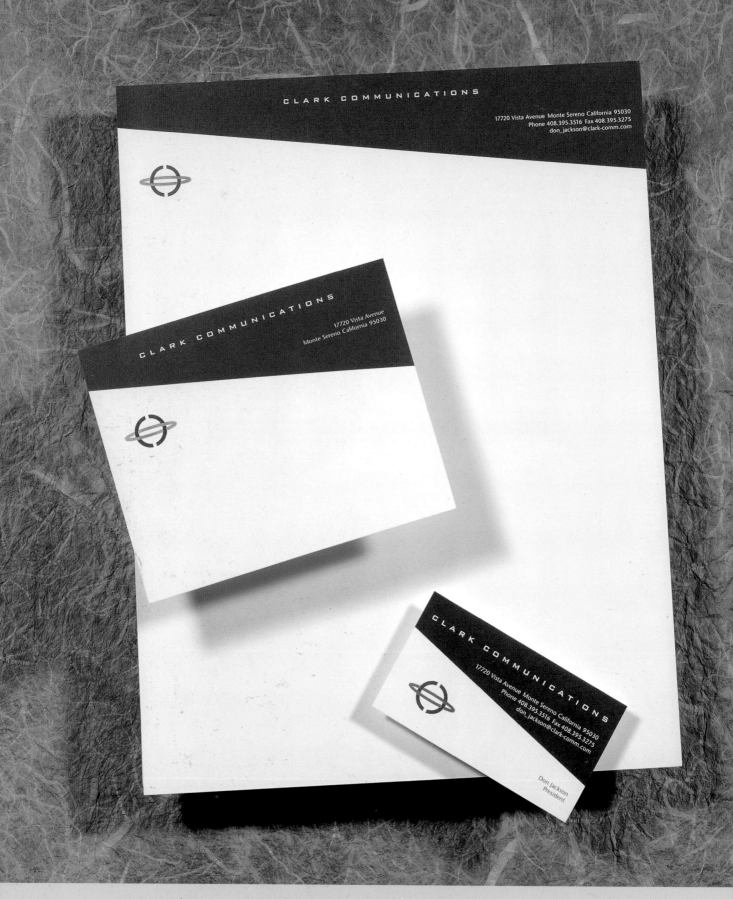

CLARK COMMUNICATIONS

17720 Vista Avenue Monte Sereno California 95030
Phone 408.395.3516 Fax 408.395.3275
don_jackson@clark-comm.com

CLARK COMMUNICATIONS

17720 Vista Avenue
Monte Sereno California 95030

CLARK COMMUNICATIONS

17720 Vista Avenue Monte Sereno
California 95030
Phone 408.395.3516 Fax 408.395.3275
don_jackson@clark-comm.com

Don Jackson
President

DESIGN FIRM | MELISSA PASSEHL DESIGN
ART DIRECTOR/DESIGNER | MELISSA PASSEHL
CLIENT | CLARK COMMUNICATIONS

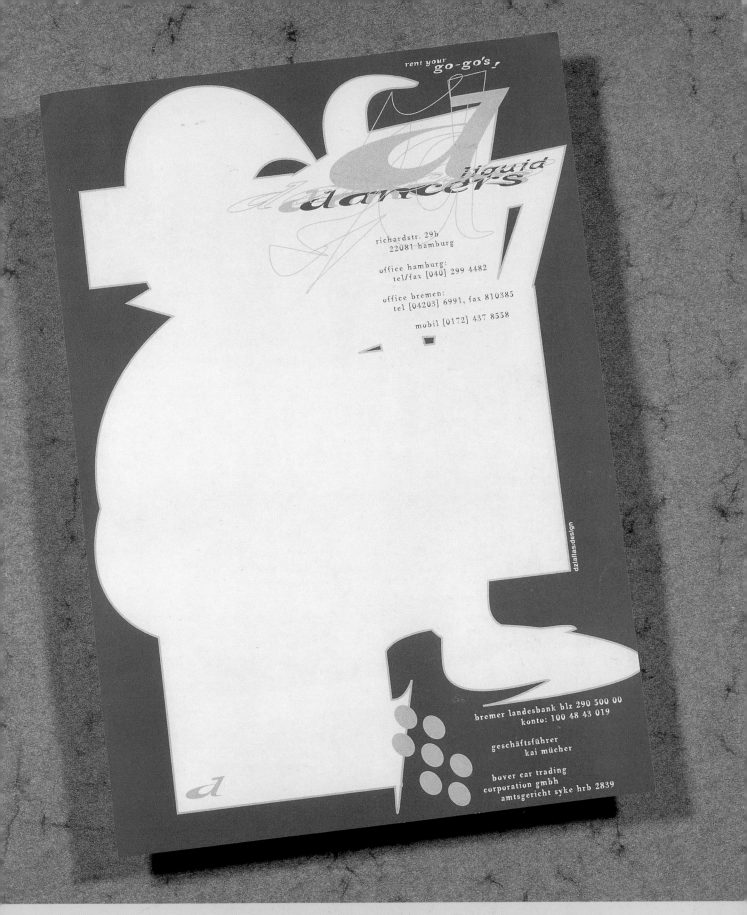

rent your go-go's!

liquid dancers

richardstr. 29b
22081 hamburg

office hamburg:
tel/fax [040] 299 4482

office bremen:
tel [04203] 6991, fax 810385

mobil [0172] 437 8558

dziallas.design

bremer landesbank blz 290 500 00
konto: 100 48 43 019

geschäftsführer
kai mücher

bover car trading
corporation gmbh
amtsgericht syke hrb 2839

DESIGN FIRM | STEFAN DZIALLAS DESIGN
DESIGNER/ILLUSTRATOR | STEFAN DZIALLAS
CLIENT | STEFAN DZIALLAS
TOOLS | ADOBE ILLUSTRATOR, QUARKXPRESS,
MACINTOSH

ALCAROTTI
CENTRO SPORTIVO

DESIGN FIRM | TANGRAM STRATEGIC DESIGN
ART DIRECTOR/DESIGNER | ANTONELLA TREVISAN
CLIENT | CENTRO SPORTIVO ALCAROTTI
TOOLS | POWER MACINTOSH

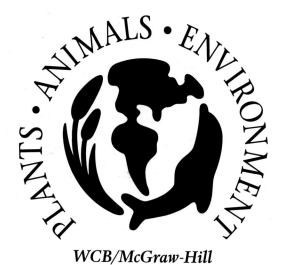

WCB/McGraw-Hill

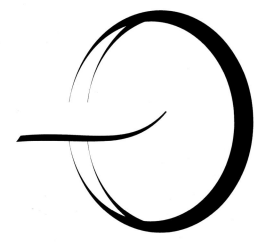

DESIGN FIRM | GET SMART DESIGN COMPANY
ART DIRECTOR | JEFF MACFARLANE
DESIGNER/ILLUSTRATOR | TOM CULBERTSON
CLIENT | WCB/McGRAW-HILL PUBLISHERS
TOOLS | MACROMEDIA FREEHAND

DESIGN FIRM | EYE DESIGN INCORPORATED
ALL DESIGN | ROBIN MEYERS
CLIENT | DYNAMIC DECISIONS/PEI-O
TOOLS | ADOBE ILLUSTRATOR
PAPER/PRINTING | PMS 485

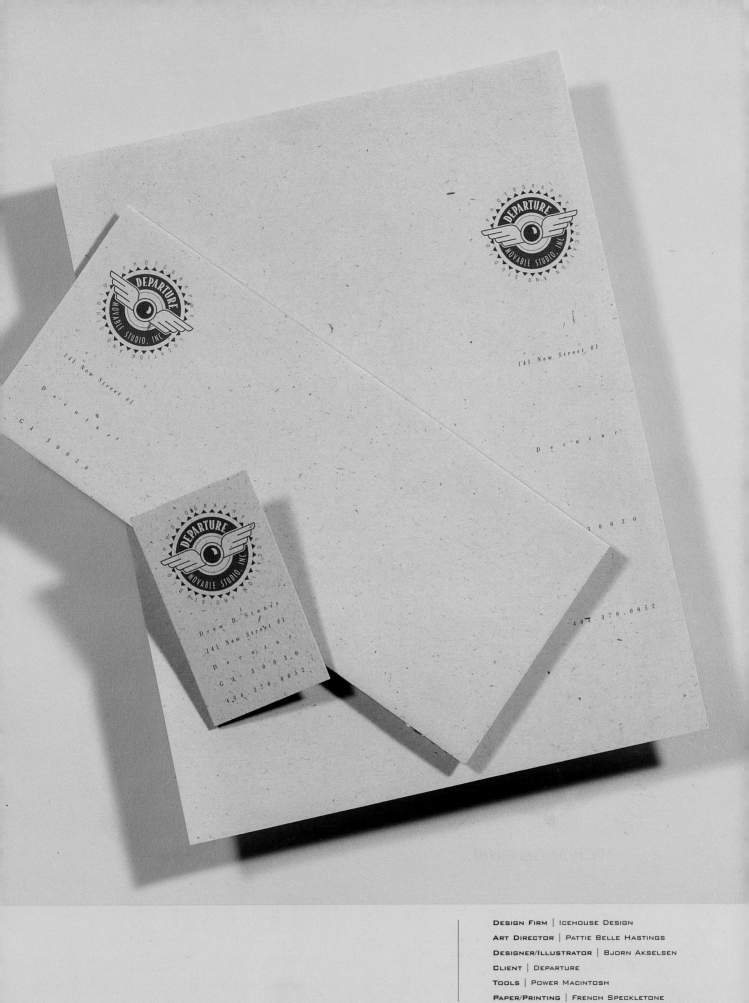

DESIGN FIRM | ICEHOUSE DESIGN
ART DIRECTOR | PATTIE BELLE HASTINGS
DESIGNER/ILLUSTRATOR | BJORN AKSELSEN
CLIENT | DEPARTURE
TOOLS | POWER MACINTOSH
PAPER/PRINTING | FRENCH SPECKLETONE

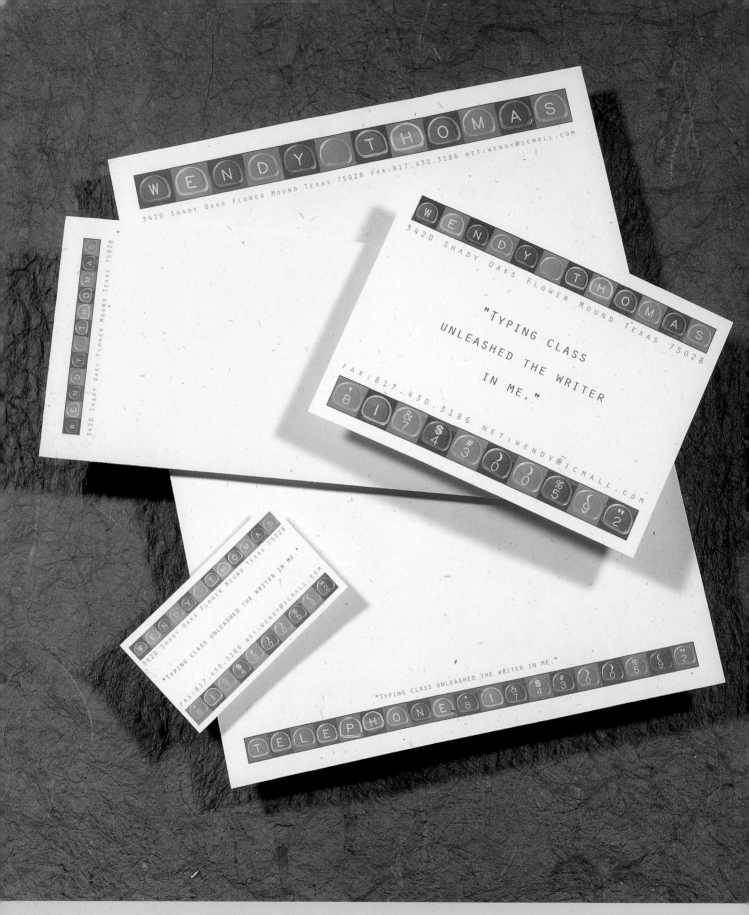

DESIGN FIRM | ELENA DESIGN

ART DIRECTOR/DESIGNER | ELENA BACA

ILLUSTRATOR | PHOTOTONE ALPHABETS

CLIENT | WENDY THOMAS

TOOLS | QUARKXPRESS

PAPER/PRINTING | FRENCH SPECKELTONE

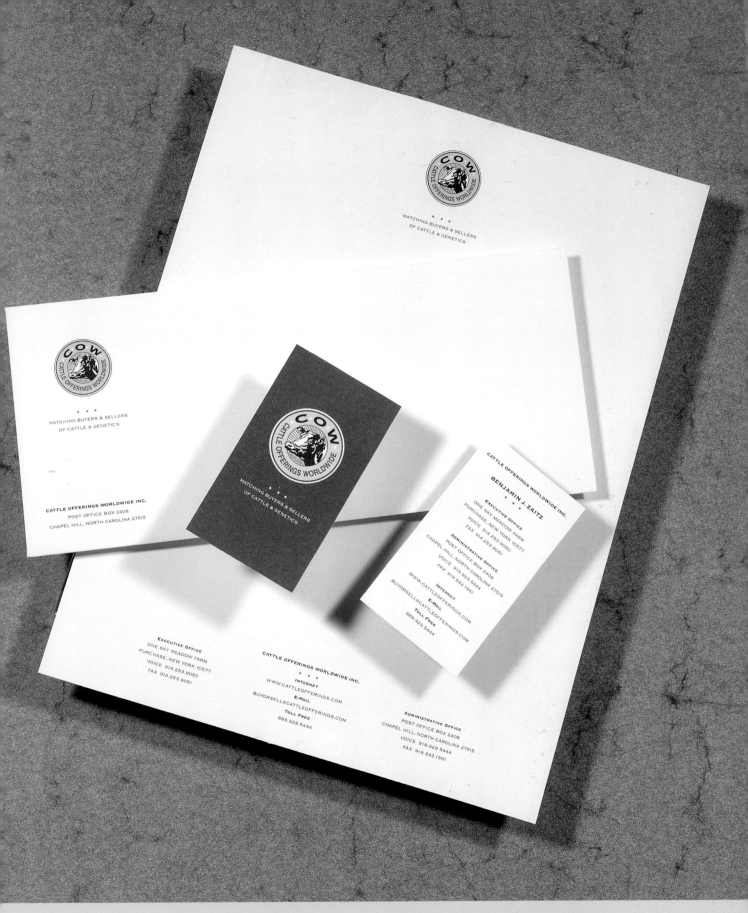

CATTLE OFFERINGS WORLDWIDE INC.

BENJAMIN J. ZAITZ

EXECUTIVE OFFICE
ONE SKY MEADOW FARM
PURCHASE, NEW YORK 10577
VOICE 914.253.9050
FAX 914.253.9051

ADMINISTRATIVE OFFICE
POST OFFICE BOX 2408
CHAPEL HILL, NORTH CAROLINA 27515
VOICE 919.929.5444
FAX 919.942.1561

INTERNET
WWW.CATTLEOFFERINGS.COM
E-MAIL
BUYORSELL@CATTLEOFFERINGS.COM
TOLL FREE
888.929.5444

C O W
CATTLE OFFERINGS WORLDWIDE

MATCHING BUYERS & SELLERS
OF CATTLE & GENETICS

CATTLE OFFERINGS WORLDWIDE INC.
POST OFFICE BOX 2408
CHAPEL HILL, NORTH CAROLINA 27515

EXECUTIVE OFFICE
ONE SKY MEADOW FARM
PURCHASE, NEW YORK 10577
VOICE 914.253.9050
FAX 914.253.9051

CATTLE OFFERINGS WORLDWIDE INC.
INTERNET
WWW.CATTLEOFFERINGS.COM
E-MAIL
BUYORSELL@CATTLEOFFERINGS.COM
TOLL FREE
888.929.5444

ADMINISTRATIVE OFFICE
POST OFFICE BOX 2408
CHAPEL HILL, NORTH CAROLINA 27515
VOICE 919.929.5444
FAX 919.942.1561

DESIGN FIRM | MICHAEL STANARD DESIGN, INC.

ART DIRECTOR | MICHAEL STANARD

DESIGNER/ILLUSTRATOR | KRISTY VANDEKERCKHOVE

CLIENT | CATTLE OFFERINGS WORLDWIDE

TOOLS | MACINTOSH, ADOBE ILLUSTRATOR

PAPER/PRINTING | STRATHMORE WRITING

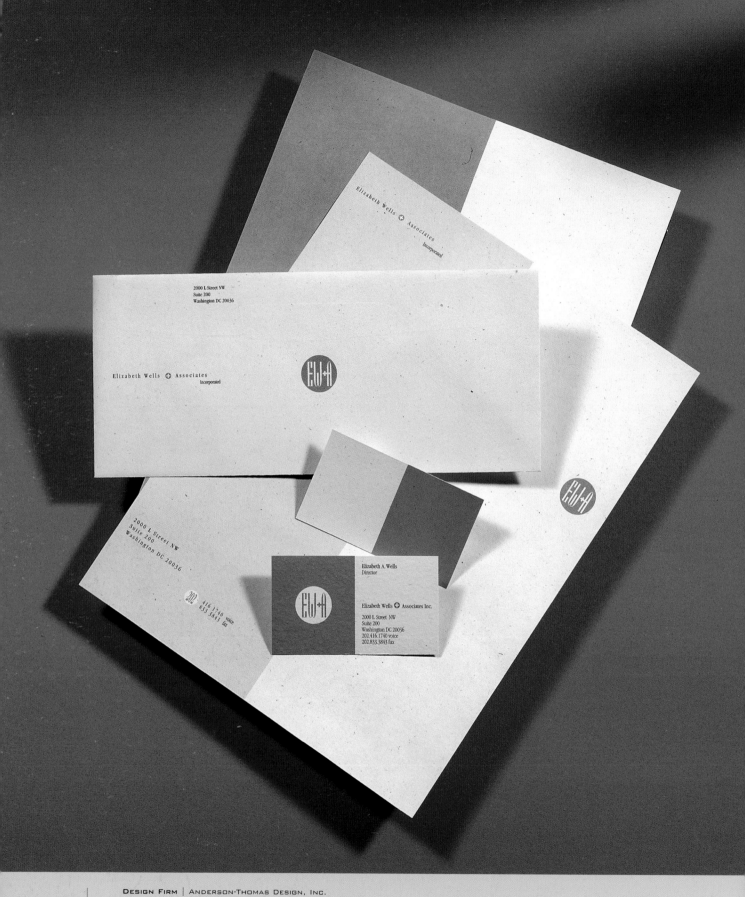

DESIGN FIRM | ANDERSON-THOMAS DESIGN, INC.

ART DIRECTOR/DESIGNER | JOEL ANDERSON

CLIENT | STAR SONG COMMUNICATIONS

TOOLS | QUARKXPRESS, ADOBE ILLUSTRATOR

PAPER/PRINTING | CLASSIC CREST/BLACK PLUS ONE PMS

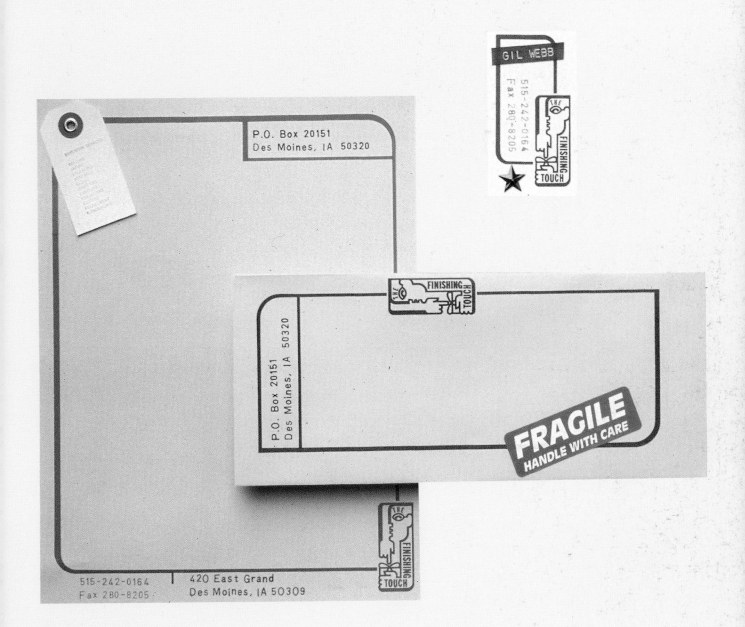

GIL WEBB

515-242-0164
Fax 280-8205

THE FINISHING TOUCH

P.O. Box 20151
Des Moines, IA 50320

THE FINISHING TOUCH

P.O. Box 20151
Des Moines, IA 50320

FRAGILE
HANDLE WITH CARE

THE FINISHING TOUCH

515-242-0164
Fax 280-8205

420 East Grand
Des Moines, IA 50309

DESIGN FIRM | SAYLES GRAPHIC DESIGN
ALL DESIGN | JOHN SAYLES
CLIENT | THE FINISHING TOUCH
PAPER/PRINTING | INCENTIVE 100 LB. AND
MANILA TAG/ OFFSET AND RUBBER STAMP

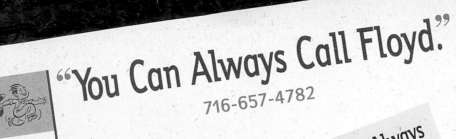

"You Can Always Call Floyd."
716-657-4782

HEATING

PLUMBING

CARPENTRY

ELECTRIC

ROOFING

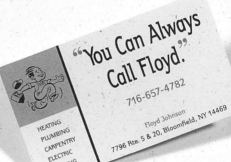

"You Can Always Call Floyd."
716-657-4782

HEATING
PLUMBING
CARPENTRY
ELECTRIC
ROOFING

Floyd Johnson
7796 Rte. 5 & 20, Bloomfield, NY 14469

"You Can Always Call Floyd."
716-657-4782

HEATING
PLUMBING
CARPENTRY
ELECTRIC
ROOFING

Floyd Johnson
7796 Rte. 5 & 20
Bloomfield, NY
14469

Floyd Johnson

7796 Rte. 5 & 20

Bloomfield, NY

14469

DESIGN FIRM | LYNN WOOD DESIGN

ART DIRECTOR/DESIGNER | LYNN WOOD

ILLUSTRATOR | MODIFIED CLIP ART

CLIENT | FLOYD JOHNSON

TOOLS | QUARKXPRESS, ADOBE ILLUSTRATOR, POWER MACINTOSH

PAPER/PRINTING | BENEFIT/GRAPHIC BROKERAGE

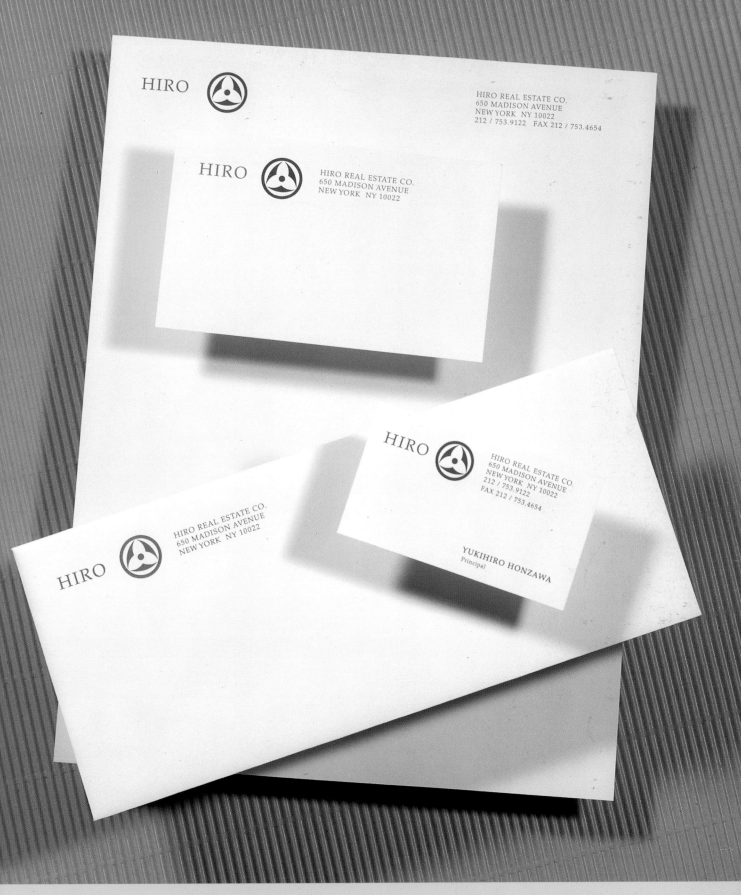

HIRO

HIRO REAL ESTATE CO.
650 MADISON AVENUE
NEW YORK NY 10022
212 / 753.9122   FAX 212 / 753.4654

HIRO

HIRO REAL ESTATE CO.
650 MADISON AVENUE
NEW YORK NY 10022

HIRO

HIRO REAL ESTATE CO.
650 MADISON AVENUE
NEW YORK NY 10022
212 / 753.9122
FAX 212 / 753.4654

YUKIHIRO HONZAWA
Principal

HIRO

HIRO REAL ESTATE CO.
650 MADISON AVENUE
NEW YORK NY 10022

DESIGN FIRM │ E. CHRISTOPHER KLUMB ASSOCIATES, INC.

ALL DESIGN │ CHRISTOPHER KLUMB

CLIENT │ HIRO REAL ESTATE COMPANY

TOOLS │ QUARKXPRESS, MACINTOSH

PAPER/PRINTING │ STRATHMORE

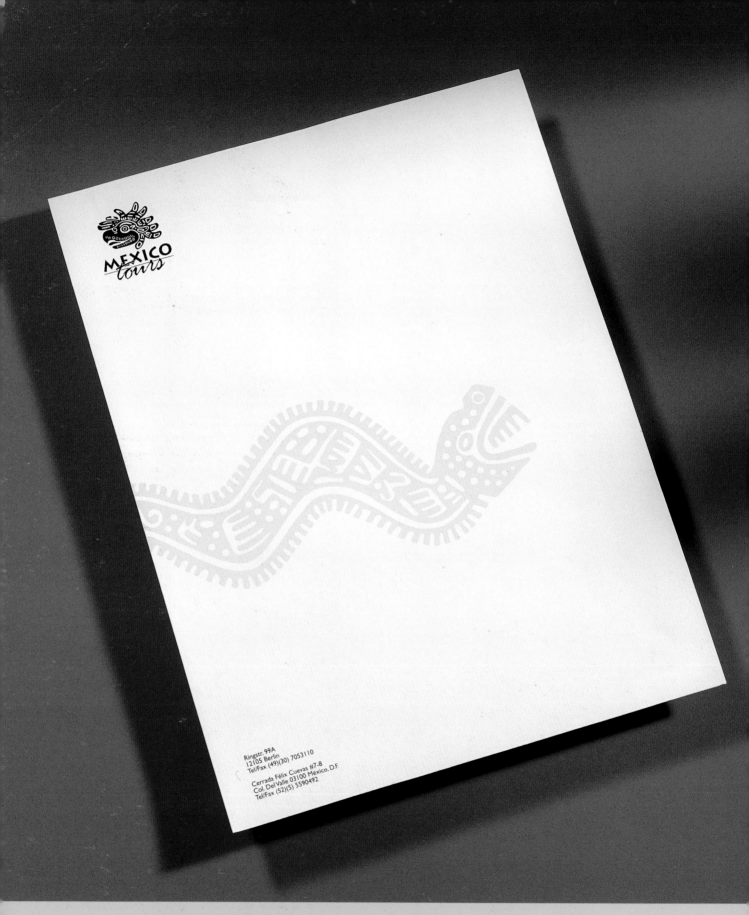

Ringstr. 99A
12105 Berlin
Tel/Fax (49)(30) 7053110

Cerrada Félix Cuevas #7-8
Col. Del Valle 03100 Mexico, D.F.
Tel/Fax (52)(5) 5590492

DESIGN FIRM | ZAPPATA DESIGNERS

ART DIRECTOR/DESIGNER | IBO ANGULO

CLIENT | MEXICO TOURS (TOURIST AGENCY IN GERMANY)

TOOLS | MACROMEDIA FREEHAND

PAPER/PRINTING | RECYCLED/SILKSCREEN

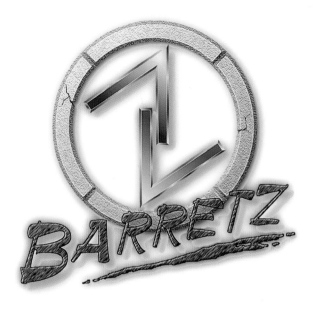

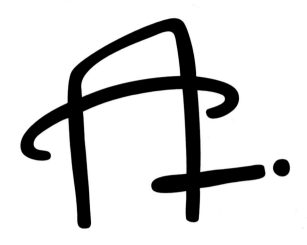

DESIGN FIRM | XSNRG ILLUSTRATION AND DESIGN

ALL DESIGN | KEVIN BALL

CLIENT | BARRETZ

TOOLS | CORELDRAW, PICTURE PUBLISHER

DESIGN FIRM | DOGSTAR

ART DIRECTOR | MARTIN LEEDS/CIGAR AFICIONADO

DESIGNER/ILLUSTRATOR | RODNEY DAVIDSON

CLIENT | CIGAR AFICIONADO

TOOLS | ADOBE ILLUSTRATOR, STREAMLINE, MACROMEDIA FREEHAND

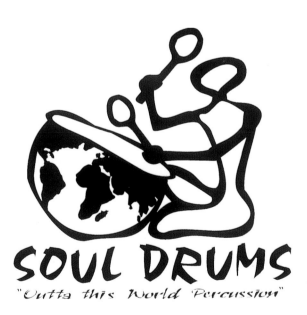

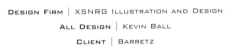

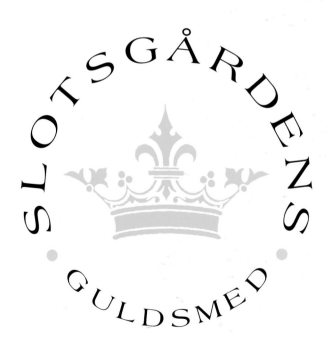

DESIGN FIRM | XSNRG ILLUSTRATION AND DESIGN

ALL DESIGN | KEVIN BALL

CLIENT | SOUL DRUMS

TOOLS | CORELDRAW

ART DIRECTOR/DESIGNER | ATHENA WINDELEV

CLIENT | SLOTSGÅRDENS GULDSMED, GOLDSMITH

DESIGN FIRM | RAMONA HUTKO DESIGN

ART DIRECTOR/DESIGNER | RAMONA HUTKO

PHOTOGRAPHER | SHAWN HUTKO

CLIENT | PINNACLE ALLIANCE

TOOLS | ADOBE PHOTOSHOP, QUARKXPRESS

PAPER/PRINTING | MOHAWK SUPERFINE WHITE ESS SHELL
FINISH 80 LB. TEXT

DESIGN FIRM | ICEHOUSE DESIGN
ART DIRECTOR/DESIGNER | PATTIE BELLE HASTINGS
CLIENT | JOHN HOWARD/BENJAMIN RODEN-LUPTON
TOOLS | POWER MACINTOSH
PAPER/PRINTING | CLASSIC CREST

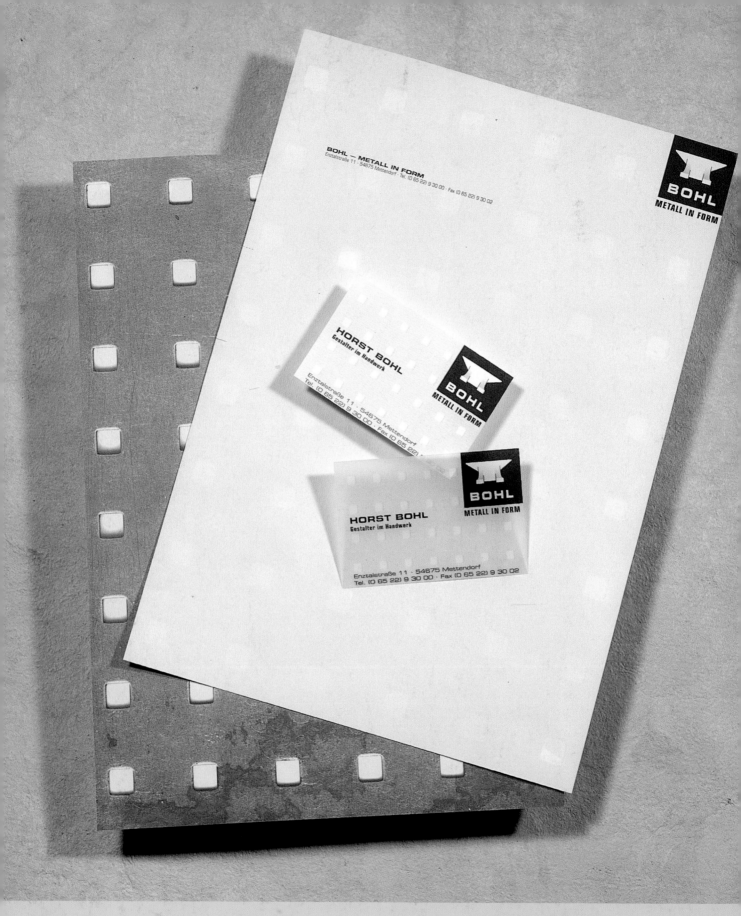

DESIGN FIRM | BOHL
ART DIRECTOR | STEFAN BOHL
CLIENT | BOHL METALL IN FORM
TOOLS | MACINTOSH

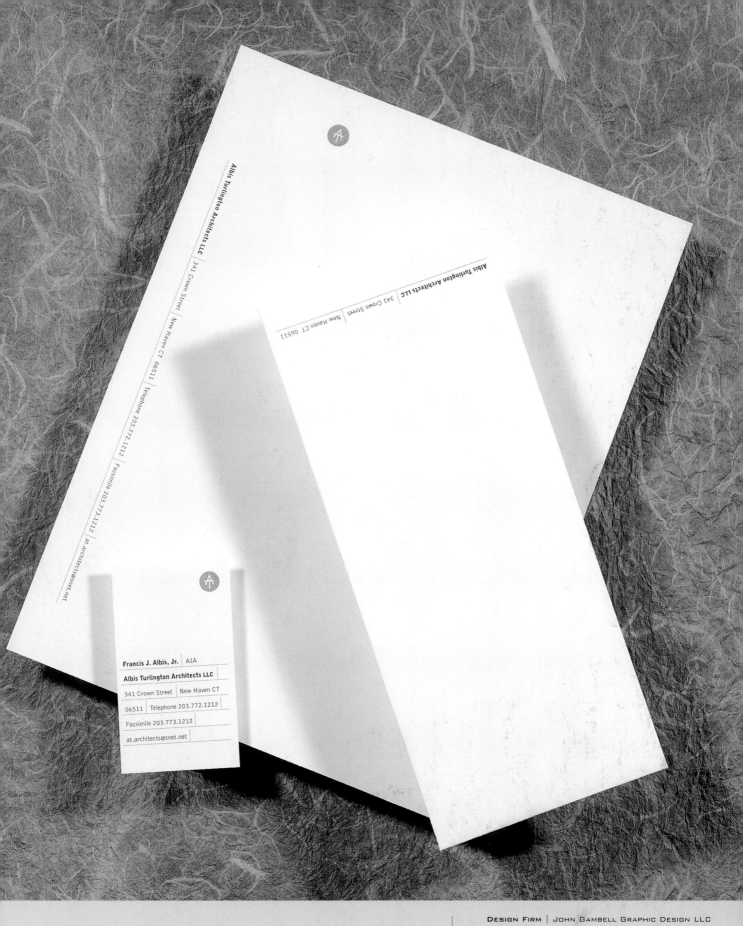

Albis Turlington Architects LLC

341 Crown Street

New Haven CT 06511

Telephone 203.772.1212

Facsimile 203.773.1212

at.architects@snet.net

Albis Turlington Architects LLC | 341 Crown Street | New Haven CT 06511

Francis J. Albis, Jr. | AIA

Albis Turlington Architects LLC

341 Crown Street | New Haven CT

06511 | Telephone 203.772.1212

Facsimile 203.773.1212

at.architects@snet.net

DESIGN FIRM | JOHN GAMBELL GRAPHIC DESIGN LLC

ART DIRECTOR | JOHN GAMBELL

DESIGNERS | JOHN GAMBELL, CHARLES ROUTHIER

CLIENT | ALBIS TURLINGTON ARCHITECTS LLC

TOOLS | QUARKXPRESS, ADOBE ILLUSTRATOR

PAPER/PRINTING | CRANES CREST 28 LB. FLOUR

WHITE/LEHAMN BROTHERS, INC., NEW HAVEN

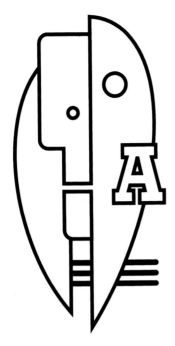

DESIGN FIRM | VOSS DESIGN
ALL DESIGN | AXEL VOSS
CLIENT | ART 'N STUFF

DESIGN FIRM | JEFF FISHER LOGOMOTIVES
ALL DESIGN | JEFF FISHER
CLIENT | SHLEIFER MARKETING COMMUNICATIONS, AGENCY FOR
SAMUELS YOELIN KANTOR SEYMOUR AND SPINRAD
TOOLS | MACROMEDIA FREEHAND

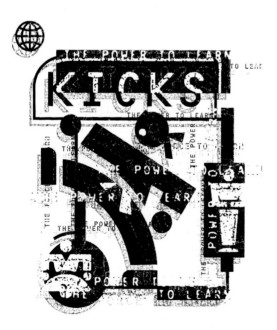

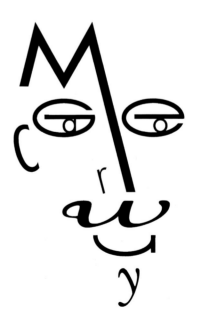

DESIGN FIRM | INSIGHT DESIGN COMMUNICATIONS
ALL DESIGNS | SHERRIE AND TRACY HOLDEMAN
CLIENT | KICKS
TOOLS | POWER MACINTOSH, MACROMEDIA FREEHAND,
ADOBE PHOTOSHOP

DESIGN FIRM | COMMONWEALTH CREATIVE ASSOCIATES
ART DIRECTOR/DESIGNER | ADAM RUDIKOFF
CLIENT | McGOWAN EYECARE
TOOLS | MACINTOSH

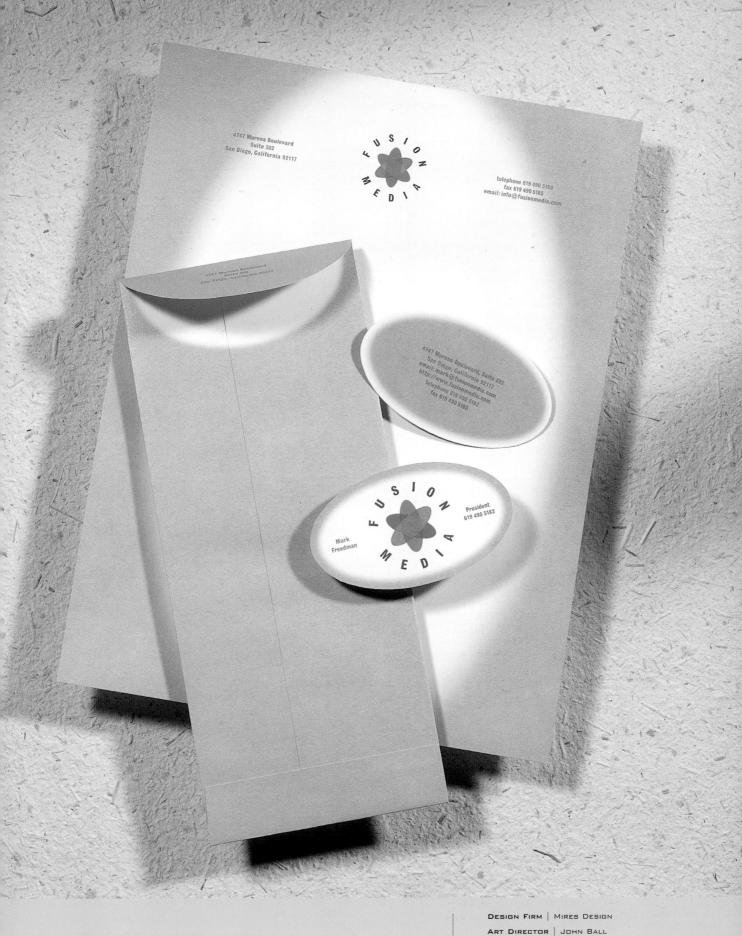

4747 Morena Boulevard
Suite 302
San Diego, California 92117

FUSION
MEDIA

telephone 619 490 5160
fax 619 490 5185
email: info@fusionmedia.com

4747 Morena Boulevard
Suite 302
San Diego, California 92117

4747 Morena Boulevard, Suite 302,
San Diego, California 92117
email: mark@fusionmedia.com
http://www.fusionmedia.com
telephone 619 490 5182
fax 619 490 5185

FUSION
MEDIA

Mark
Freedman

President
619 490 5182

DESIGN FIRM | MIRES DESIGN
ART DIRECTOR | JOHN BALL
DESIGNERS | JOHN BALL, DOBORAH HORN
CLIENT | FUSION MEDIA
PAPER/PRINTING | STARWHITE

725 Cowper Street, Suite 45 • Palo Alto, California 94301 • (415) 326-8337 Fax (415) 323-8111 • Internet bwqc20a@prodigy.com

ACUMEN
GROUP

725 Cowper Street, Suite 45 • Palo Alto, California 94301

ACUMEN
GROUP

London • Portland • "MARKETING YOUR PRODUCTS TO THE WORLD" •San Francisco • Santiago

DESIGN FIRM | SAYLES GRAPHIC DESIGN

ALL DESIGN | JOHN SAYLES

CLIENT | ACUMEN GROUP

PAPER/PRINTING | GRAPHIKA WHITE PARCHMENT/OFFSET

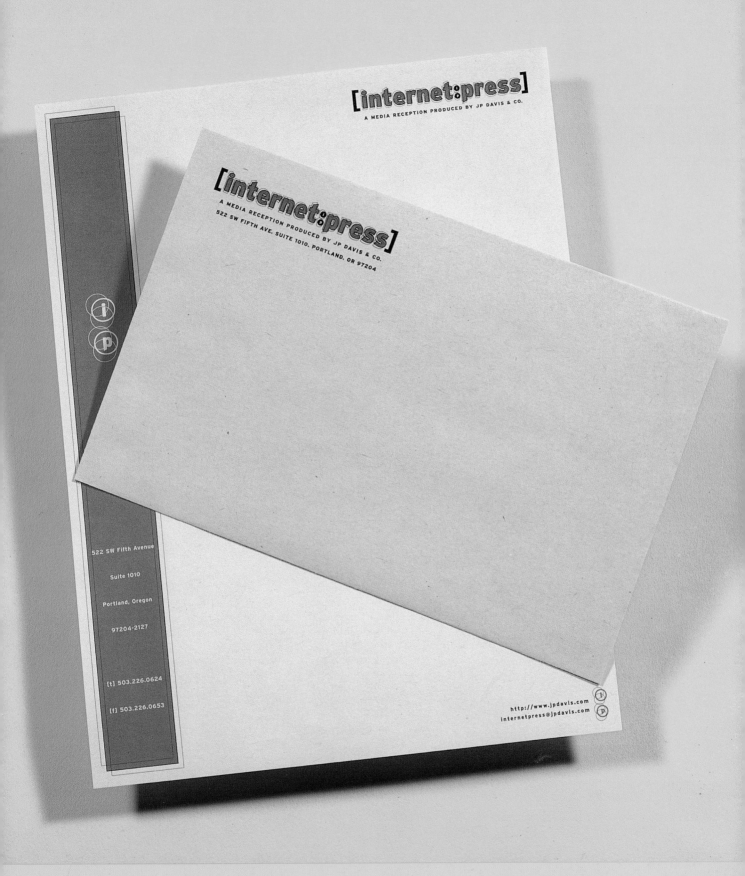

[internet:press]
A MEDIA RECEPTION PRODUCED BY JP DAVIS & CO.

[internet:press]
A MEDIA RECEPTION PRODUCED BY JP DAVIS & CO.
522 SW FIFTH AVE. SUITE 1010, PORTLAND, OR 97204

522 SW Fifth Avenue

Suite 1010

Portland, Oregon

97204-2127

[t] 503.226.0624

[f] 503.226.0653

http://www.jpdavis.com
internetpress@jpdavis.com

DESIGN FIRM | LSL INDUSTRIES
DESIGNER | ELISABETH SPITALNY
CLIENT | JP DAVIS & COMPANY, INTERNET PRESS
TOOLS | QuarkXPress, ADOBE ILLUSTRATOR
PAPER/PRINTING | FRENCH NEWSPRINT AGED/OFFSET

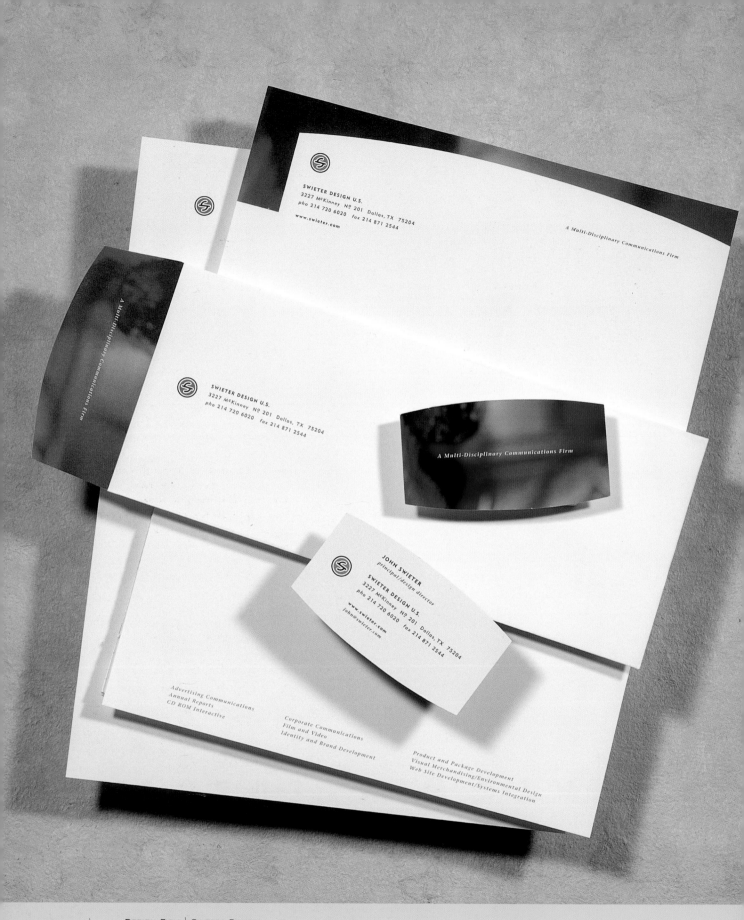

SWIETER DESIGN U.S.
3227 McKinney № 201 Dallas, TX 75204
pho 214 720 6020 fax 214 871 2544
www.swieter.com

A Multi-Disciplinary Communications Firm

A Multi-Disciplinary Communications Firm

SWIETER DESIGN U.S.
3227 McKinney № 201 Dallas, TX 75204
pho 214 720 6020 fax 214 871 2544

A Multi-Disciplinary Communications Firm

JOHN SWIETER
principal/design director
SWIETER DESIGN U.S.
3227 McKinney № 201 Dallas, TX 75204
pho 214 720 6020 fax 214 871 2544
www.swieter.com
john@swieter.com

Advertising Communications
Annual Reports
CD ROM Interactive

Corporate Communications
Film and Video
Identity and Brand Development

Product and Package Development
Visual Merchandising/Environmental Design
Web Site Development/Systems Integration

DESIGN FIRM | SWIETER DESIGN

ART DIRECTOR | JOHN SWIETER

DESIGNER | MARK FORD

CLIENT | SWIETER DESIGN

TOOLS | ADOBE PHOTOSHOP

PAPER/PRINTING | COATED/FOUR COLOR

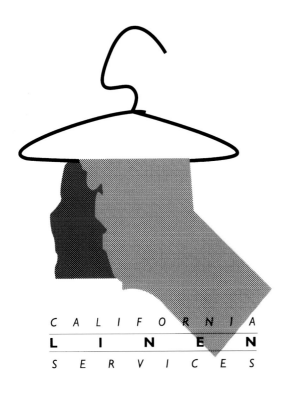

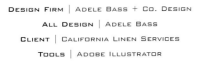

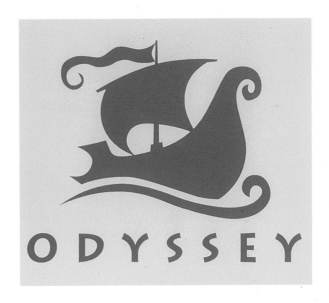

DESIGN FIRM | ADELE BASS + CO. DESIGN

ALL DESIGN | ADELE BASS

CLIENT | CALIFORNIA LINEN SERVICES

TOOLS | ADOBE ILLUSTRATOR

DESIGN FIRM | TRACY SABIN GRAPHIC DESIGN

ART DIRECTOR | ELISABETH PETERS

DESIGNER/ILLUSTRATOR | TRACY SABIN

CLIENT | HARCOURT BRACE & COMPANY/ODYSSEY

TOOLS | ADOBE ILLUSTRATOR

CHALMER ⊕ HVEDEHAVE

DESIGN FIRM | TRANSPARENT OFFICE

ART DIRECTOR/DESIGNER | VIBEKE NØDSKOV

CLIENT | CHALMER + HVEDEHAVE

TOOLS | QUARKXPRESS, ADOBE ILLUSTRATOR

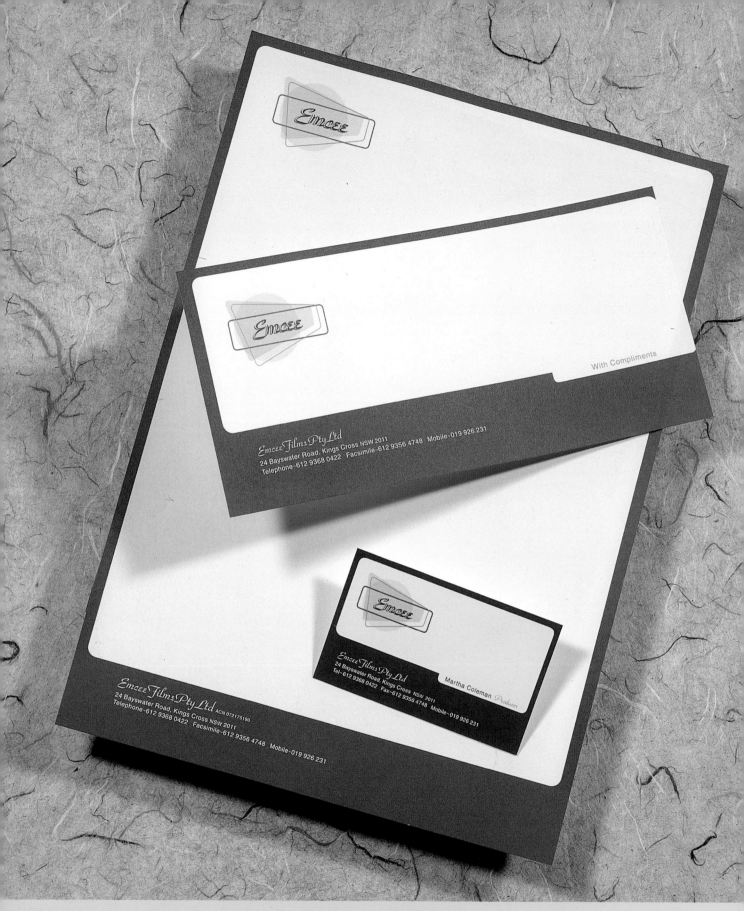

DESIGN FIRM | LUCY WALKER GRAPHIC DESIGN

ART DIRECTOR/DESIGNER | LUCY WALKER

CLIENT | EMCEE FILMS PTY. LTD.

TOOLS | ADOBE ILLUSTRATOR

PAPER/PRINTING | OCM IVORY WOVE

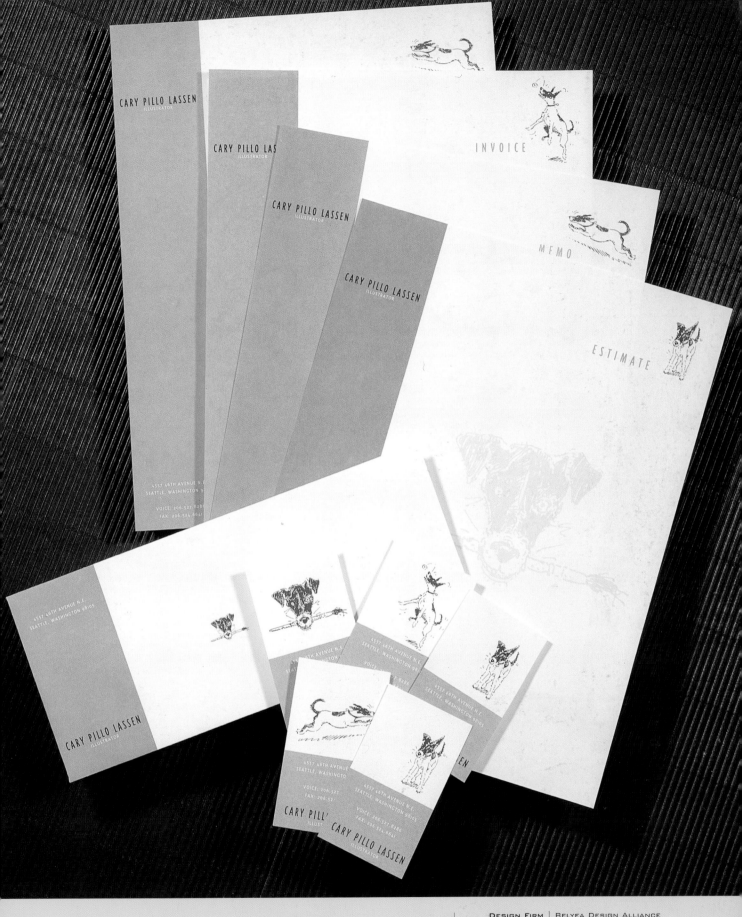

INVOICE

MEMO

ESTIMATE

CARY PILLO LASSEN
ILLUSTRATOR

DESIGN FIRM | BELYEA DESIGN ALLIANCE
ART DIRECTOR | PATRICIA BELYEA
DESIGNER | TIM RUSZEL
ILLUSTRATOR | CARY PILLO LASSEN
CLIENT | CARY PILLO LASSEN

DESIGN FIRM | TANAGRAM

DESIGNER/ILLUSTRATOR | ANTHONY MA

CLIENT | LANKMAR CORPORATION

TOOLS | MACROMEDIA FREEHAND, ADOBE PHOTOSHOP

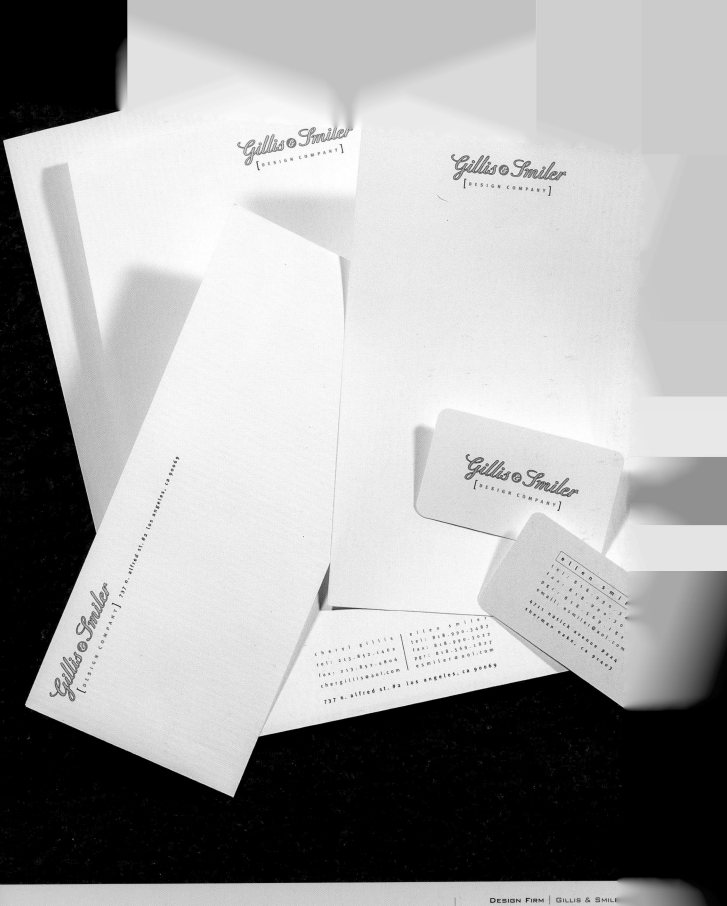

Gillis & Smiler
[DESIGN COMPANY]

Gillis & Smiler
[DESIGN COMPANY]

Gillis & Smiler
[DESIGN COMPANY]

Gillis & Smiler
[DESIGN COMPANY] 737 n. alfred st. #2 los angeles, ca 90069

cheryl gillis
tel: 213.852.1462
fax: 213.852.4806
chergillis@aol.com

ellen smiler
tel: 818.990.3487
fax: 818.990.3022
pgr: 818.569.1827
esmiler@aol.com

737 n. alfred st. #2 los angeles, ca 90069

ellen smiler
tel: 818.990.3
fax: 818.990.3
pgr: 818.569.182
email: esmiler@aol.com
4711 natick avenue #224
sherman oaks, ca 91403

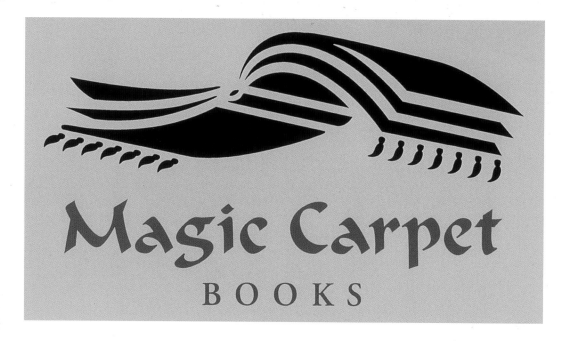

DESIGN FIRM | MIRES DESIGN
ART DIRECTOR | JOSÉ SERRANO
ILLUSTRATOR | TRACY SABIN
CLIENT | HARCOURT BRACE & COMPANY/MAGIC CARPET BOOKS
TOOLS | ADOBE ILLUSTRATOR

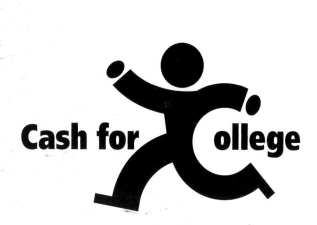

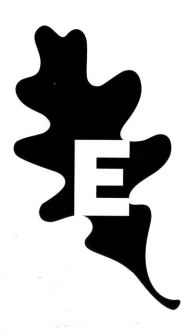

DESIGN FIRM | TIM NOONAN DESIGN
DESIGNER | TIM NOONAN
CLIENT | FIRSTAR BANK
TOOLS | ADOBE ILLUSTRATOR, QUARKXPRESS

DESIGN FIRM | MICHAEL STANARD DESIGN, INC.
ART DIRECTOR | MICHAEL STANARD
DESIGNERS | MICHAEL STANARD, KRISTY VANDEKERCKHOVE
ILLUSTRATOR | KRISTY VANDEKERCKHOVE
CLIENT | CITY OF EVANSTON
TOOLS | MACINTOSH, ADOBE ILLUSTRATOR

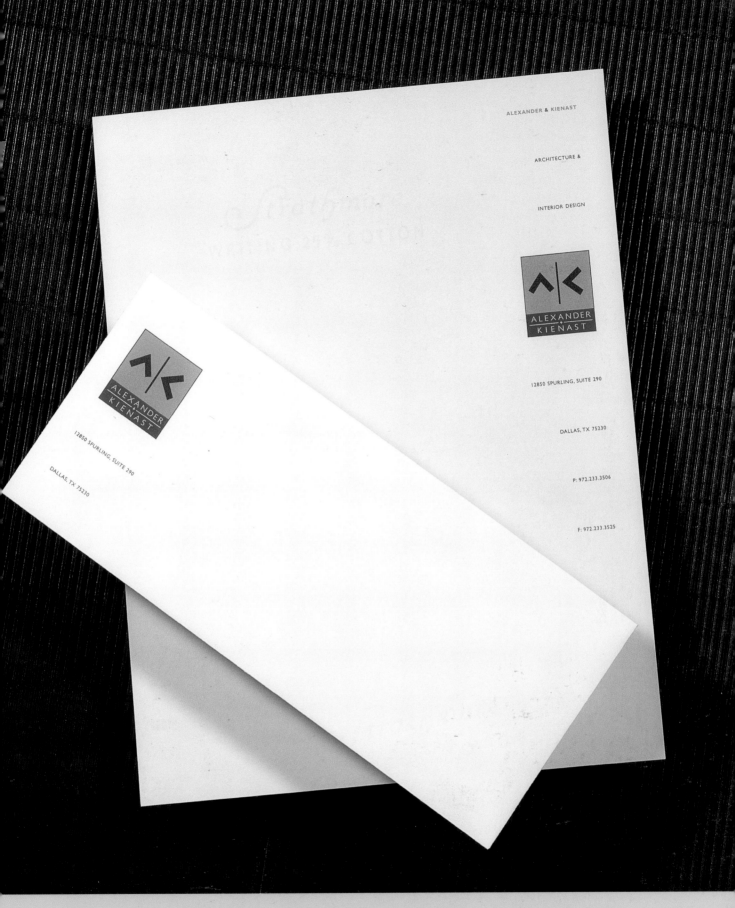

ALEXANDER & KIENAST

ARCHITECTURE &

INTERIOR DESIGN

12850 SPURLING, SUITE 290

DALLAS, TX 75230

P: 972.233.3506

F: 972.233.3525

12850 SPURLING, SUITE 290

DALLAS, TX 75230

DESIGN FIRM | SULLIVAN PERKINS
ART DIRECTOR/DESIGNER | MARCUS DICKERSON
CLIENT | ALEXANDER + KIENAST
TOOLS | MACINTOSH

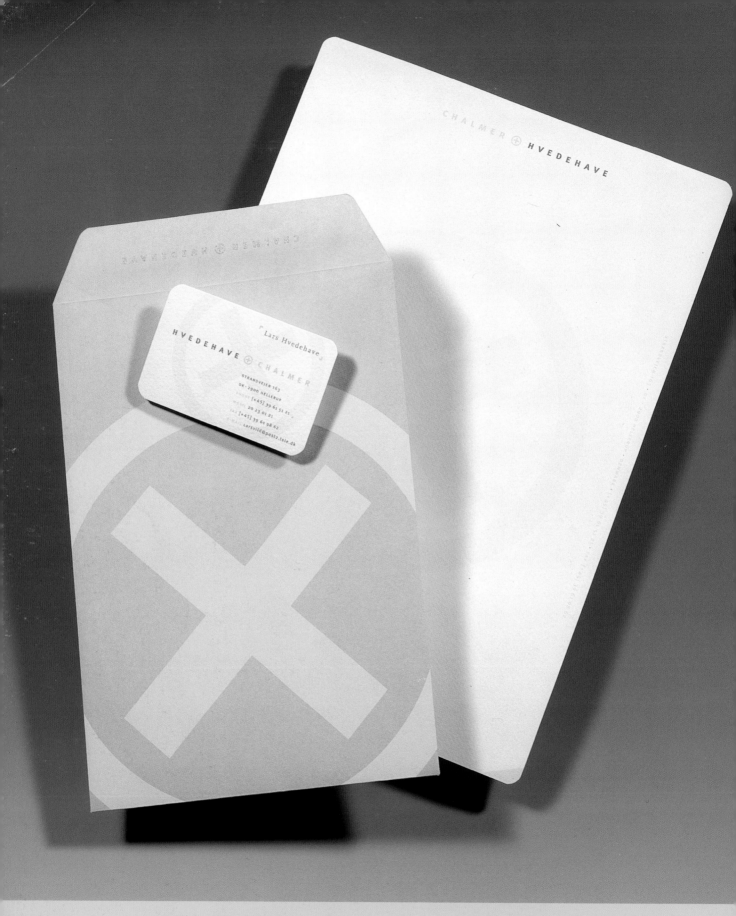

DESIGN FIRM | TRANSPARENT OFFICE

ART DIRECTOR/DESIGNER | VIBEKE NØDSKOV

CLIENT | CHALMER + HVEDEHAVE

TOOLS | QUARKXPRESS, ADOBE ILLUSTRATOR

PAPER/PRINTING | FAUNA RC 100G. IVORY/COLOR IT GREY

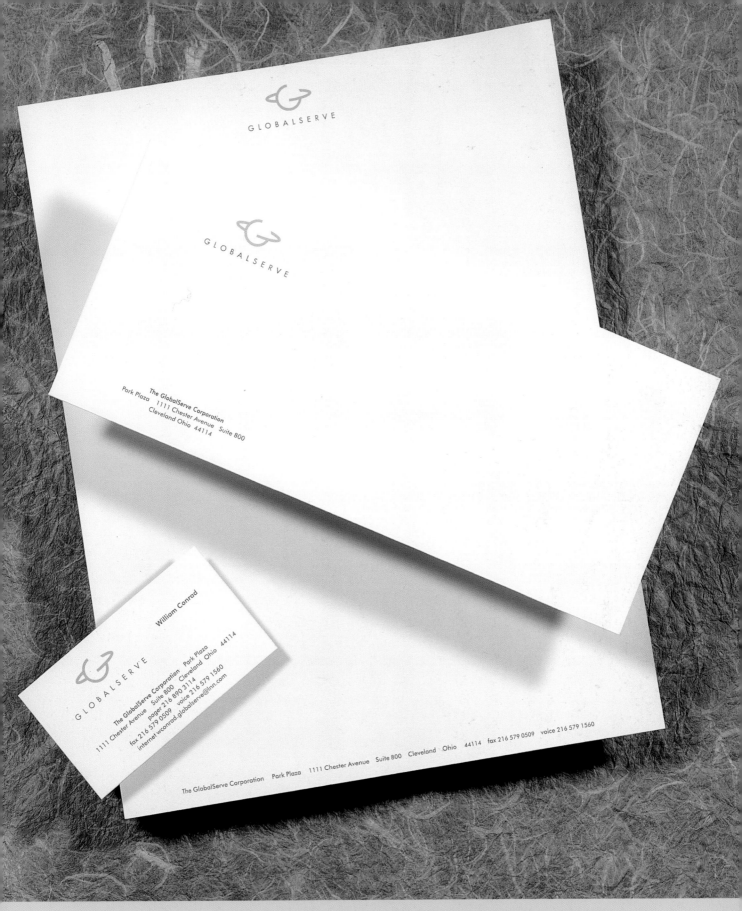

GLOBALSERVE

GLOBALSERVE

The GlobalServe Corporation
Park Plaza 1111 Chester Avenue Suite 800
Cleveland Ohio 44114

William Conrad

GLOBALSERVE

The GlobalServe Corporation Park Plaza
1111 Chester Avenue Suite 800 Cleveland Ohio 44114
pager 216 890 3114 voice 216 579 1560
fax 216 579 0509 internet wconrad.globalserve@lnn.com

The GlobalServe Corporation Park Plaza 1111 Chester Avenue Suite 800 Cleveland Ohio 44114 fax 216 579 0509 voice 216 579 1560

DESIGN FIRM | NESNADNY + SCHWARTZ

ALL DESIGN | GREGORY OZNOWICH

CLIENT | THE GLOBALSERVE CORPORATION

PAPER/PRINTING | MANADNOCK

STROLITE/HEXAGRAPHICS

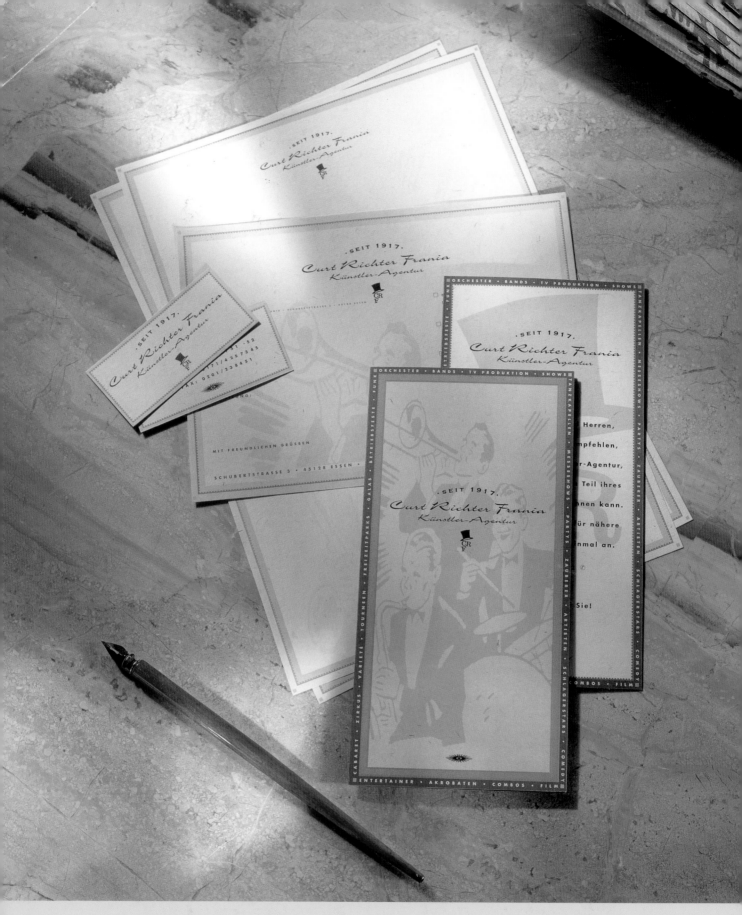

DESIGN FIRM | VOSS DESIGN

ART DIRECTOR/DESIGNER | AXEL VOSS

CLIENT | CURT RICHTER FANIA, ARTIST-AGENCY

PAPER/PRINTING | GMUND SILENCIUM

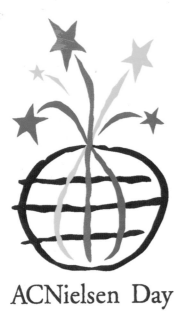

ACNielsen Day

DESIGN FIRM | WEBSTER DESIGN ASSOCIATES
ART DIRECTOR | DAVE WEBSTER
DESIGNER/ILLUSTRATOR | ANDREY NAGORNEY
CLIENT | ACNIELSEN
TOOLS | ADOBE ILLUSTRATOR

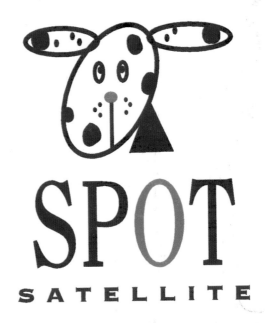

SPOT
SATELLITE

DESIGN FIRM | BARBARA BROWN MARKETING & DESIGN
ART DIRECTOR/DESIGNER | BARBARA BROWN
CLIENT | SPOT SATELLITE

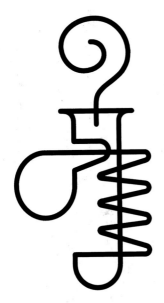

DESIGN FIRM | DESIGN CENTER
ART DIRECTOR | JOHN REGER
DESIGNER | SHERWIN SCHWARTZROCK
CLIENT | McGINLEY ASSOCIATES
TOOLS | MACINTOSH

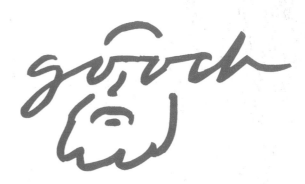

DESIGN FIRM | DOGSTAR
DESIGNER/ILLUSTRATOR | RODNEY DAVIDSON
CLIENT | MARK GOOCH PHOTOGRAPHY
TOOLS | ADOBE ILLUSTRATOR, STREAMLINE, MACROMEDIA FREEHAND

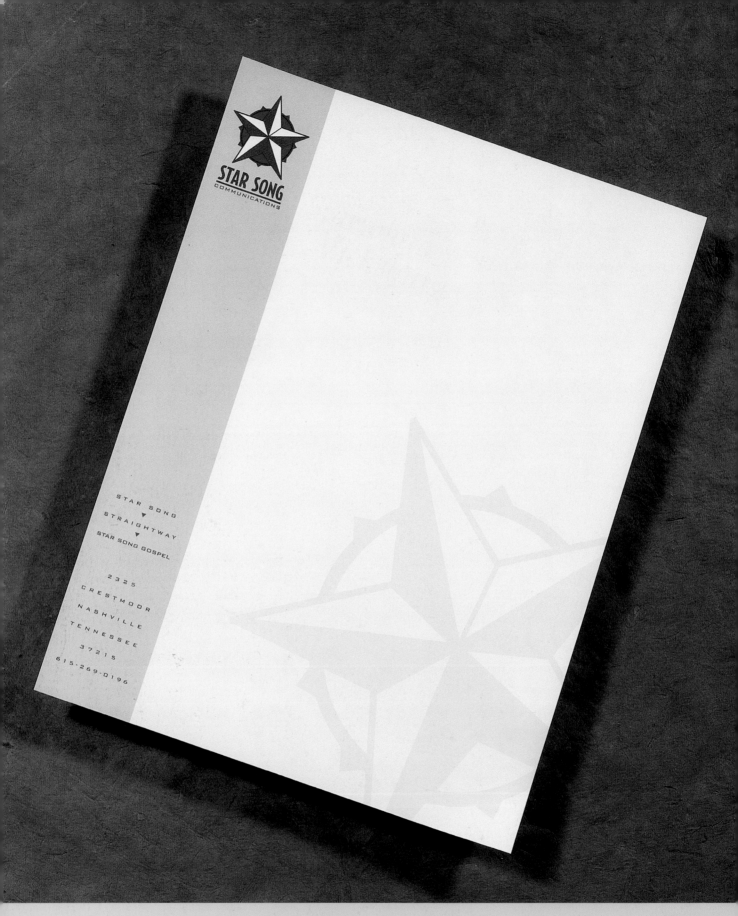

STAR SONG
▼
STRAIGHTWAY
▼
STAR SONG GOSPEL

2325
CRESTMOOR
NASHVILLE
TENNESSEE
37215
615-269-0196

DESIGN FIRM | ANDERSON-THOMAS DESIGN, INC.

ART DIRECTOR/DESIGNER | JOEL ANDERSON

CLIENT | STAR SONG COMMUNICATIONS

TOOLS | QUARKXPRESS, ADOBE ILLUSTRATOR

PAPER/PRINTING | CLASSIC CREST/BLACK AND 1 PMS

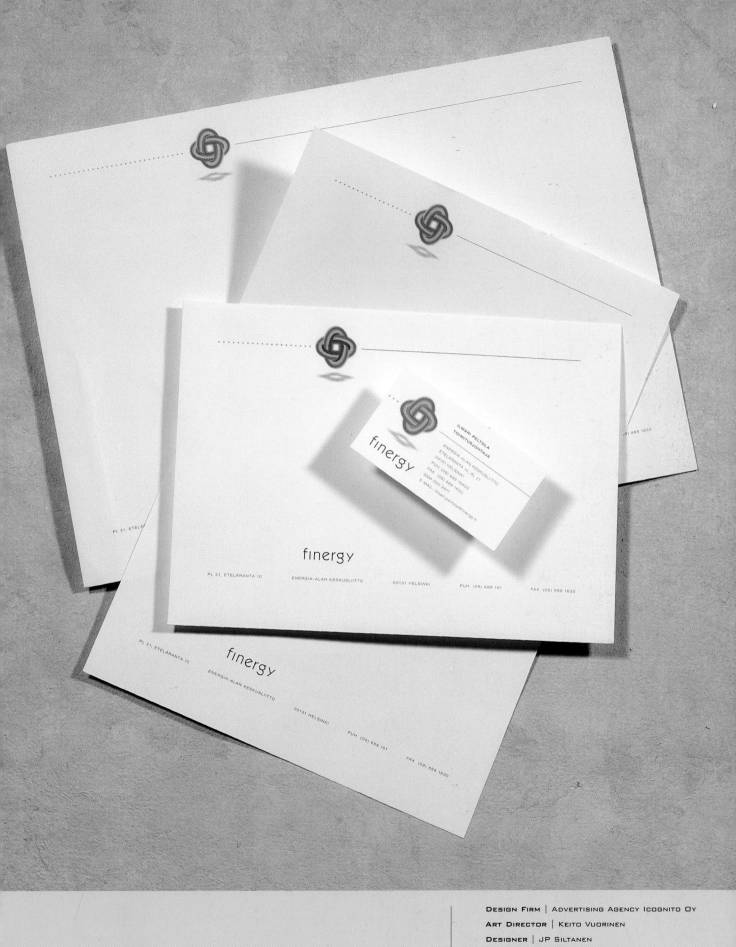

finergy

DESIGN FIRM | ADVERTISING AGENCY ICOGNITO OY

ART DIRECTOR | KEITO VUORINEN

DESIGNER | JP SILTANEN

ILLUSTRATOR | KEITO VUORINEN

CLIENT | ENERGIA-ALAN KESKUSLIITTO

TOOLS | MACROMEDIA FREEHAND, ADOBE PHOTOSHOP

PAPER/PRINTING | F. G. LÖNNBERG

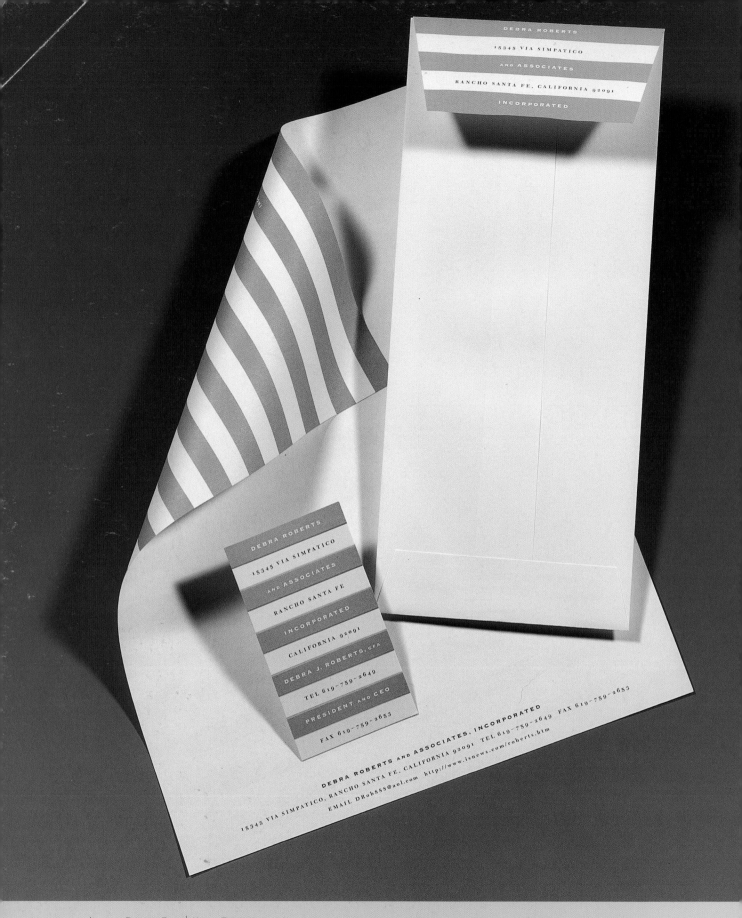

DESIGN FIRM | MIRES DESIGN
ART DIRECTOR | SCOTT MIRES
DESIGNERS | DEBORAH HORN, SCOTT MIRES
CLIENT | DEBRA ROBERTS AND ASSOCIATES

BEST CASE SOLUTIONS

BEST CASE SOLUTIONS

BEST CASE SOLUTIONS

BEST CASE SOLUTIONS

JOHN J. MANCINI
President

BEST CASE SOLUTIONS, INC.
635 CHICAGO AVENUE, SUITE 110
EVANSTON, ILLINOIS 60202
708.492.8037 TELEPHONE
708.492.8038 FACSIMILE
800.492.8037 TOLL FREE

BEST CASE SOLUTIONS, INC.
635 CHICAGO AVENUE, SUITE 110, EVANSTON, ILLINOIS 60202
708.492.8037 TELEPHONE, 708.492.8038 FACSIMILE, 800.492.8037 TOLL FREE

DESIGN FIRM | MICHAEL STANARD DESIGN, INC.
ART DIRECTOR | MICHAEL STANARD
DESIGNER | KRISTY VANDEKERCKHOVE
CLIENT | JOHN MANCINI
TOOLS | MACINTOSH, ADOBE ILLUSTRATOR
PAPER/PRINTING | STRATHMORE WRITING

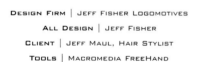

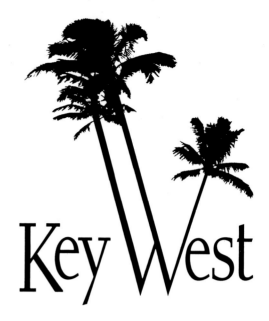

DESIGN FIRM | JEFF FISHER LOGOMOTIVES

ALL DESIGN | JEFF FISHER

CLIENT | JEFF MAUL, HAIR STYLIST

TOOLS | MACROMEDIA FREEHAND

DESIGN FIRM | MacVicar Design & Communications

ALL DESIGN | William A. Gordon

CLIENT | Federal Data Corporation

TOOLS | Pen, ink; Adobe Illustrator

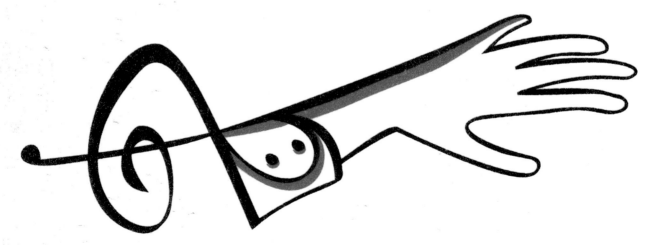

Vladimir Svoysky

DESIGN FIRM | CECILY ROBERTS DESIGN

ALL DESIGN | CECILY ROBERTS

CLIENT | VLADIMIR SVOYSKY

TOOLS | MACROMEDIA FREEHAND, QUARKXPRESS

PAPER/PRINTING | 80 LB. COVER ESSE, WHITE SMOOTH

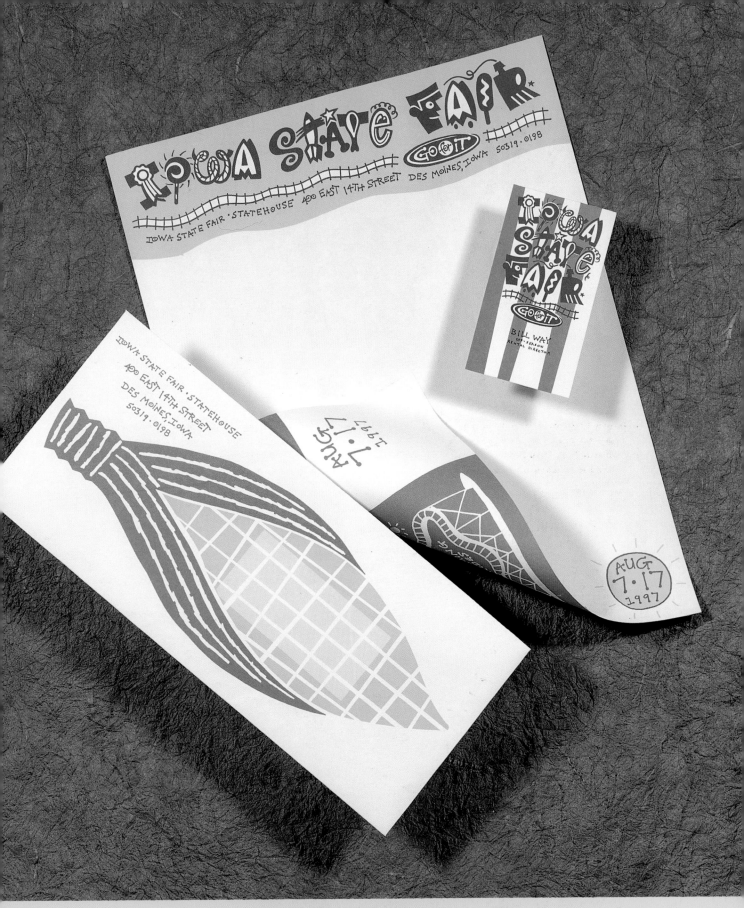

DESIGN FIRM │ SAYLES GRAPHIC DESIGN
ART DIRECTOR/ILLUSTRATOR │ JOHN SAYLES
DESIGNER │ JOHN SAYLES, JENNIFER ELLIOTT
CLIENT │ IOWA STATE FAIR

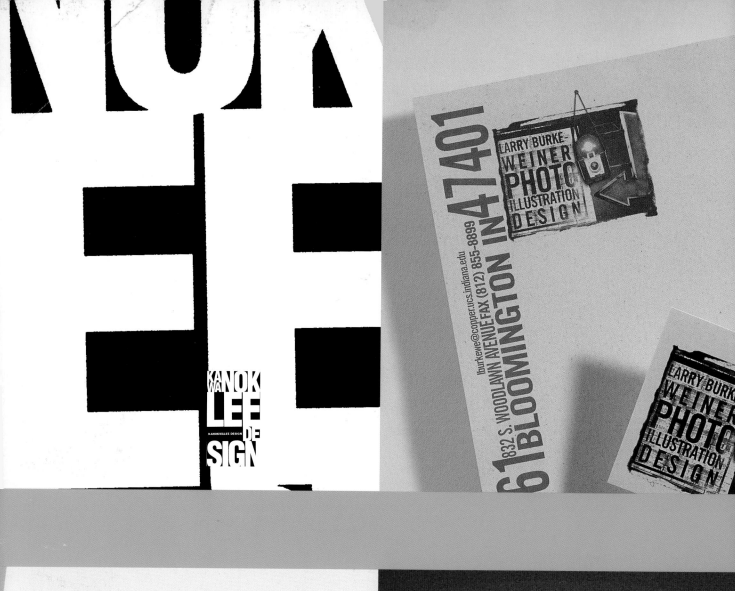

NOR
LEE

KANOKWA
NOK
LEE
DE
SIGN

KANOKWALEE DESIGN

LARRY BURKE-
WEINER
PHOTO
ILLUSTRATION
DESIGN

47401

lburkewe@copper.ucs.indiana.edu

(812) 855-8899

AVENUE FAX

1832 S. WOODLAWN

61 BLOOMINGTON IN

LARRY BURKE-
WEINER
PHOTO
ILLUSTRATION
DESIGN

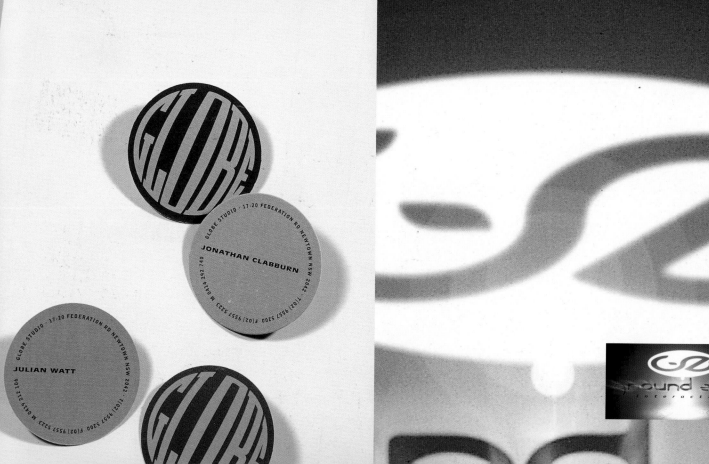

GLOBE

GLOBE STUDIO · 17-20 FEDERATION RD NEWTOWN NSW 2042
JONATHAN CLABBURN
T [02] 9557 5200 F [02] 9557 5223 M 0414 242 740

GLOBE STUDIO · 17-20 FEDERATION RD NEWTOWN NSW 2042
JULIAN WATT
T [02] 9557 5200 F [02] 9557 5223 M 0419 212 106

GLOBE

ground zero
interactive

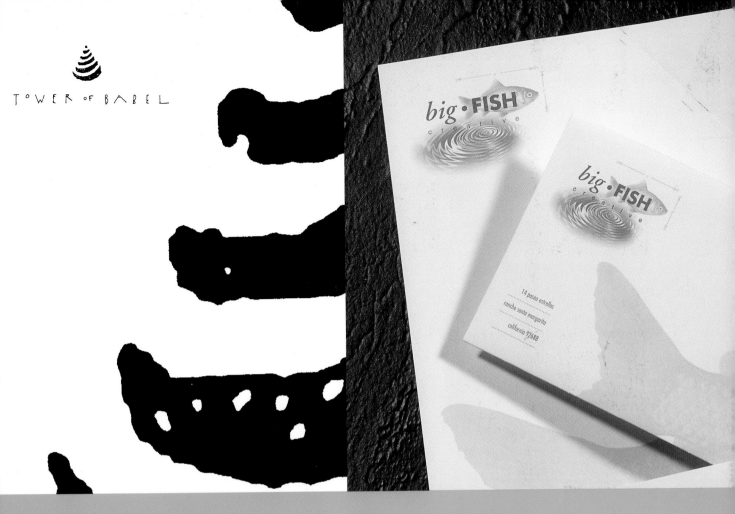

TOWER OF BABEL

big•FISH
creative

14 paseo estrellas
rancho santa margarita
california 92688

CREATIVE SERVICES

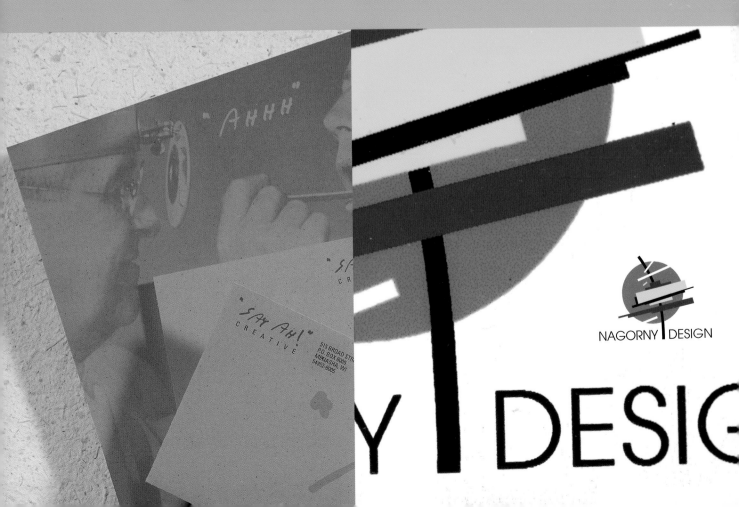

"AHHH

"SAY AH!"
CREATIVE

"SAY AH!"
CREATIVE
515 BROAD STR
P.O. BOX 800
MENASHA, WI
54952-8005

NAGORNY DESIGN

Y DESIG

KANOK
WA
LEE
KANOKWALEE DESIGN
DE
SIGN

DESIGN FIRM | KANOKWALEE DESIGN
ART DIRECTOR/DESIGNER | KANOKWALEE LEE
CLIENT | KANOKWALEE DESIGN
TOOLS | ADOBE ILLUSTRATOR, QUARKXPRESS

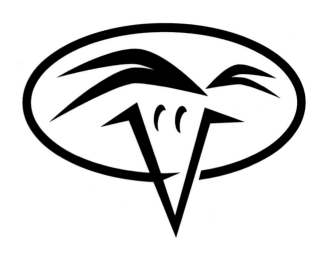

DESIGN FIRM | GET SMART DESIGN COMPANY
DESIGNER/ILLUSTRATOR | TOM CULBERTSON
CLIENT | JODY VANDERAH/"V" MAN
TOOLS | MACROMEDIA FREEHAND

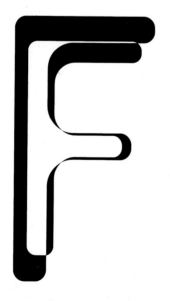

DESIGN FIRM | FORDESIGN
ALL DESIGN | FRANK FORD
CLIENT | FORDESIGN
TOOLS | ADOBE ILLUSTRATOR

JEFF FISHER
LOGO
MOTIVES

DESIGN FIRM | JEFF FISHER LOGOMOTIVES
ALL DESIGN | JEFF FISHER
CLIENT | LOGOMOTIVES
TOOLS | MACROMEDIA FREEHAND

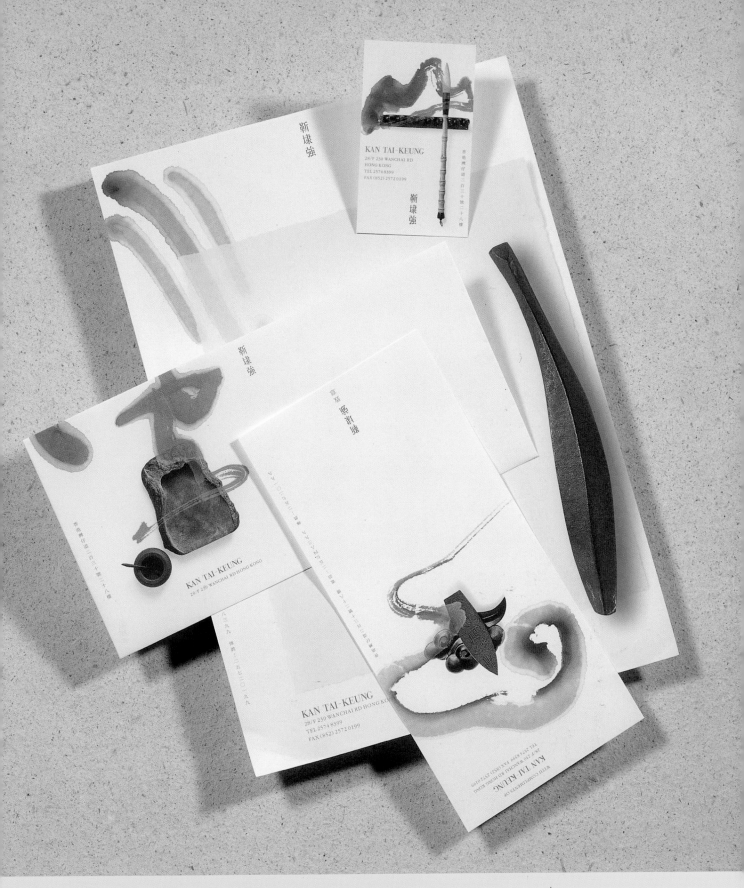

KAN TAI-KEUNG
28/F 250 WANCHAI RD
HONG KONG
TEL 2574 8399
FAX (852) 2572 0199

靳埭強

KAN TAI-KEUNG
28/F 250 WANCHAI RD HONG KONG

KAN TAI-KEUNG
28/F 250 WANCHAI RD HONG KONG
TEL 2574 8399
FAX (852) 2572 0199

DESIGN FIRM | KAN & LAU DESIGN CONSULTANTS

ART DIRECTOR/DESIGNER | KAN TAI-KEUNG

CLIENT | KAN TAI-KEUNG

TOOLS | NAME CARD: CONQUEROR DIAMOND WHITE CX22 250GSM; LETTERHEAD: CONQUEROR DIAMOND WHITE CX22 100GSM; ENVELOPE: CONQUEROR HIGHWHITE WOVE 100GSM/OFFSET

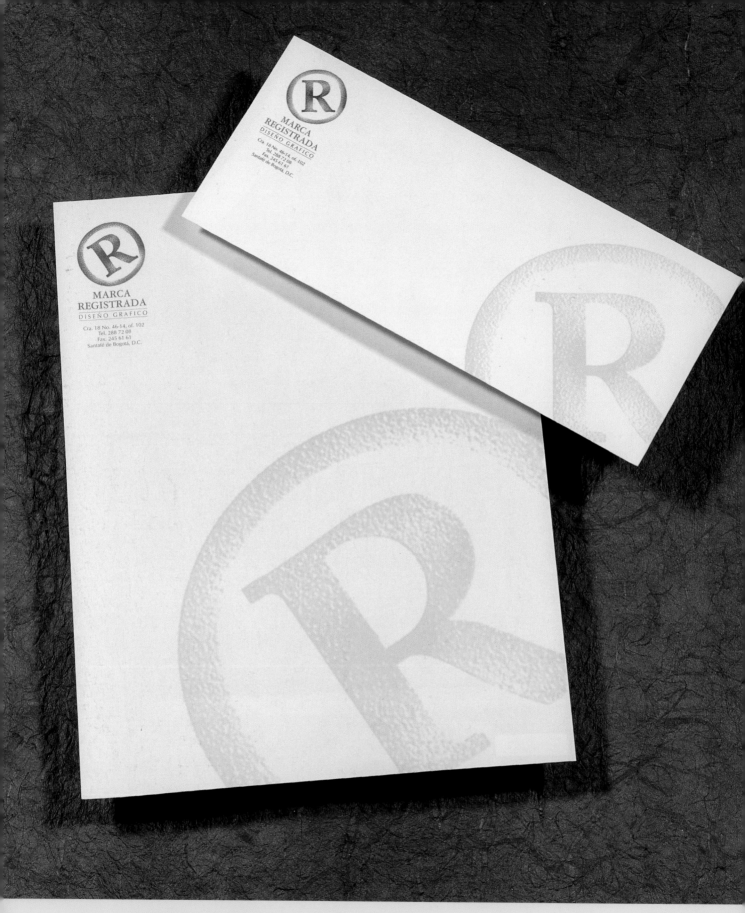

DESIGN FIRM | MARCA REGISTRADA DISEÑO GRAFICO

ART DIRECTOR | IVÁN CORREA

DESIGNER | MARTHA CADENA

ILLUSTRATOR | HENRY GONZÁLEZ

CLIENT | MARCA REGISTRADA DISEÑO GRAFICO

TOOLS | ADOBE PHOTOSHOP, MACINTOSH

PAPER/PRINTING | EDICIONES ANTROPOS (TORREÓN OFFSET)

DESIGN FIRM | GAF ADVERTISING DESIGN

ALL DESIGN | GREGG A. FLOYD

CLIENT | GAF ADVERTISING DESIGN

TOOLS | WOODCUT, QUARKXPRESS

PAPER/PRINTING | CONCRET/TWO COLOR SPOT LITHO

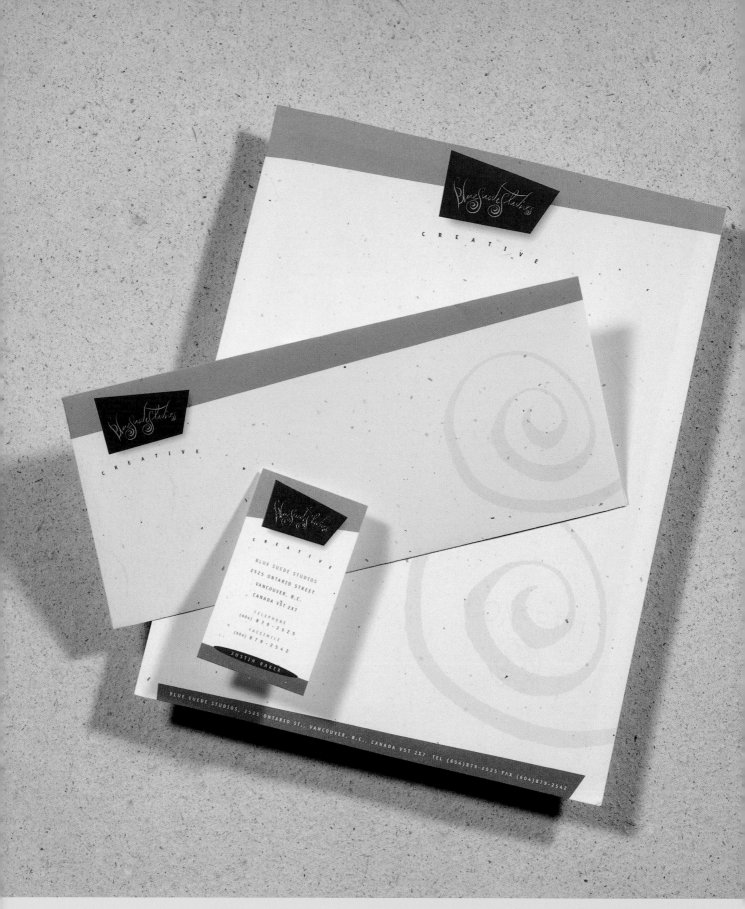

DESIGN FIRM | BLUE SUEDE STUDIOS
ART DIRECTOR | DAVE KENNEDY
DESIGNER/ILLUSTRATOR | JUSTIN BAKER
CLIENT | BLUE SUEDE STUDIOS
PAPER/PRINTING | CONFETTI/ULTRATECH PRINTERS

DESIGN FIRM | ABLE DESIGN, INC.

ART DIRECTORS | STUART HARVEY LEE, MARTHA DAVIS

DESIGNER | MARTIN PERRIN

CLIENT | ABLE DESIGN, INC.

TOOLS | POWER MACINTOSH, QUARKXPRESS

PAPER/PRINTING | BECKETT EXPRESSION, ICEBERG, 24 LB.

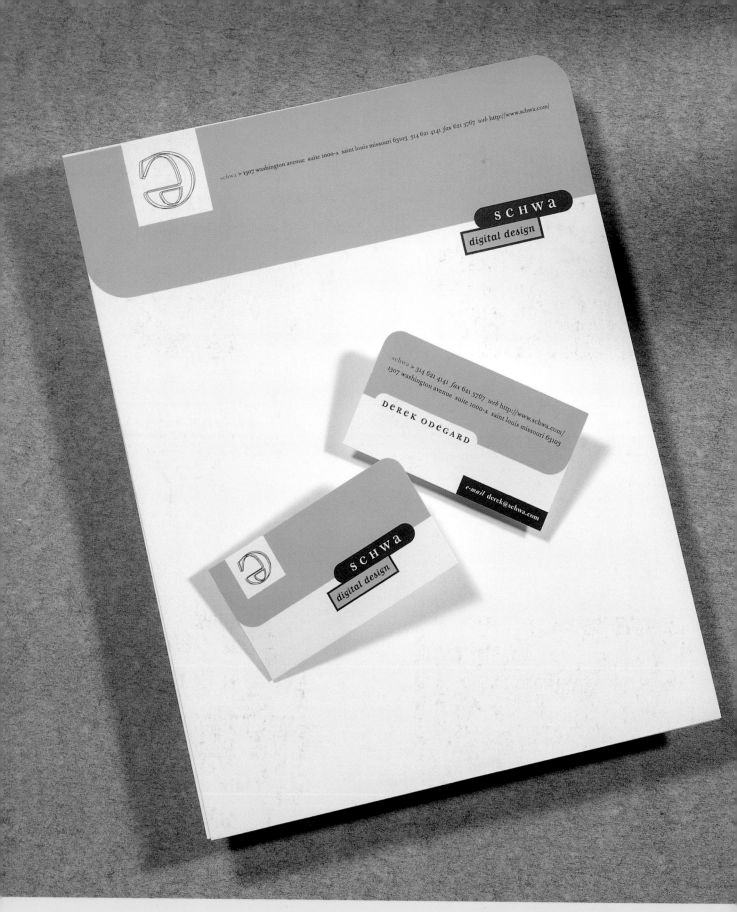

DESIGN FIRM | PHOENIX CREATIVE
ART DIRECTOR | ERIC THOELKE
DESIGNERS/ILLUSTRATORS | ERIC THOELKE, STEVE WIENKE
CLIENT | SCHWA DIGITAL DESIGN
TOOLS | ADOBE ILLUSTRATOR, QUARKXPRESS

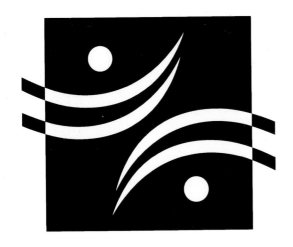

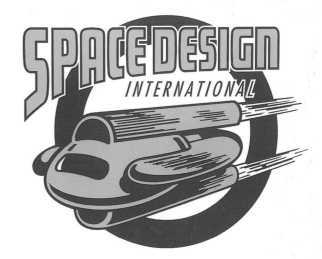

DESIGN FIRM | STEWART MONDERER DESIGN, INC.
ART DIRECTOR | STEWART MONDERER
DESIGNERS | AIME LECUSAY, STEWART MONDERER
ILLUSTRATOR | AIME LECUSAY
CLIENT | CORPORATE COMMUNICATIONS, INC.
TOOLS | ADOBE ILLUSTRATOR

DESIGN FIRM | SPACE DESIGN INTERNATIONAL
ALL DESIGN | TIM A. FRAME
CLIENT | SPACE DESIGN INTERNATIONAL
TOOLS | ADOBE ILLUSTRATOR

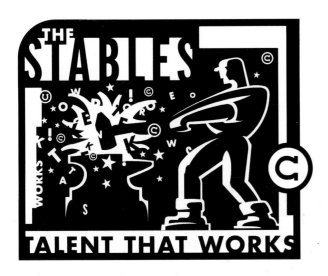

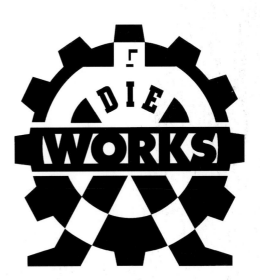

DESIGN FIRM | INSIGHT DESIGN COMMUNICATIONS
ALL DESIGN | SHERRIE HOLDEMAN, TRACY HOLDEMAN
CLIENT | THE STABLES
TOOLS | POWER MACINTOSH, MACROMEDIA FREEHAND

DESIGN FIRM | WEBSTER DESIGN ASSOCIATES
ART DIRECTOR | DAVE WEBSTER
DESIGNER/ILLUSTRATOR | ANDREY NAGORNY
CLIENT | DIE WORKS
TOOLS | MACROMEDIA FREEHAND

www.mmasia.com

MULTIMEDIA
A S I A
22

Multimedia Asia Inc.

USA
P.O. Box 18416
San Jose, California
95158

Asia
P.O. Box 1345
Ortigas Center
Metro Manila
PHILIPPINES
1653

Asia: P.O. Box 1345 Ortigas Center Metro Manila, PHILIPPINES 1653 • Tel: (63-2) 7160670 Fax: (63-2) 7135182 **USA:** P.O. Box 18416 San Jose, California 95158 • Tel/Auto Fax: (408) 264-7799

DESIGN FIRM | MULTIMEDIA ASIA, INC.

ART DIRECTOR | G. LEE

CLIENT | MULTIMEDIA ASIA, INC.

TOOLS | ADOBE PAGEMAKER

PAPER/PRINTING | 80 LB. MILKWEED GENESIS

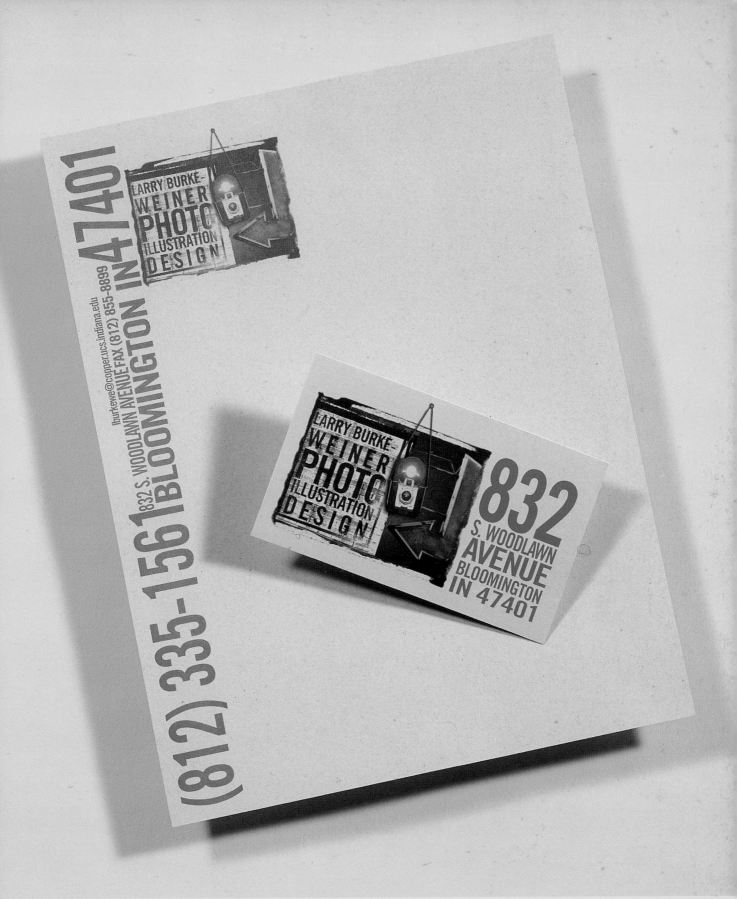

LARRY BURKE WEINER PHOTO ILLUSTRATION DESIGN

lburkewe@copper.ucs.indiana.edu
832 S. WOODLAWN AVENUE FAX (812) 855-8899
832 S. WOODLAWN BLOOMINGTON IN 47401
(812) 335-1561

832 S. WOODLAWN AVENUE BLOOMINGTON IN 47401

DESIGN FIRM | LARRY BURKE-WEINER DESIGN

ALL DESIGN | LARRY BURKE-WEINER

CLIENT | LARRY BURKE-WEINER

TOOLS | ADOBE PHOTOSHOP, PAINTER,

ADOBE ILLUSTRATOR, QUARKXPRESS

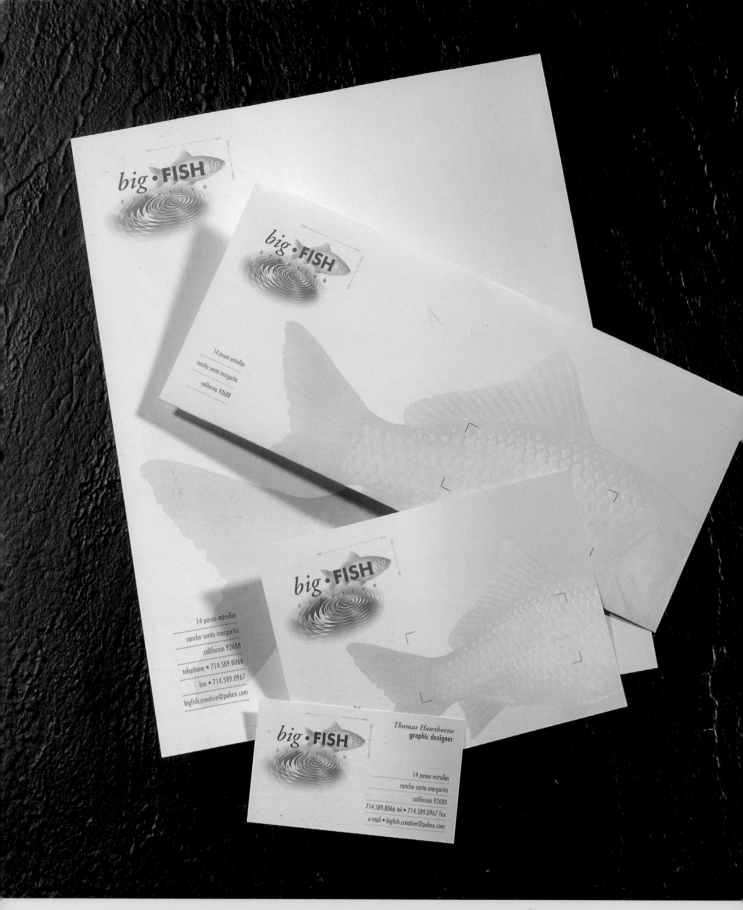

DESIGN FIRM | BIG FISH CREATIVE

ALL DESIGN | THOMAS HAWTHORNE

CLIENT | BIG FISH CREATIVE

TOOLS | QUARKXPRESS, ADOBE PHOTOSHOP, MACINTOSH

PAPER/PRINTING | STRATHMORE ELEMENTS

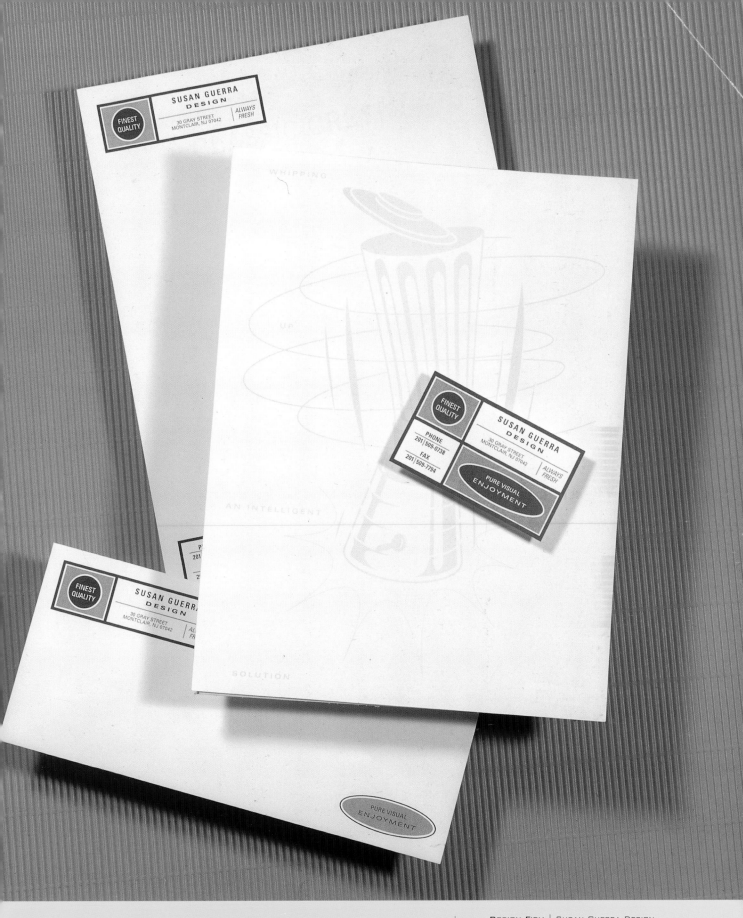

DESIGN FIRM | SUSAN GUERRA DESIGN

ART DIRECTOR/DESIGNER | SUSAN GUERRA

ILLUSTRATOR | METAL STUDIOS CLIP ART

CLIENT | SUSAN GUERRA DESIGN

TOOLS | QUARKXPRESS, ADOBE ILLUSTRATOR

PAPER/PRINTING | CLASSIC CREST/TWO COLOR

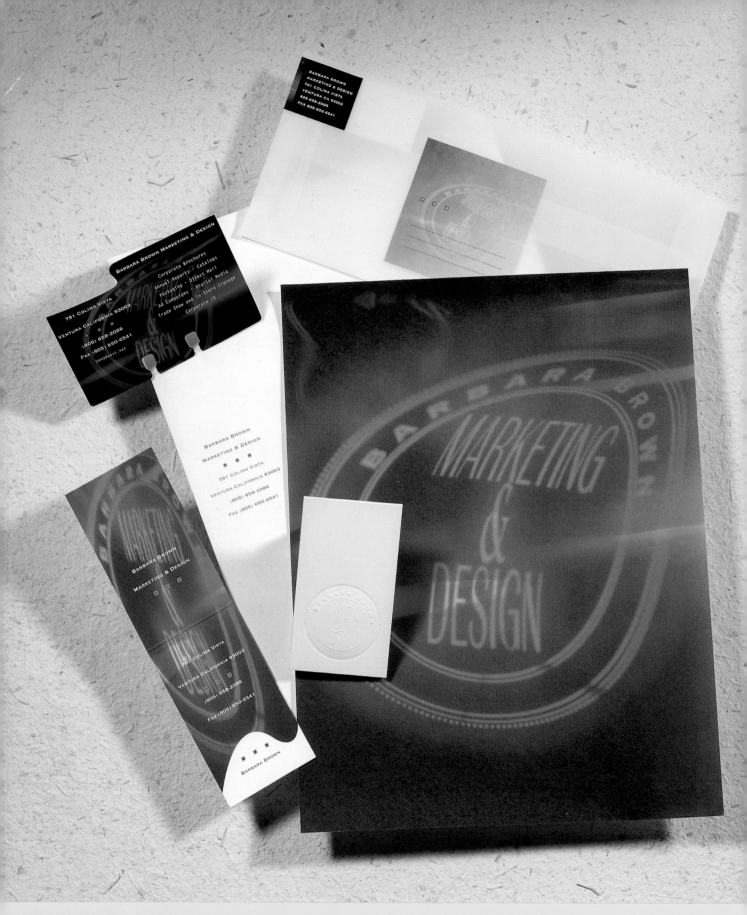

DESIGN FIRM | BARBARA BROWN MARKETING & DESIGN

ART DIRECTOR | BARBARA BROWN

DESIGNER | LANA CURTIN, PRODUCTION ARTIST

PHOTOGRAPHER | SCHAF PHOTO

CLIENT | BARBARA BROWN MARKETING & DESIGN

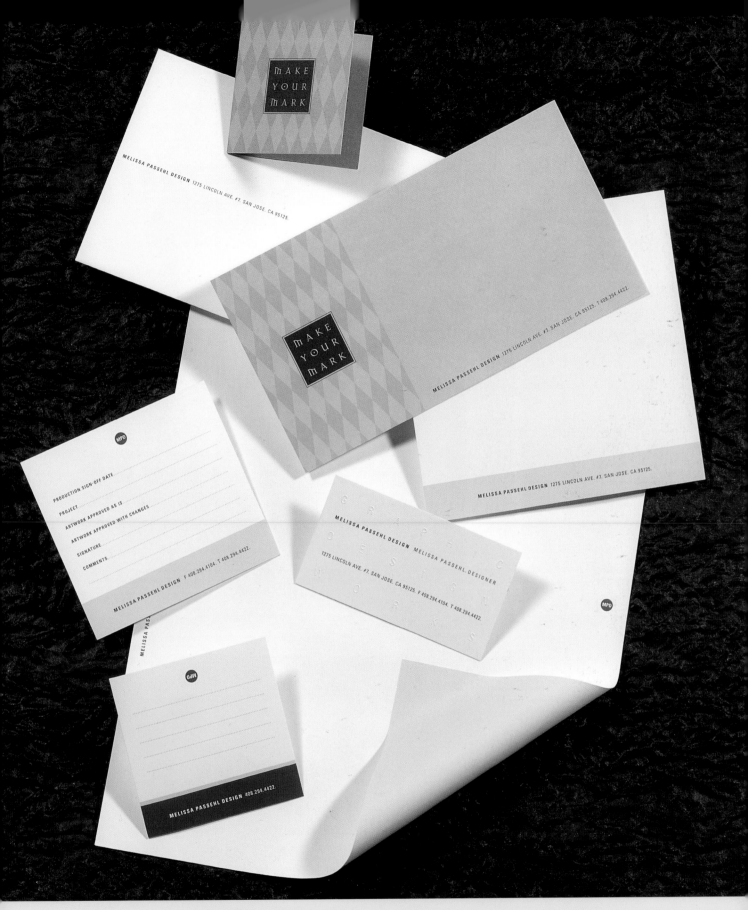

MAKE YOUR MARK

MELISSA PASSEHL DESIGN 1275 LINCOLN AVE. #7, SAN JOSE, CA 95125.

MELISSA PASSEHL DESIGN 1275 LINCOLN AVE. #7, SAN JOSE, CA 95125. T 408.294.4422.

MELISSA PASSEHL DESIGN 1275 LINCOLN AVE. #7, SAN JOSE, CA 95125.

PRODUCTION SIGN-OFF DATE

PROJECT

ARTWORK APPROVED AS IS

ARTWORK APPROVED WITH CHANGES

SIGNATURE

COMMENTS

MELISSA PASSEHL DESIGN F 408.294.4104. T 408.294.4422.

MELISSA PASSEHL DESIGN MELISSA PASSEHL, DESIGNER
1275 LINCOLN AVE. #7, SAN JOSE, CA 95125. F 408.294.4104. T 408.294.4422.

MELISSA PASSEHL DESIGN 408.294.4422.

DESIGN FIRM | MELISSA PASSEHL DESIGN
ART DIRECTOR | MELISSA PASSEHL
DESIGNERS | MELISSA PASSEHL, CHARLOTTE LAMBRECHTS
CLIENT | MELISSA PASSEHL DESIGN

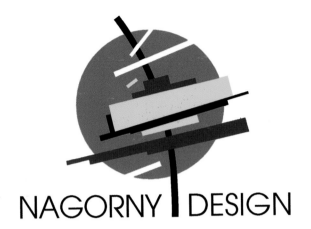

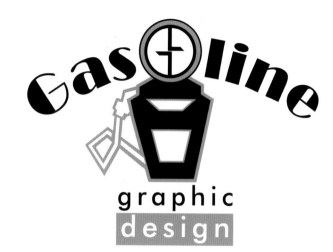

DESIGN FIRM | Nagorny Design
ALL DESIGN | Andrey Nagorny
CLIENT | Nagorny Design
TOOLS | Macromedia FreeHand

DESIGN FIRM | Gasoline Graphic Design
ART DIRECTORS | Angeline Beckley, Zane Vredenburg
DESIGNERS | Zane Vredenburg, Angeline Beckley
CLIENT | Gasoline Graphic Design
TOOLS | Adobe Illustrator

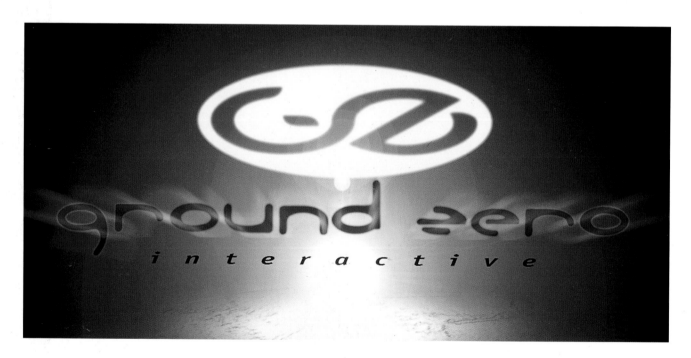

DESIGN FIRM | MBBIUS
ALL DESIGN | Chip Taylor
CLIENT | Ground Zero Interactive
TOOLS | Macintosh, Adobe Photoshop, Adobe Illustrator

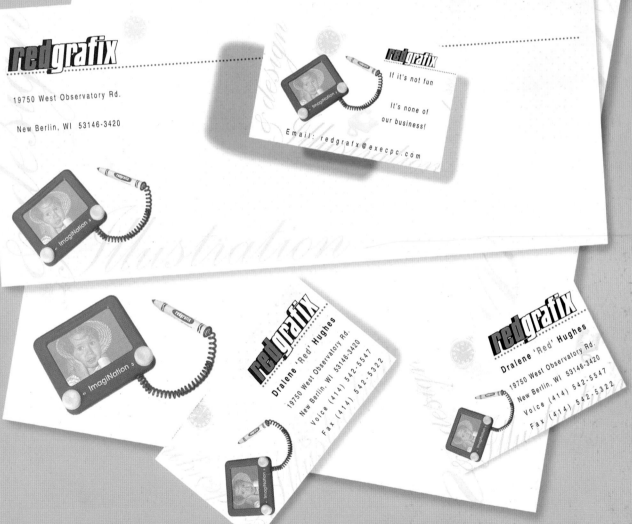

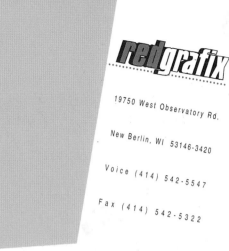

redgrafix

19750 West Observatory Rd.

New Berlin, WI 53146-3420

Voice (414) 542-5547

Fax (414) 542-5322

redgrafix

19750 West Observatory Rd.

New Berlin, WI 53146-3420

redgrafix

If it's not fun

It's none of

our business!

Email: redgrafx@execpc.com

redgrafix

Dralene "Red" Hughes

19750 West Observatory Rd.

New Berlin, WI 53146-3420

Voice (414) 542-5547

Fax (414) 542-5322

redgrafix

Dralene 'Red' Hughes

19750 West Observatory Rd.

New Berlin, WI 53146-3420

Voice (414) 542-5547

Fax (414) 542-5322

DESIGN FIRM | REDGRAFIX DESIGN & ILLUSTRATION

ALL DESIGN | DRALENE "RED" HUGHES

CLIENT | REDGRAFIX DESIGN & ILLUSTRATION

TOOLS | ADOBE PHOTOSHOP, ADOBE ILLUSTRATOR,
QUARKXPRESS

PAPER/PRINTING | STRATHMORE ELEMENTS
WHITE/FOUR COLOR, TI PRINTING

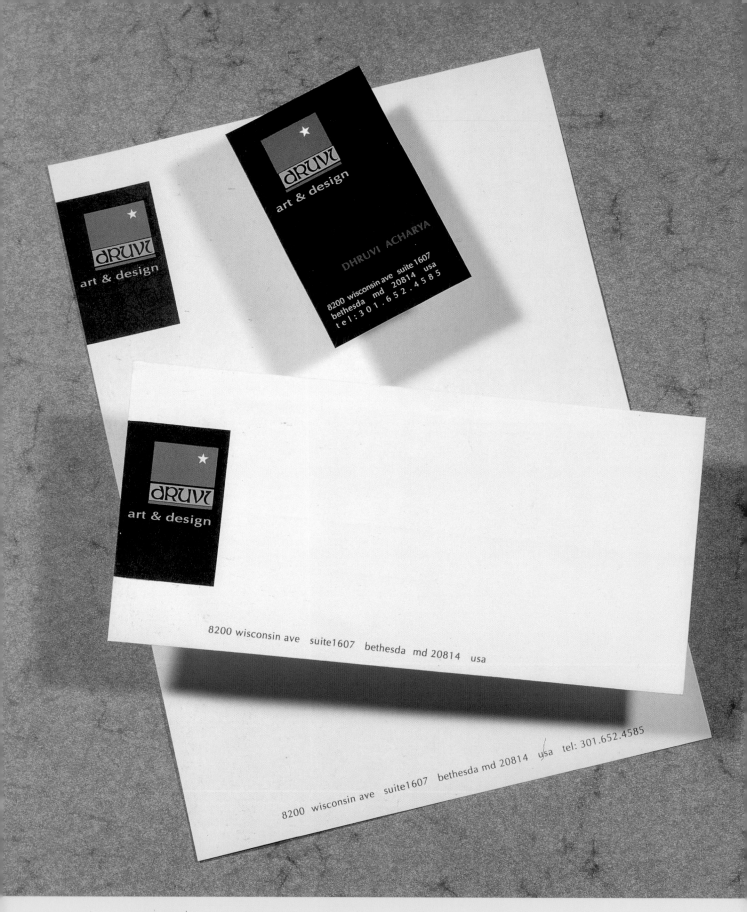

DESIGN FIRM │ DRUVI ART AND DESIGN

ALL DESIGN │ DRUVI ACHARYA

CLIENT │ DRUVI ART AND DESIGN

PAPER/PRINTING │ 80/100 LBS. CARD STOCK,

BOND PAPER/SCREENPRINTING

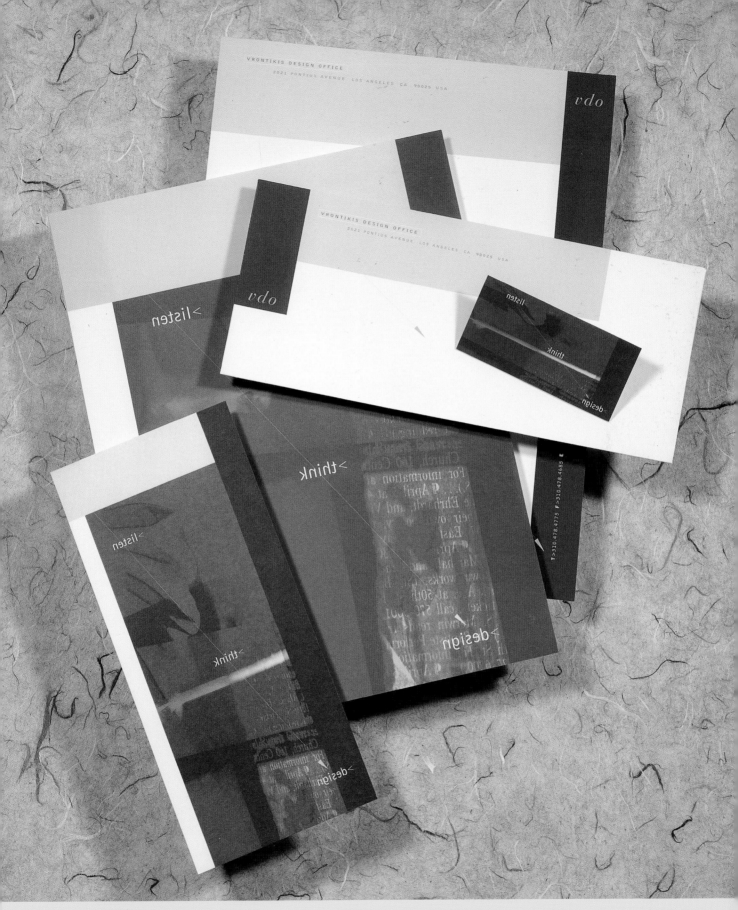

DESIGN FIRM | VRONTIKIS DESIGN OFFICE

ART DIRECTOR/DESIGNER | PETRULA VRONTIKIS

CLIENT | VRONTIKIS DESIGN OFFICE

TOOLS | QUARKXPRESS, ADOBE PHOTOSHOP

PAPER/PRINTING | NEENAH CLASSIC CREST/LOGIN PRINTING

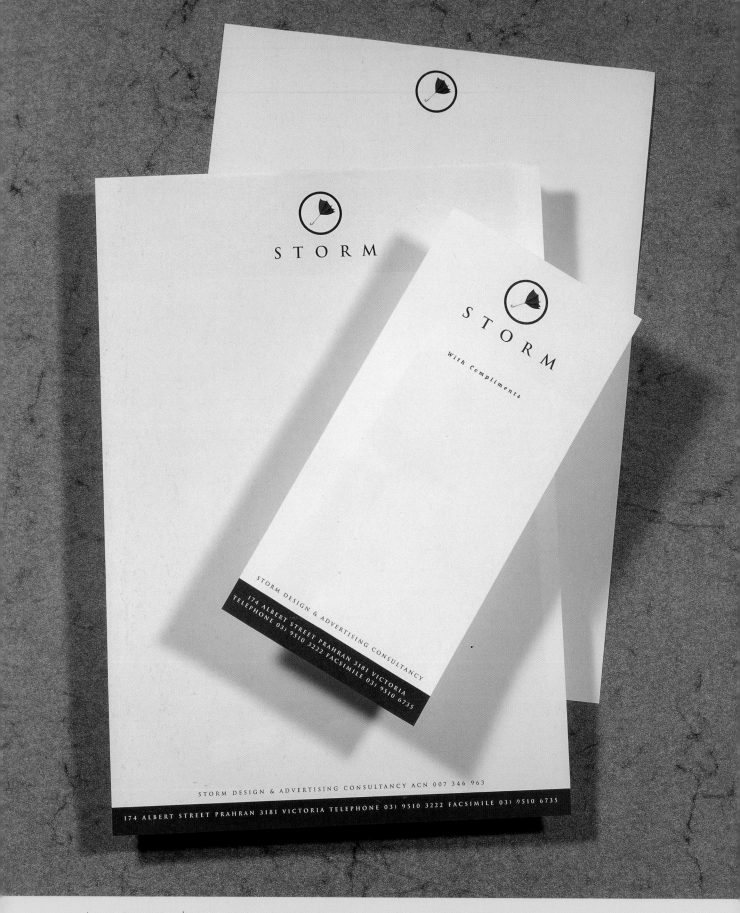

DESIGN FIRM │ STORM DESIGN & ADVERTISING CONSULTANCY

ART DIRECTORS/DESIGNERS │ DAVID ANSETT, DEAN BUTLER, JULIA JARVIS

PHOTOGRAPHER │ MARCUS STRUZINA

CLIENT │ STORM DESIGN & ADVERTISING CONSULTANCY

TOOLS │ ADOBE PHOTOSHOP

PAPER/PRINTING │ SAXTON SMOOTHE/FOUR COLOR PROCESS PLUS ONE

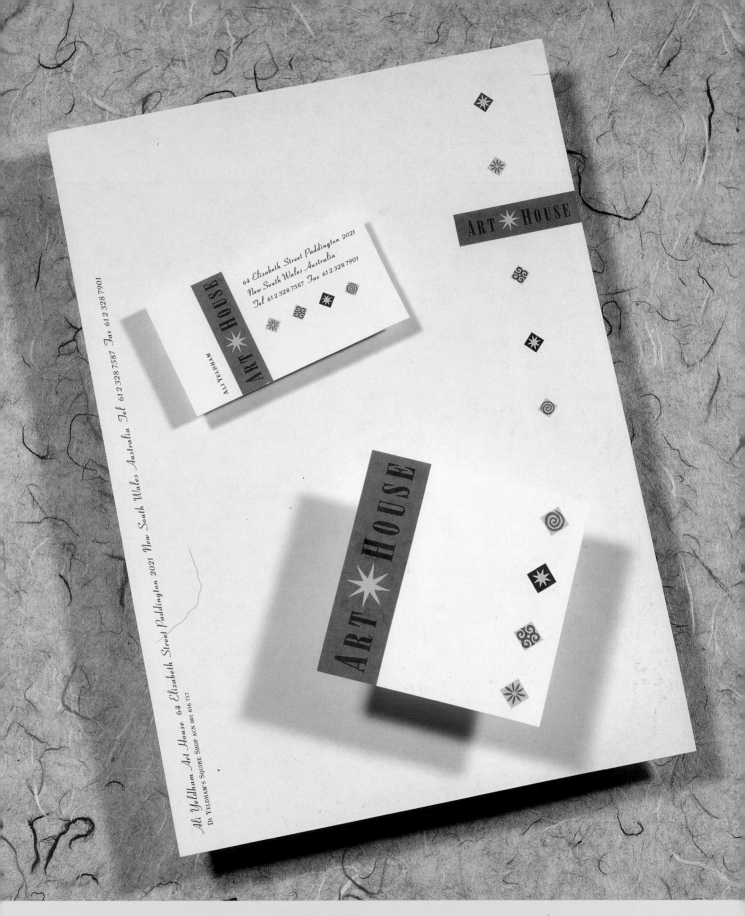

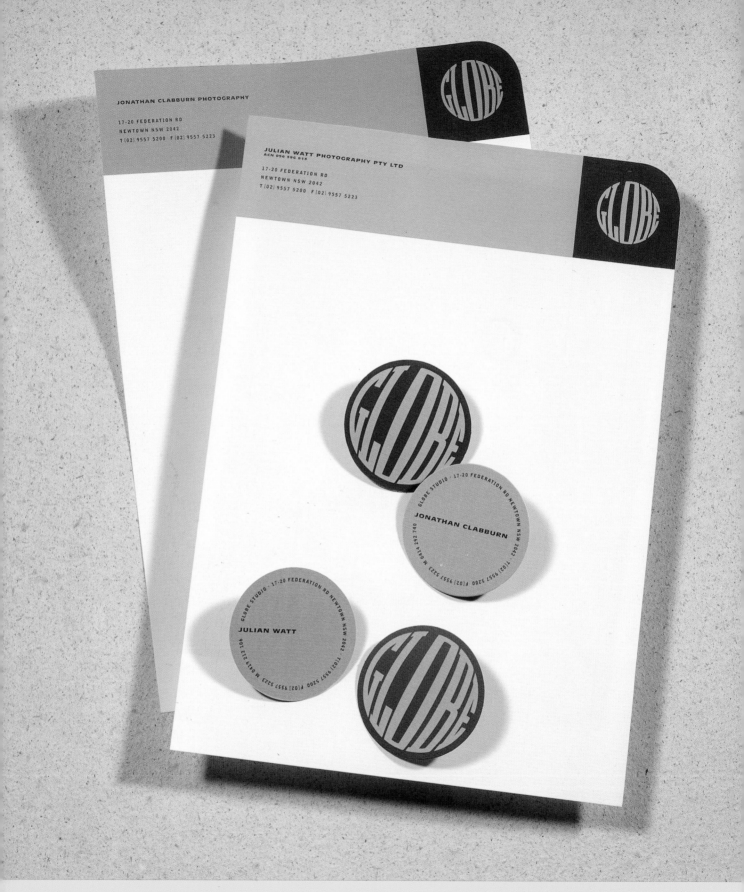

JONATHAN CLABBURN PHOTOGRAPHY

17-20 FEDERATION RD
NEWTOWN NSW 2042
T (02) 9557 5200 F (02) 9557 5223

JULIAN WATT PHOTOGRAPHY PTY LTD
ACN 056 596 819

17-20 FEDERATION RD
NEWTOWN NSW 2042
T (02) 9557 5200 F (02) 9557 5223

GLOBE STUDIO · 17-20 FEDERATION RD NEWTOWN NSW 2042 · T (02) 9557 5200 F (02) 9557 5223 M 0414 292 740

JONATHAN CLABBURN

GLOBE STUDIO · 17-20 FEDERATION RD NEWTOWN NSW 2042 · T (02) 9557 5200 F (02) 9557 5223 M 0419 213 106

JULIAN WATT

DESIGN FIRM | MOTHER GRAPHIC DESIGN
ART DIRECTOR/DESIGNER | KRISTIN THIEME
CLIENT | GLOBE STUDIO

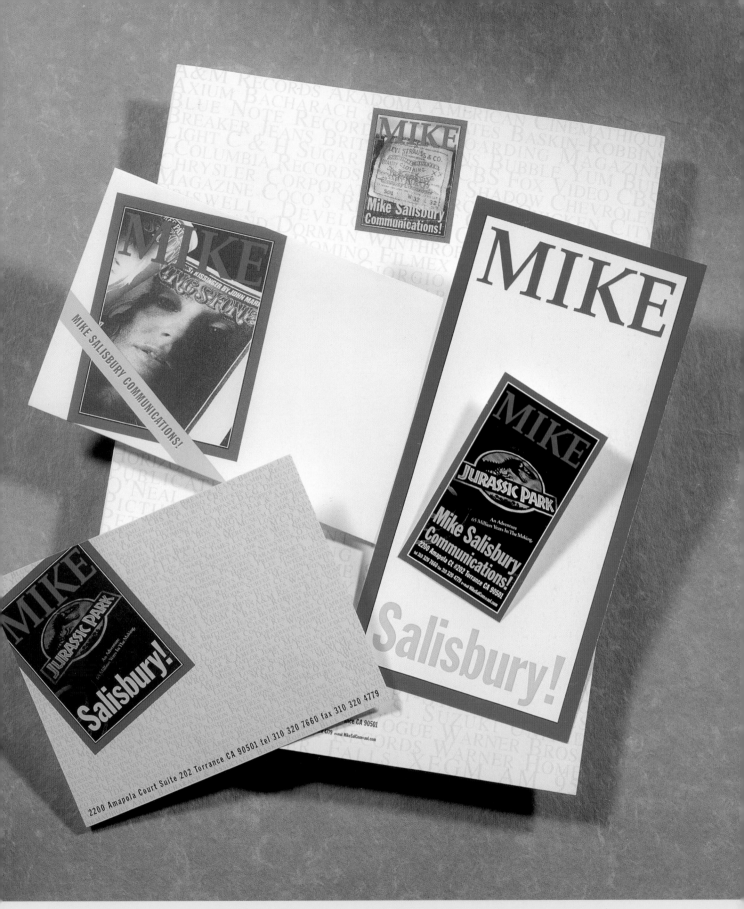

DESIGN FIRM | MIKE SALISBURY COMMUNICATIONS, INC.

ART DIRECTOR | MIKE SALISBURY

DESIGNER | MARY EVELYN MCGOUGH

CLIENT | MIKE SALISBURY COMMUNICATIONS

PLATINUM DESIGN, INC.
14 West 23rd St., New York, NY 10010
tel: 212-366-4000 fax: 212-366-4046

PLATINUM

PLATINUM DESIGN, INC.
14 West 23rd St., New York, NY 10010

PLATINUM

DESIGN FIRM | PLATINUM DESIGN, INC.

ART DIRECTOR/DESIGNER | VICTORIA STAMM

CLIENT | PLATINUM DESIGN, INC.

TOOLS | POWER MACINTOSH 8100

PAPER/PRINTING | CLR/STARWHITE VICKSBURG

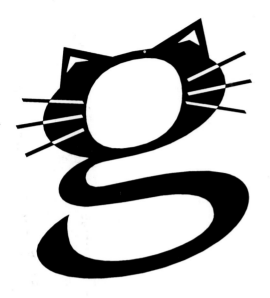

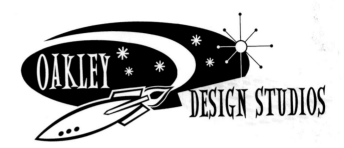

DESIGN FIRM | GRAY CAT DESIGN
DESIGNER | LISA SCALISE
CLIENT | GRAY CAT DESIGN
PAPER/PRINTING | MOHAWK SUPERFINE/LAKE PRINTERS

DESIGN FIRM | OAKLEY DESIGN STUDIOS
ALL DESIGN | TIM OAKLEY
CLIENT | OAKLEY DESIGN STUDIOS
TOOLS | ADOBE ILLUSTRATOR

JUICE

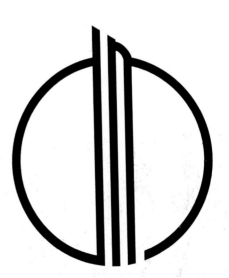

DESIGN FIRM | JUICE DESIGN
ART DIRECTOR | BRETT M. CRITCHLOW
DESIGNERS | BRETT M. CRITCHLOW, MATT SMIALEK, MIMI PAJO
CLIENT | JUICE DESIGN

DESIGN FIRM | MALIK DESIGN
ALL DESIGN | DONNA MALIK
CLIENT | MALIK DESIGN
TOOLS | MACROMEDIA FREEHAND
PAPER/PRINTING | STRATHMORE RENEWAL

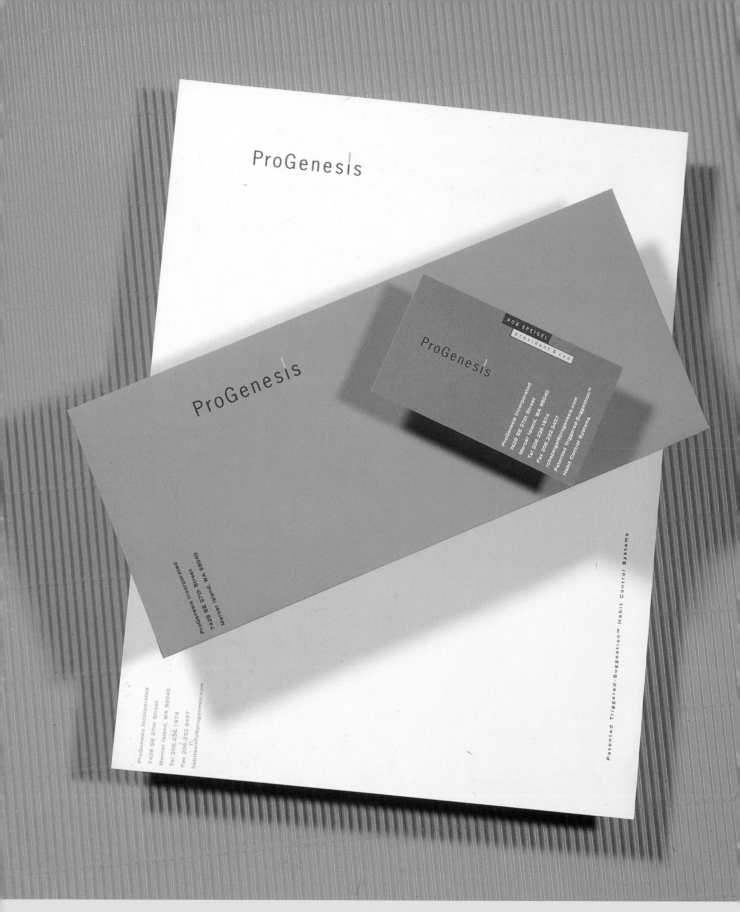

ProGenesis

ProGenesis

ProGenesis

ROB SPEIGEL
president & ceo

ProGenesis Incorporated
7429 SE 27th Street
Mercer Island, WA 98040
Tel 206.236.1974
Fax 206.232.9437
robspeigel@progenesis.com
Patented Triggered-Suggestion™
Habit Control Systems

ProGenesis Incorporated
7429 SE 27th Street,
Mercer Island, WA 98040

ProGenesis Incorporated
7429 SE 27th Street
Mercer Island, WA 98040
Tel 206.236.1974
Fax 206.232.9437
habitaxinfo@progenesis.com

Patented Triggered-Suggestion™ Habit Control Systems

DESIGN FIRM | WIDMEYER DESIGN

ART DIRECTORS | KEN WIDMEYER, DALE HART

DESIGNER | DALE HART

CLIENT | PROGENESIS

TOOLS | POWER MACINTOSH, MACROMEDIA FREEHAND

PAPER/PRINTING | ENVIRONMENT/OFFSET

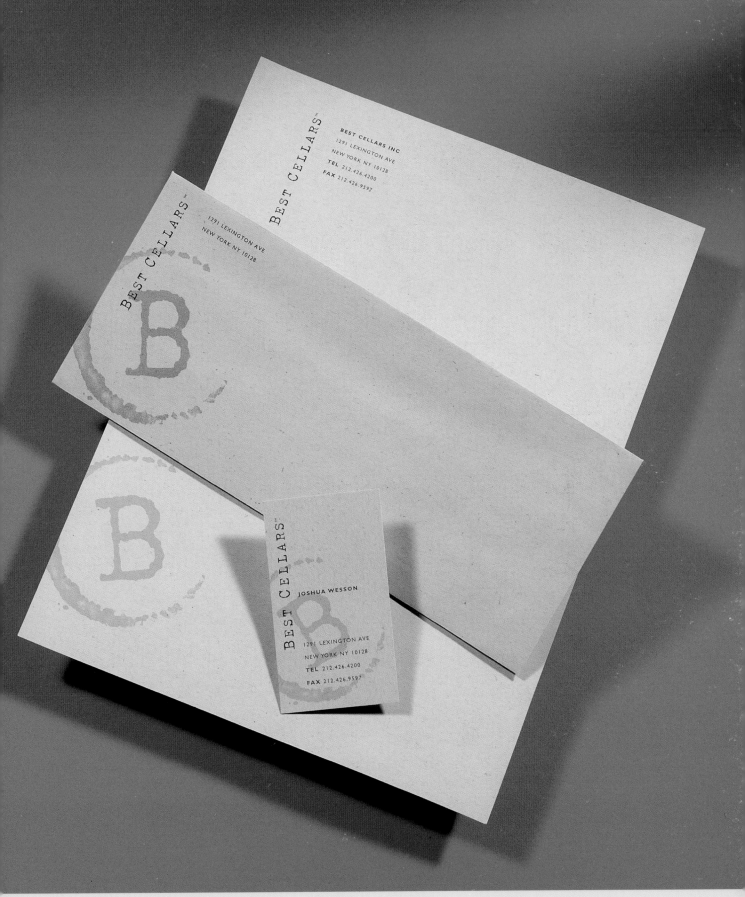

BEST CELLARS™

BEST CELLARS INC
1291 LEXINGTON AVE
NEW YORK NY 10128
TEL 212.426.4200
FAX 212.426.9597

BEST CELLARS™

1291 LEXINGTON AVE
NEW YORK NY 10128

B

B

BEST CELLARS™

JOSHUA WESSON

B

1291 LEXINGTON AVE
NEW YORK NY 10128
TEL 212.426.4200
FAX 212.426.9597

DESIGN FIRM | HORNALL ANDERSON DESIGN WORKS, INC.
ART DIRECTOR | JACK ANDERSON
DESIGNERS | JACK ANDERSON, LISA CERVENY,
JANA WILSON, DAVID BATES
CLIENT | BEST CELLARS

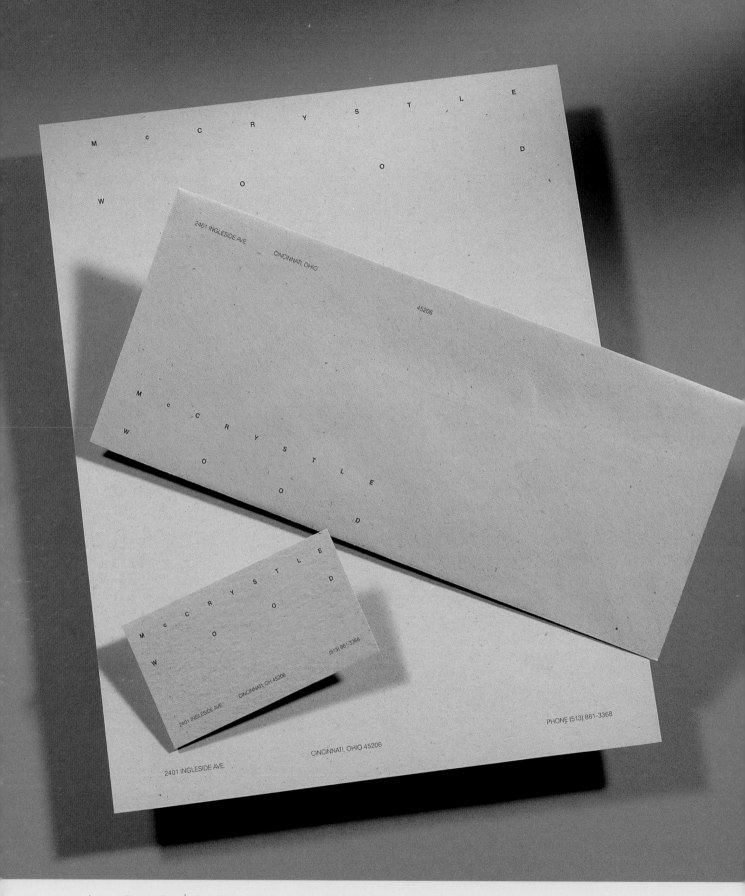

DESIGN FIRM │ WOOD/BROD DESIGN

ART DIRECTOR/DESIGNER │ STAN BROD

CLIENT │ STAN BROD, MCCRYSTLE WOOD

TOOLS │ ADOBE ILLUSTRATOR

PAPER/PRINTING │ SPECKLETONE/BERMAN PRINTING COMPANY

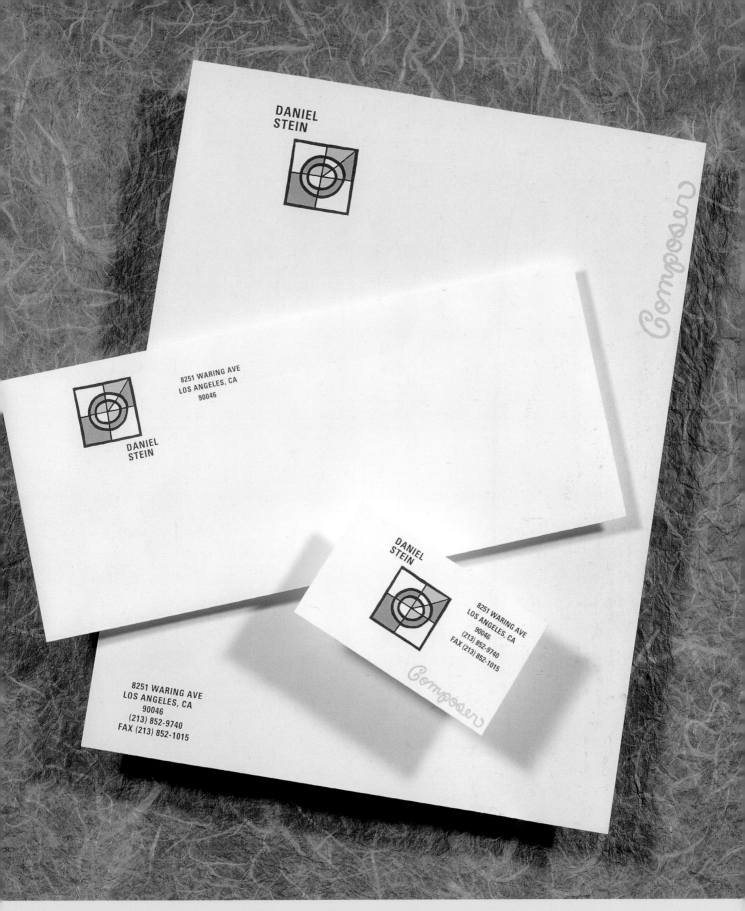

DANIEL
STEIN

Composer

8251 WARING AVE
LOS ANGELES, CA
90046

DANIEL
STEIN

DANIEL
STEIN

8251 WARING AVE
LOS ANGELES, CA
90046
(213) 852-9740
FAX (213) 852-1015

Composer

8251 WARING AVE
LOS ANGELES, CA
90046
(213) 852-9740
FAX (213) 852-1015

DESIGN FIRM | SUSAN GUERRA DESIGN

ALL DESIGN | SUSAN GUERRA DESIGN

CLIENT | DANIEL STEIN

TOOLS | ADOBE ILLUSTRATOR

PAPER/PRINTING | CLASSIC CREST/TWO COLOR

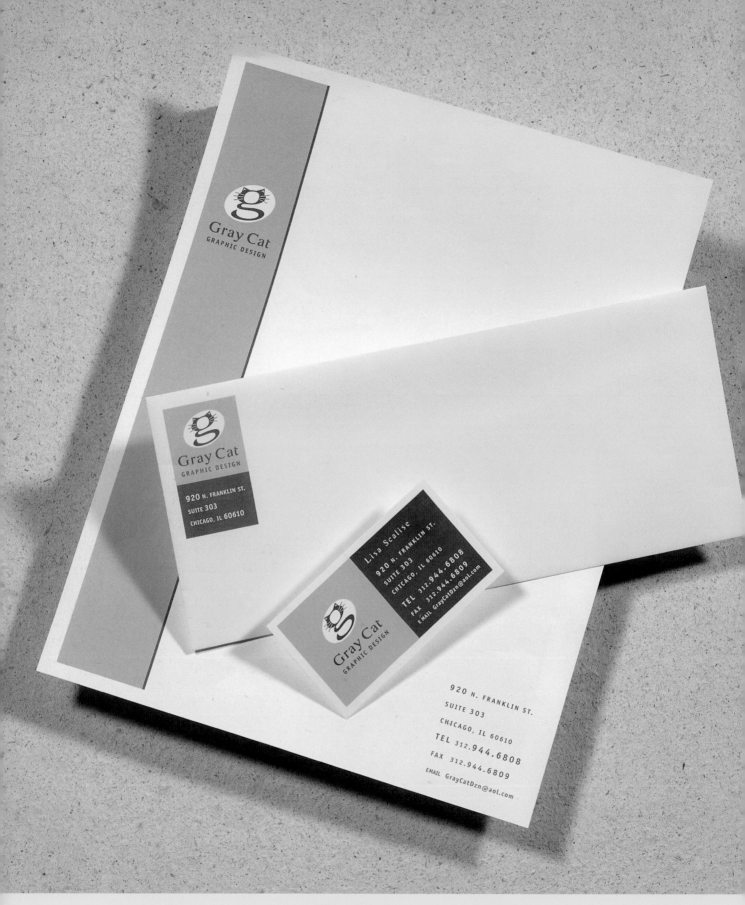

DESIGN FIRM | GRAY CAT DESIGN

DESIGNER | LISA SCALISE

CLIENT | GRAY CAT DESIGN

PAPER/PRINTING | MOHAWK SUPERFINE/LAKE PRINTERS

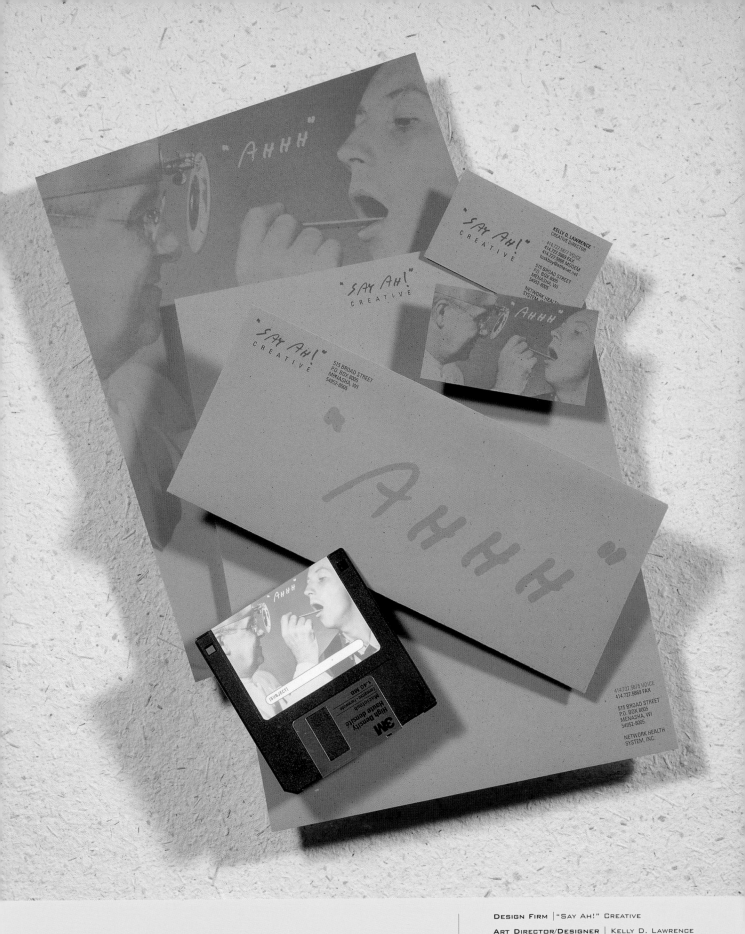

DESIGN FIRM | "SAY AH!" CREATIVE

ART DIRECTOR/DESIGNER | KELLY D. LAWRENCE

PHOTOGRAPHY | SUPERSTOCK

PRODUCTION | JON EMPEY, VICKIE MARTIN

CLIENT | "SAY AH!" CREATIVE

TOOLS | QUARKXPRESS, ADOBE PHOTOSHOP,
ADOBE ILLUSTRATOR

PAPER/PRINTING | SIMPSON QUEST-BRONZE/OFFSET

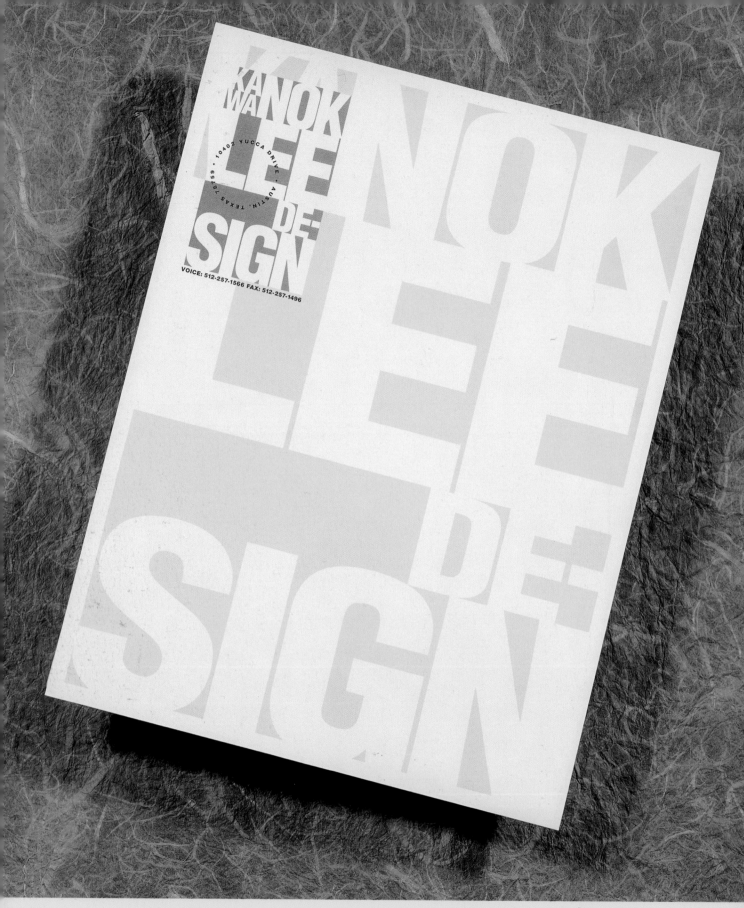

DESIGN FIRM | KANOKWALEE DESIGN

ART DIRECTOR/DESIGNER | KANOKWALEE LEE

CLIENT | KANOKWALEE DESIGN

TOOLS | ADOBE ILLUSTRATOR, QUARKXPRESS

PAPER/PRINTING | STRATHMORE KRAFT/OFFSET

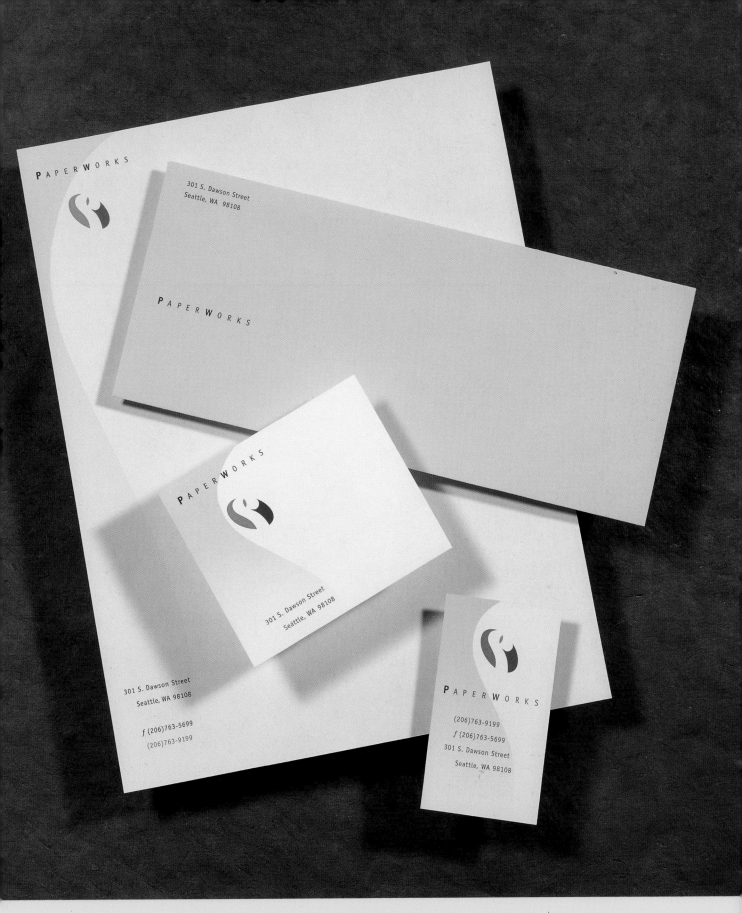

DESIGN FIRM | BELYEA DESIGN ALLIANCE
ART DIRECTOR | PATRICIA BELYEA
DESIGNER | CHRISTIAN SALAS
CLIENT | PAPERWORKS

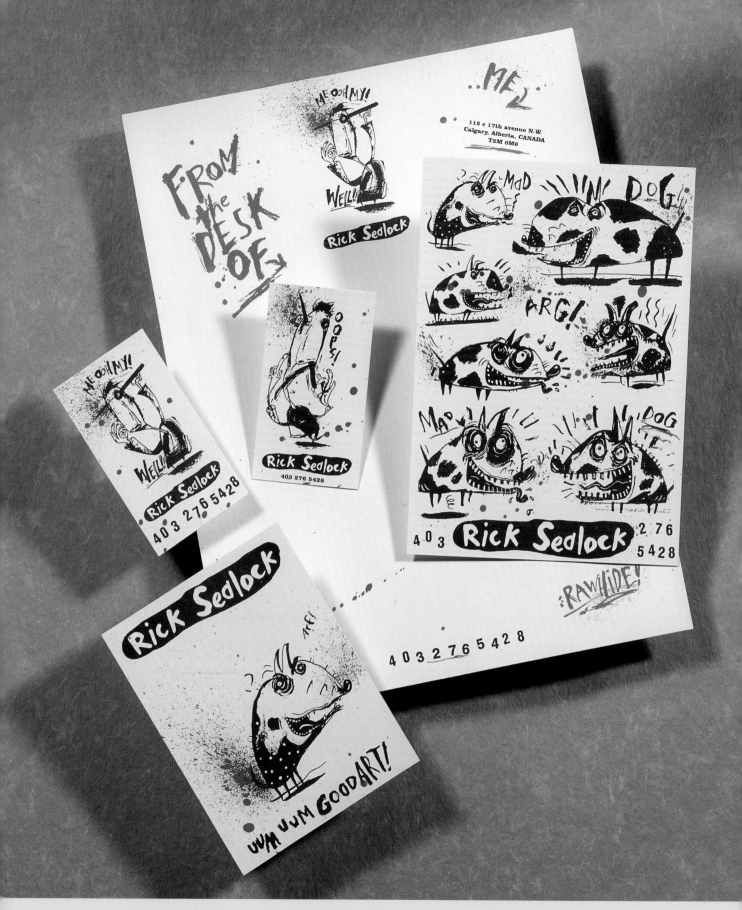

DESIGN FIRM | RICK SEALOCK ILLUSTRATION

ALL DESIGN | RICK SEALOCK

CLIENT | RICK SEALOCK

TOOLS | FOUND TYPE/PHOTOCOPIER

PAPER/PRINTING | CLASSIC COLUMN/OFFSET

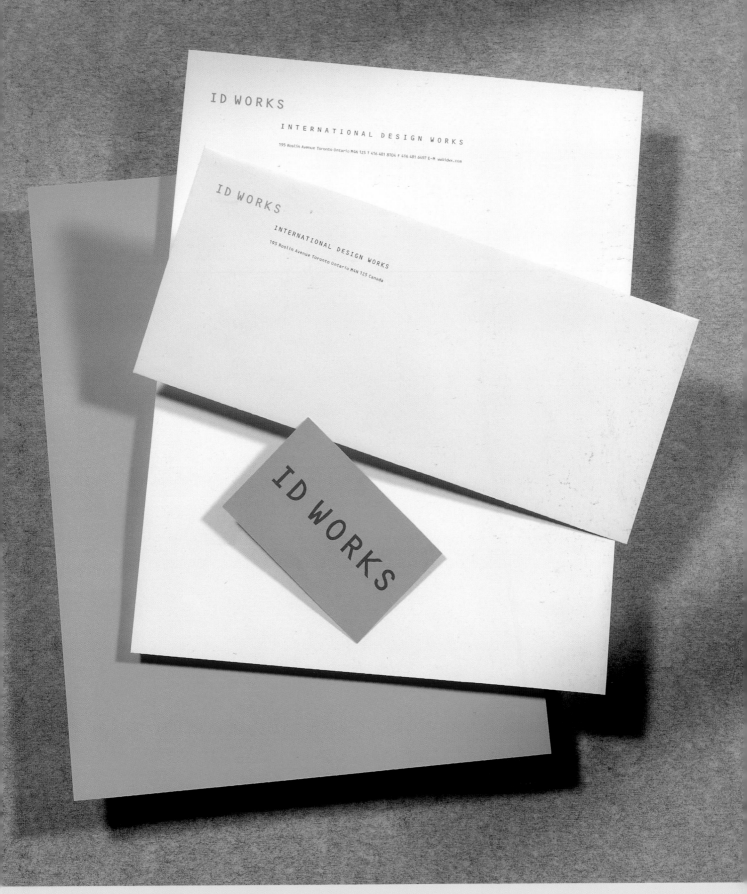

ID WORKS

INTERNATIONAL DESIGN WORKS

195 Roslin Avenue Toronto Ontario M4N 1Z5 T 416 481 8104 F 416 481 6497 E-M ww@idwx.com

ID WORKS

INTERNATIONAL DESIGN WORKS

195 Roslin Avenue Toronto Ontario M4N 1Z5 Canada

ID WORKS

DESIGN FIRM | TEIKNA

ART DIRECTOR/DESIGNER | CLAUDIA NERI

CLIENT | ID WORKS

TOOLS | QUARKXPRESS

PAPER/PRINTING | MOHAWK OPTIONS/TWO COLOR

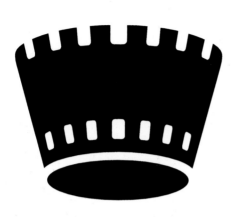

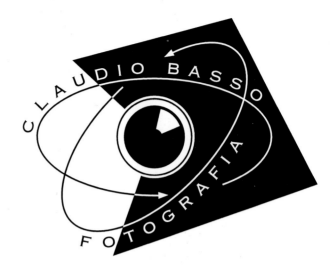

DESIGN FIRM | SIBLEY/PETEET DESIGN
DESIGNER | TOM KIRSCH
CLIENT | MIKE KING

DESIGN FIRM | VOSS DESIGN
ART DIRECTOR/DESIGNER | AXEL VOSS
CLIENT | CLAUDIO BASSO

MONKEY 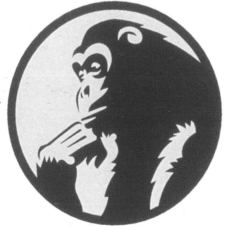 STUDIOS

DESIGN FIRM | TRACY SABIN GRAPHIC DESIGN
ART DIRECTOR | RUSSELL SABIN
ILLUSTRATOR | TRACY SABIN
CLIENT | MONKEY STUDIOS
TOOLS | ADOBE ILLUSTRATOR

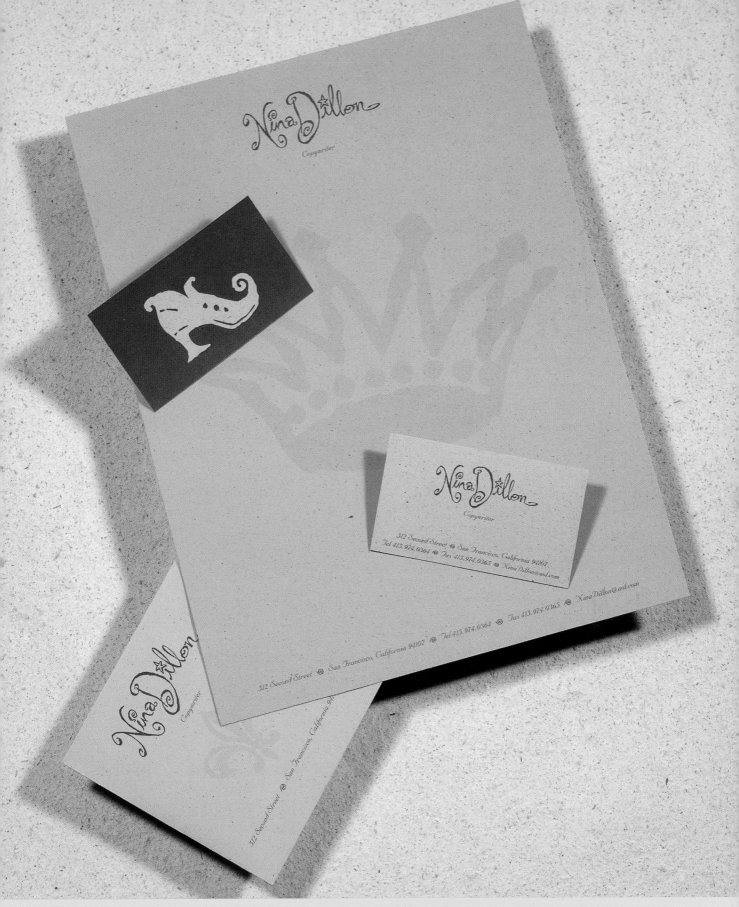

DESIGN FIRM | TIM NOONAN
DESIGNER | TIM NOONAN
CLIENT | NINA DILLON
TOOLS | QUARKXPRESS, HAND LETTERING
PAPER/PRINTING | SIMPSON QUEST/ONE PMS

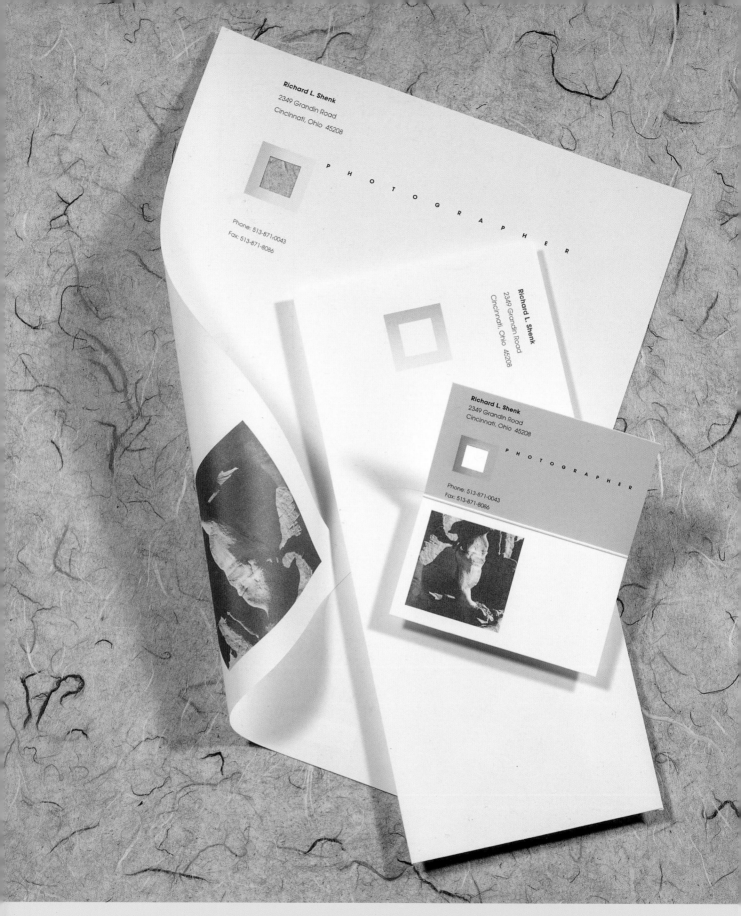

DESIGN FIRM | WOOD/BROD DESIGN

ALL DESIGN | STAN BROD

CLIENT | RICHARD L. SHENK

TOOLS | ADOBE ILLUSTRATOR

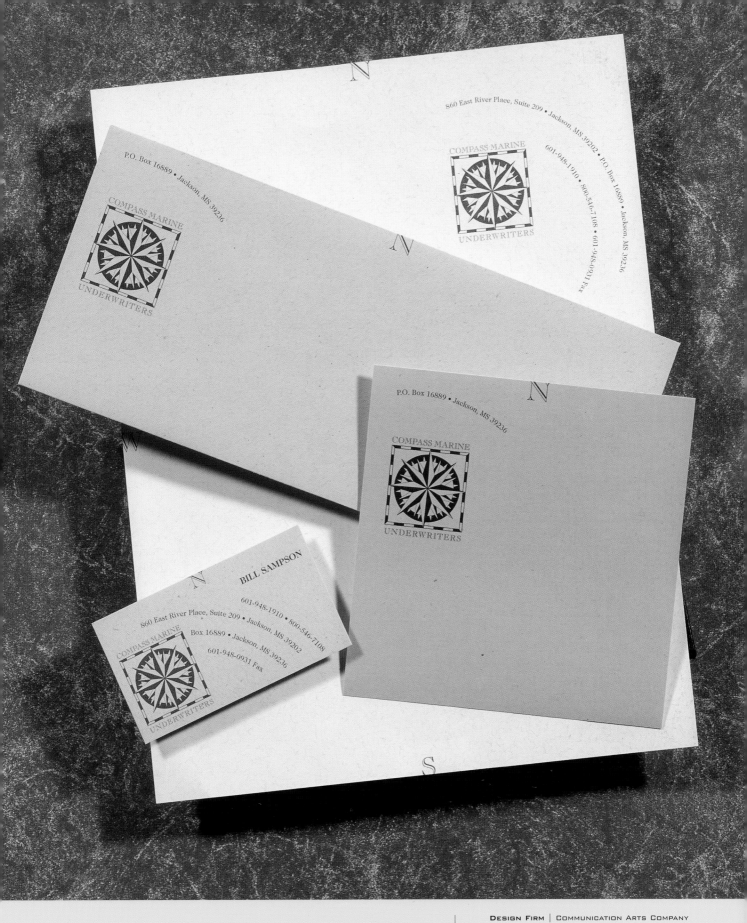

DESIGN FIRM | COMMUNICATION ARTS COMPANY

ART DIRECTOR | HAP OWEN

DESIGNER | ANNE-MARIE OTVOS

CLIENT | COMPASS MARINE UNDERWRITERS

TOOLS | MACINTOSH

PAPER/PRINTING | PROTERRA PARCHMENT &

STUCO, KRAFT/OFFSET LITHOGRAPHY

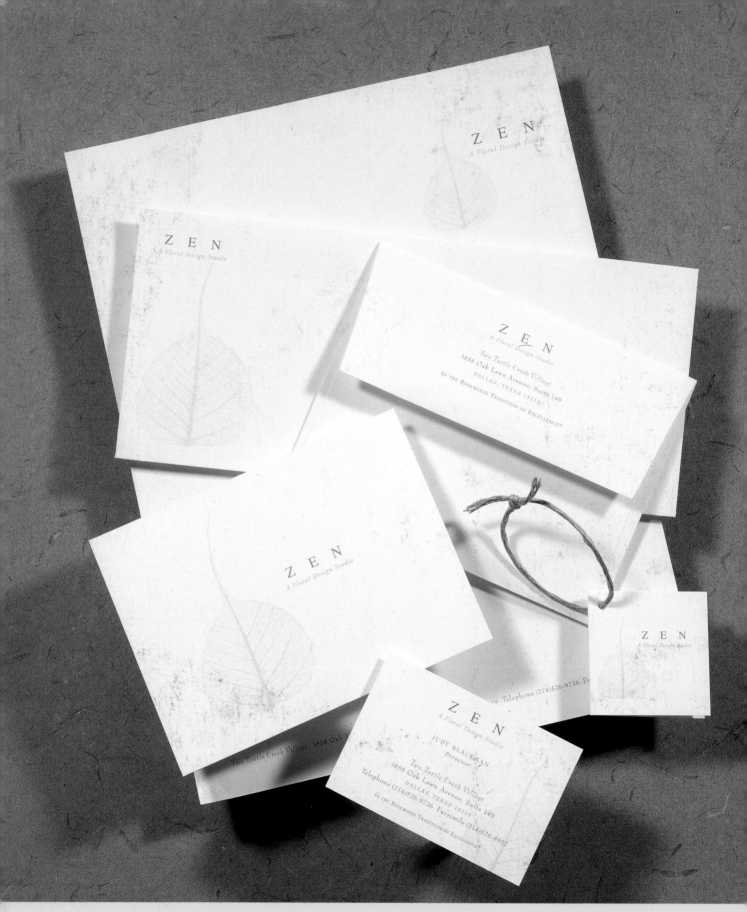

DESIGN FIRM | DAVID CARTER DESIGN

ART DIRECTORS | SHARON LEJEUNE, LORI B. WILSON

CLIENT | ZEN FLORAL DESIGN STUDIO

PAPER/PRINTING | SIMPSON EVERGREEN BIRCH/JARVIS PRESS

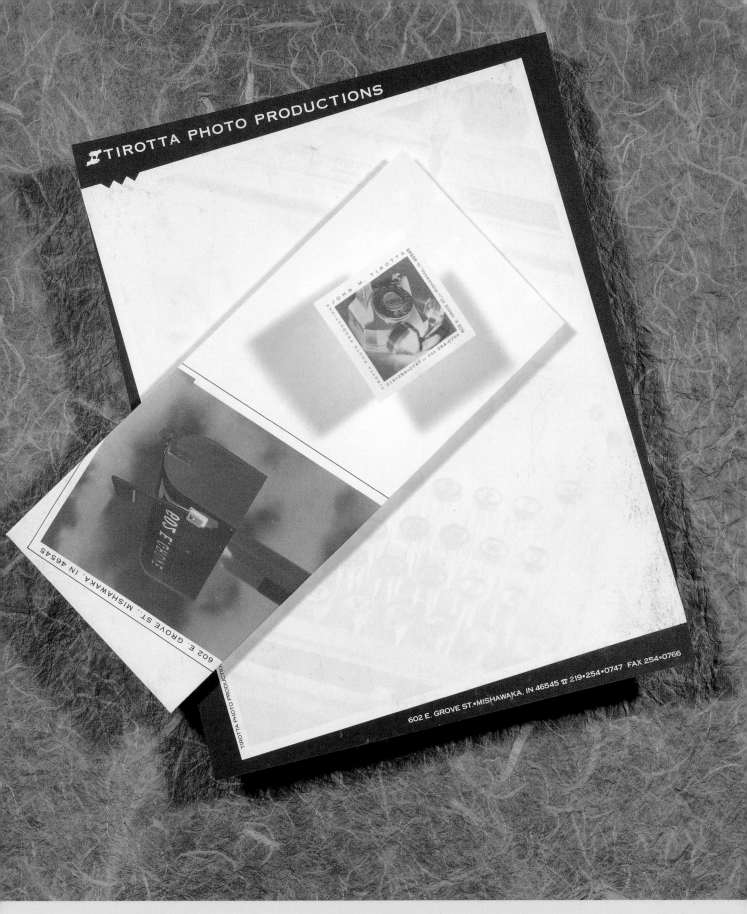

DESIGN FIRM | HIEROGLYPHICS ART & DESIGN
DESIGNER | CHRISTINE OSBORN TIROTTA
PHOTOGRAPHER | JOHN TIROTTA
CLIENT | TIROTTA PHOTO PRODUCTIONS
PAPER/PRINTING | STARWHITE VICKSBURG, UV ULTRA II

Pesona Pictures Sdn Bhd
159A Jalan Aminuddin Baki
Taman Tun Dr Ismail
60000 Kuala Lumpur *Malaysia*
Tel 603 719 1602 ✦ 718 2316
Fax 603 719 1586

Studio
24 Jalan Kemajuan 12/18
46200 Petaling Jaya
Selangor Darul Ehsan *Malaysia*
Tel 603 754 2334 ✦ 754 2276
Fax 603 754 2335

Pesona Pictures Sdn Bhd
159A Jalan Aminuddin Baki
Taman Tun Dr Ismail
60000 Kuala Lumpur *Malaysia*
Tel 603 719 1602 ✦ 718 2316
Fax 603 719 1586

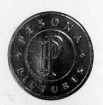

Studio
24 Jalan Kemajuan 12/18
46200 Petaling Jaya
Selangor Darul Ehsan *Malaysia*
Tel 603 754 2334 ✦ 754 2276
Fax 603 754 2335

DESIGN FIRM | WERK-HAUS

ART DIRECTOR | EZRAH RAHIM

DESIGNERS | ELRAH RAHIM, WAI MING, WEE

CLIENT | PESONA PICTURES

PAPER/PRINTING | CONCEPT WAVE SAND/ONE

COLOR, COPPER HOT STAMPING, EMBOSSING

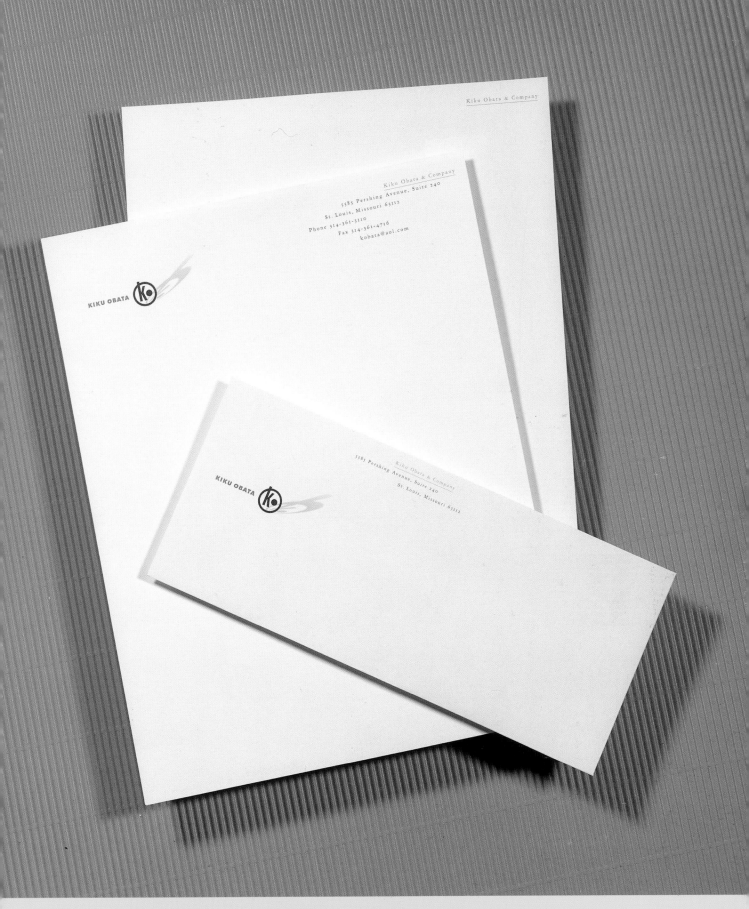

KIKU OBATA

Kiku Obata & Company

Kiku Obata & Company

5585 Pershing Avenue, Suite 240
St. Louis, Missouri 63112
Phone 314-361-3110
Fax 314-361-4716
kobata@aol.com

KIKU OBATA

Kiku Obata & Company
5585 Pershing Avenue, Suite 240
St. Louis, Missouri 63112

DESIGN FIRM │ KIKU OBATA & COMPANY
ART DIRECTOR/DESIGNER │ RICH NELSON
CLIENT │ KIKU OBATA & COMPANY
PAPER/PRINTING │ REPROX

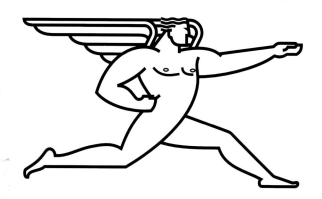

TOWER OF BABEL

DESIGN FIRM | SIBLEY/PETEET DESIGN
DESIGNER | TOM HOUGH
CLIENT | MERCURY MESSENGER

DESIGN FIRM | TOWER OF BABEL
DESIGNER | ERIC STEVENS
CLIENT | TOWER OF BABEL

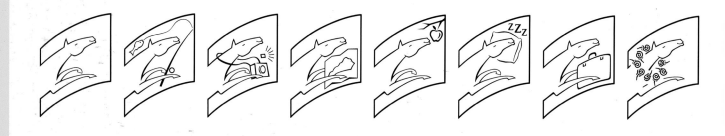

DESIGN FIRM | KIRBY STEPHENS DESIGN, INC.
ART DIRECTOR/DESIGNER | KIRBY STEPHENS
ILLUSTRATORS | DANIEL DUTTON, WILLIAM V. COX
CLIENT | KENTUCKY TOURISM COUNCIL
TOOLS | PENCIL, MACINTOSH PPC, SCANNER

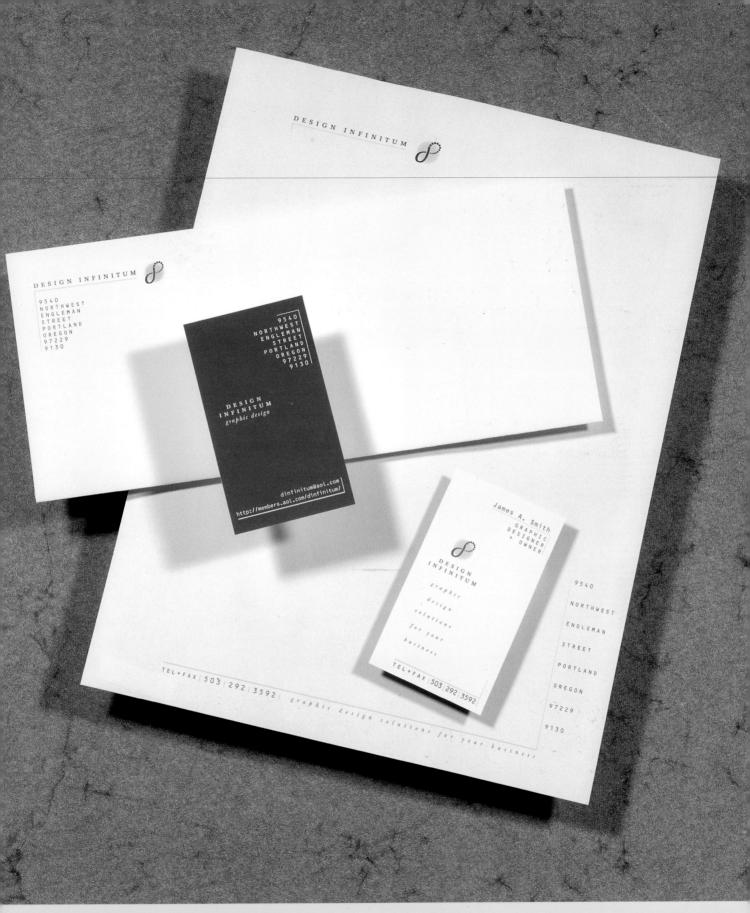

DESIGN INFINITUM

DESIGN INFINITUM

9540
NORTHWEST
ENGLEMAN
STREET
PORTLAND
OREGON
97229
9130

9540
NORTHWEST
ENGLEMAN
STREET
PORTLAND
OREGON
97229
9130

DESIGN
INFINITUM
graphic design

dinfinitum@aol.com
http://members.aol.com/dinfinitum/

James A. Smith
GRAPHIC
DESIGNER
+ OWNER

DESIGN
INFINITUM

graphic

design

solutions

for your

business

9540

NORTHWEST

ENGLEMAN

STREET

PORTLAND

OREGON

97229

9130

TEL+FAX 503 292 3592

TEL+FAX 503 292 3592

graphic design solutions for your business

DESIGN FIRM | DESIGN INFINITUM
ALL DESIGN | JAMES A. SMITH
CLIENT | DESIGN INFINITUM
TOOLS | QUARKXPRESS, ADOBE ILLUSTRATOR
PAPER/PRINTING | BECKETT EXPRESSION/
CHROMAGRAPHICS

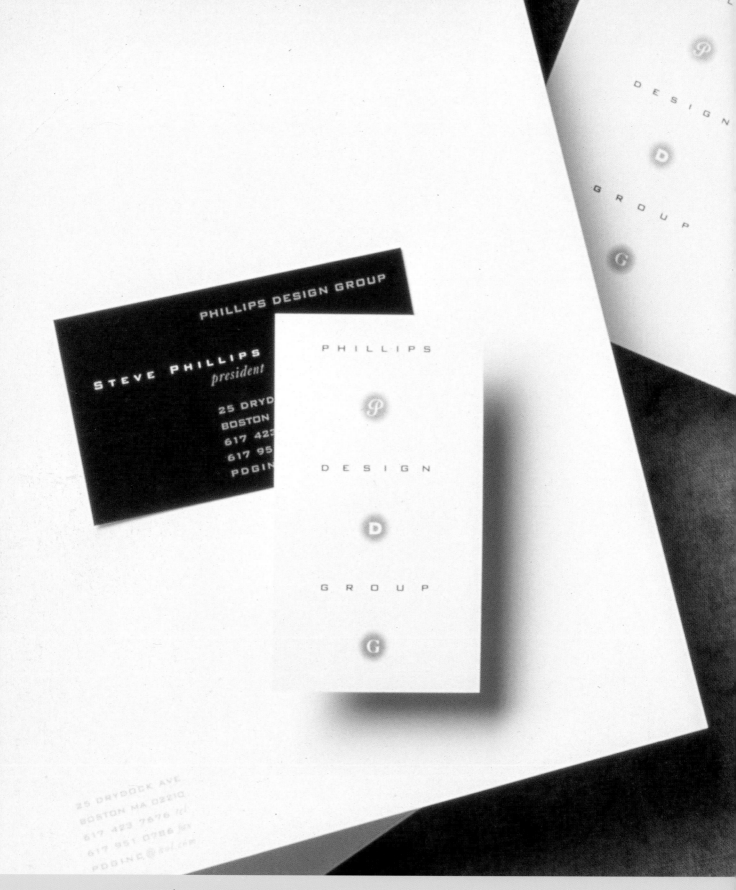

PHILLIPS DESIGN GROUP

STEVE PHILLIPS
president

25 DRYD
BOSTON
617 423
617 95
PDGIN

PHILLIPS

DESIGN

GROUP

25 DRYDOCK AVE.
BOSTON MA 02210
617 423 7676 [t]
617 951 0786 [f]
PDGINC@aol.com

DESIGN FIRM | PHILLIPS DESIGN GROUP
ART DIRECTOR | STEVE PHILLIPS
DESIGNERS | BETH PARKER, ALISON GOUDREAULT
CLIENT | PHILLIPS DESIGN GROUP
TOOLS | ADOBE ILLUSTRATOR
PAPER/PRINTING | STRATHMORE/MARAN PRINTING

DESIGN FIRM | WEBSTER DESIGN ASSOCIATES

ART DIRECTOR | DAVE WEBSTER

DESIGNER/ILLUSTRATOR | ANDREY NAGORNY

CLIENT | DIE WORKS

TOOLS | MACROMEDIA FREEHAND

PAPER/PRINTING | CROSS POINTE GENESIS FOSSIL,

FOIL STAMPED

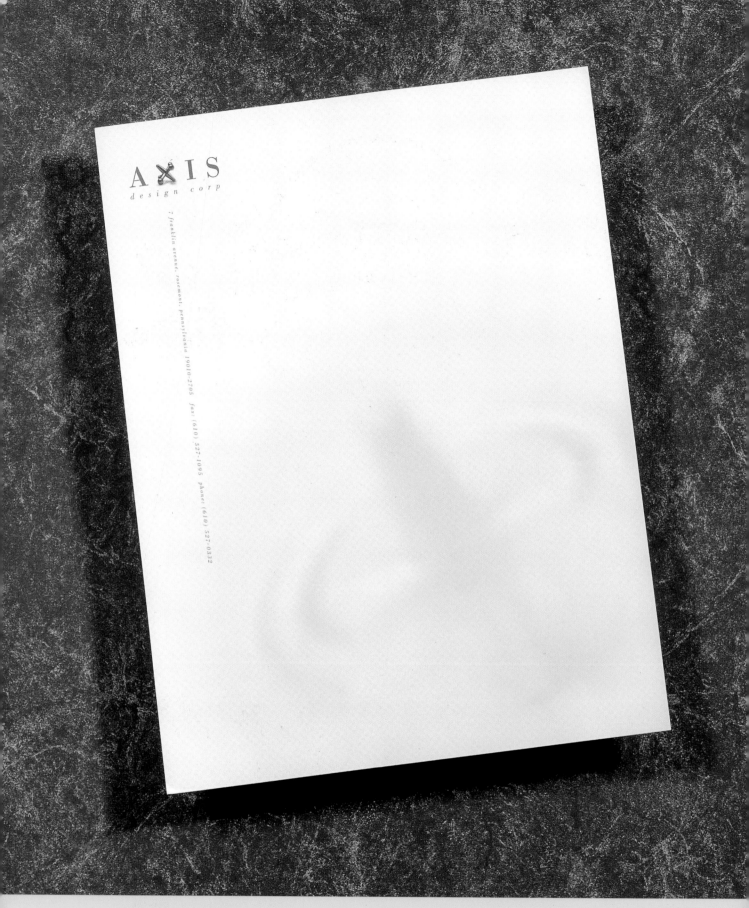

AXIS
design corp

7 franklin avenue, rosemont, pennsylvania 19010-2765   fax: (610) 527-1095   phone: (610) 527-0332

DESIGN FIRM | AXIS DESIGN
ART DIRECTOR/DESIGNER | WILLIAM MILNAZIK
CLIENT | AXIS DESIGN
PAPER/PRINTING | STRATHMORE ELEMENTS

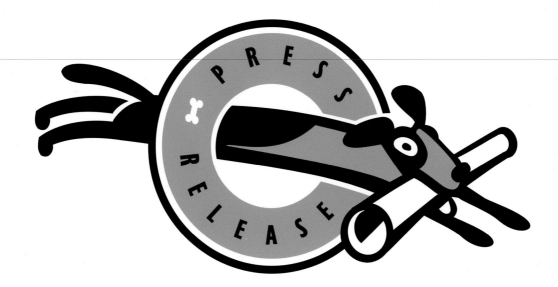

DESIGN FIRM | DOGSTAR
DESIGNER/ILLUSTRATOR | RODNEY DAVIDSON
CLIENT | DOGSTAR
TOOLS | ADOBE ILLUSTRATOR, STREAMLINE, MACROMEDIA FREEHAND

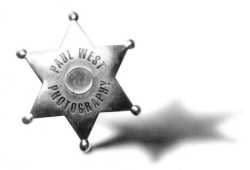

"SAY AH!"
CREATIVE

DESIGN FIRM | STORM DESIGN & ADVERTISING CONSULTANCY
ART DIRECTORS/DESIGNERS | DAVID ANSETT, DEAN BUTLER
ILLUSTRATORS | DEAN BUTLER, DAVID ANSETT
CLIENT | PAUL WEST PHOTOGRAPHY
TOOLS | ADOBE PHOTOSHOP

DESIGN FIRM | "SAY AH!" CREATIVE
ART DIRECTOR/DESIGNER | KELLY D. LAWRENCE
PHOTOGRAPHY | SUPERSTOCK
PRODUCTION | JON EMPEY, VICKIE MARTIN
CLIENT | "SAY AH!" CREATIVE
TOOLS | QUARKXPRESS, ADOBE PHOTOSHOP, ADOBE ILLUSTRATOR

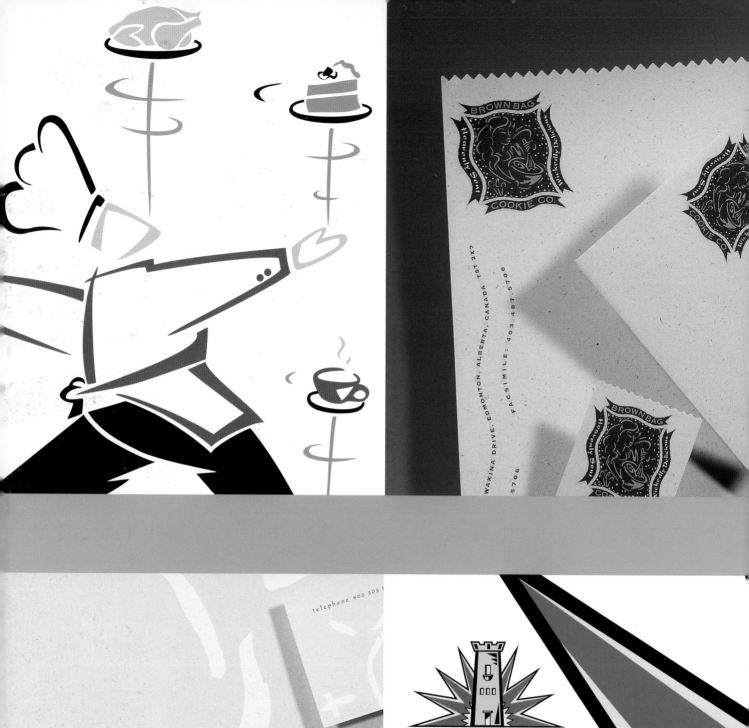

BROWN BAG
COOKIE CO

Heavenly Sent · Wickedly Delicious

WAKINA DRIVE, EDMONTON, ALBERTA, CANADA T5T 2X7

FACSIMILE: 403.487.5706

5706

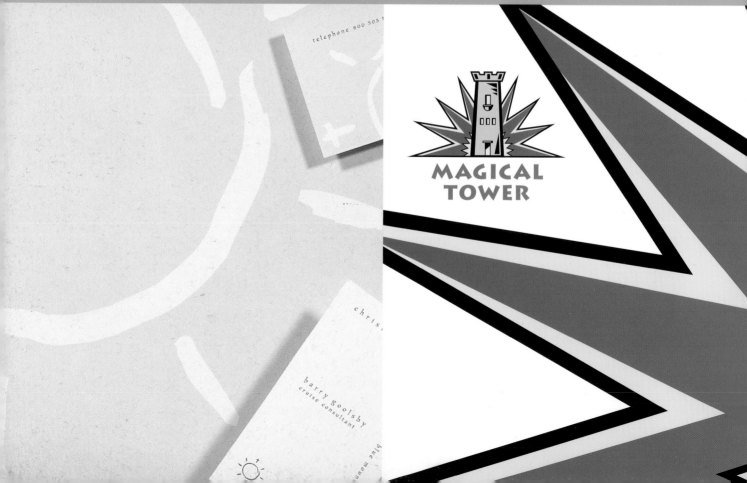

telephone 800 505

christ

barry goolsby
cruise consultant

blue mount

MAGICAL
TOWER

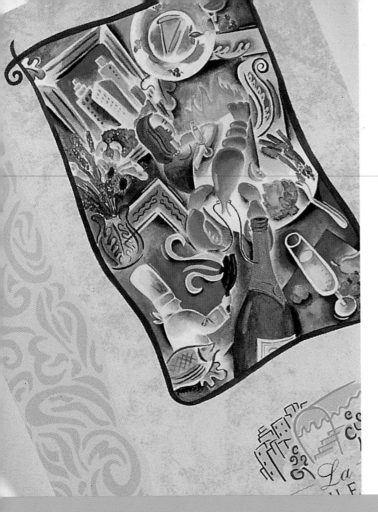

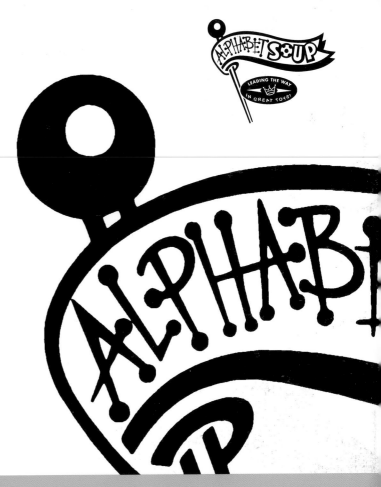

ALPHABET SOUP
LEADING THE WAY IN GREAT TOYS!

RESTAURANT, RETAIL, AND HOSPITALITY

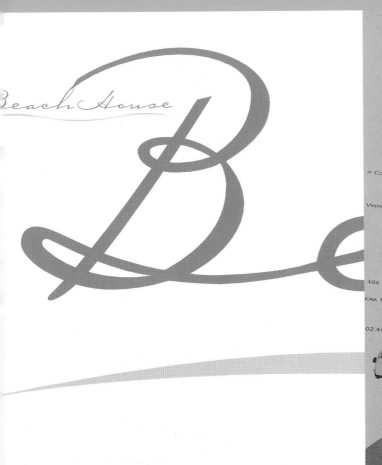

Beach House

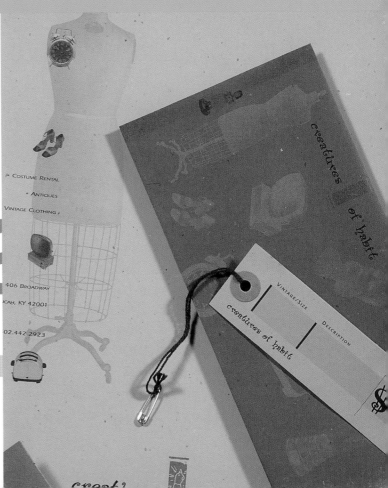

COSTUME RENTAL

ANTIQUES

VINTAGE CLOTHING

406 BROADWAY

CAH, KY 42001

02.442.2923

creatures of habit

VINTAGE/SIZE

DESCRIPTION

creatures of habit

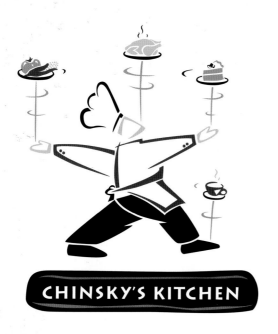

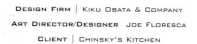

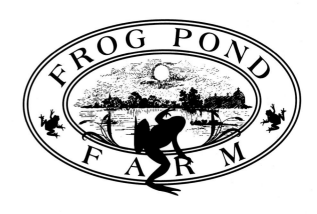

DESIGN FIRM | KIKU OBATA & COMPANY
ART DIRECTOR/DESIGNER JOE FLORESCA
CLIENT | CHINSKY'S KITCHEN

DESIGN FIRM | TURNER DESIGN
ALL DESIGN | BERT TURNER
CLIENT | FROG POND FARM

CASA de FRUTA

DESIGN FIRM | THARP DID IT
ART DIRECTOR | RICK THARP
DESIGNERS | RICK THARP, KIM TOMLINSON
CLIENT | CASA DE FRUTA
TOOLS | INK

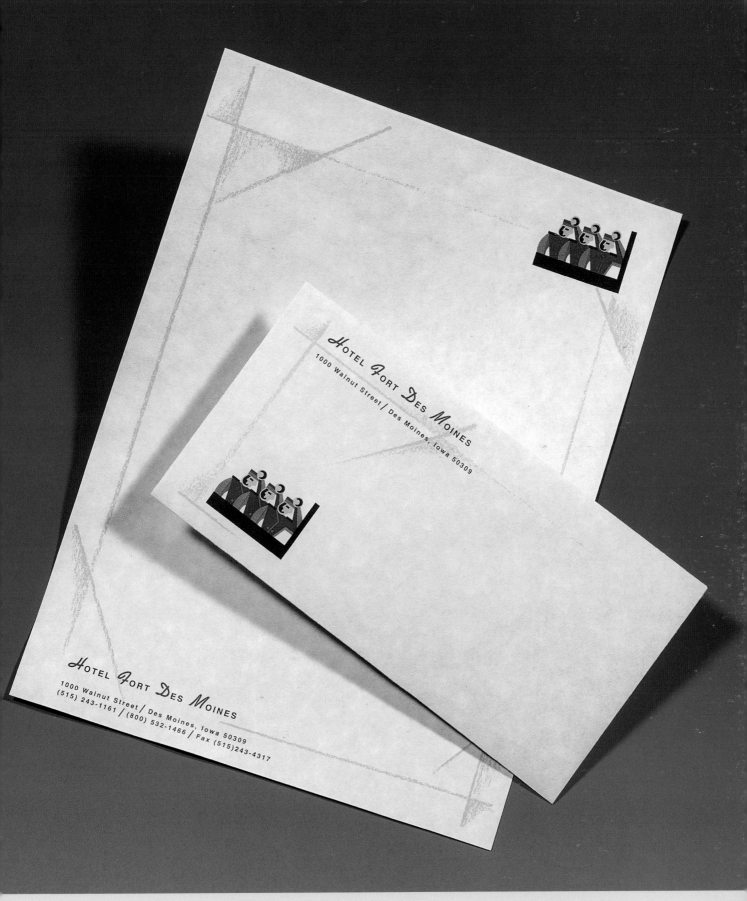

Hotel Fort Des Moines
1000 Walnut Street / Des Moines, Iowa 50309

Hotel Fort Des Moines
1000 Walnut Street / Des Moines, Iowa 50309
(515) 243-1161 / (800) 532-1466 / Fax (515)243-4317

DESIGN FIRM | SAYLES GRAPHIC DESIGN
ALL DESIGN | JOHN SAYLES
CLIENT | HOTEL FORT DES MOINES
PAPER/PRINTING | HOPPER SKYTONE NATURAL/OFFSET

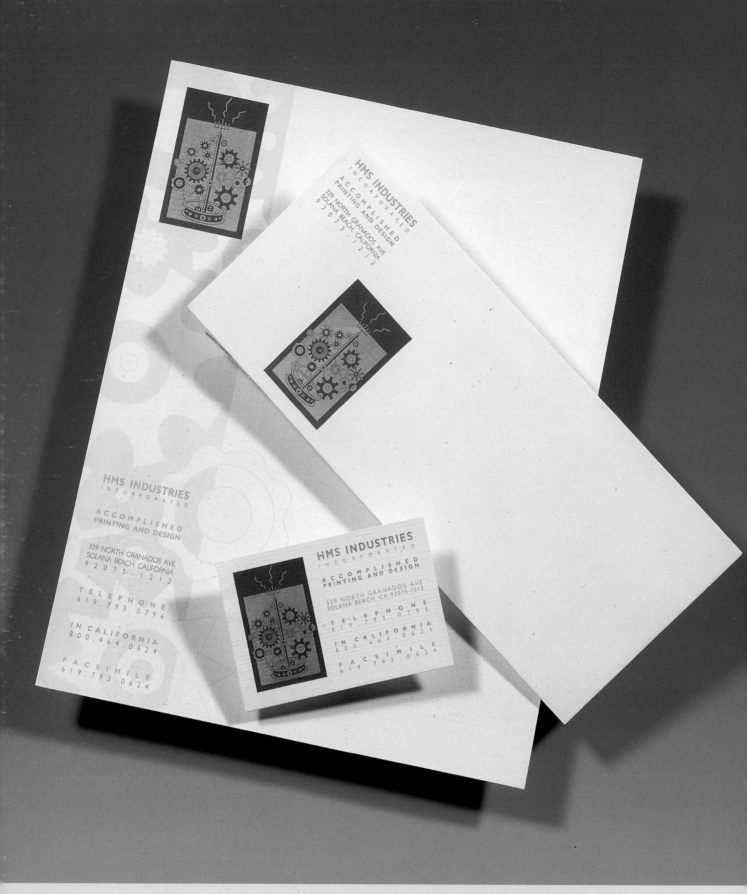

DESIGN FIRM | ICEHOUSE DESIGN

ART DIRECTOR/DESIGNER | PATTIE BELLE HASTINGS

ILLUSTRATOR | VAL TILLERY

CLIENT | HMS INDUSTRIES

TOOLS | POWER MACINTOSH

PAPER/PRINTING | CLASSIC CREST

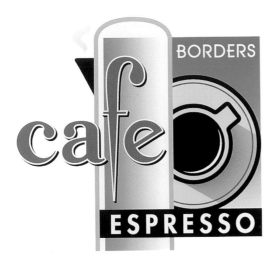

LENOX ROOM

TIP WELL AND PROSPER

DESIGN FIRM | FRCH DESIGN WORLDWIDE
ART DIRECTOR | JOAN DONNELLY
DESIGNER/ILLUSTRATOR | TIM A. FRAME
CLIENT | BORDERS BOOKS AND MUSIC
TOOLS | ADOBE ILLUSTRATOR

DESIGN FIRM | AERIAL
ART DIRECTOR/DESIGNER | TRACY MOON
PHOTOGRAPHY | R. J. MUNA
CLIENT | LENOX ROOM RESTAURANT
TOOLS | ADOBE PHOTOSHOP, QUARKXPRESS

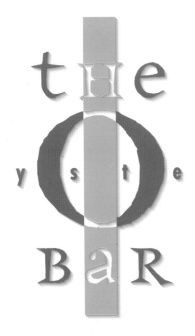

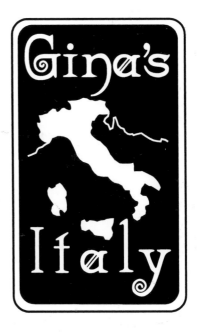

DESIGN FIRM | FLAHERTY ART & DESIGN
ALL DESIGN | MARIE FLAHERTY
CLIENT | THE O BAR OF EATING UP THE COAST
TOOLS | ADOBE ILLUSTRATOR

DESIGN FIRM | JEFF FISHER LOGOMOTIVES
ALL DESIGN | JEFF FISHER
CLIENT | TRIAD (AD AGENCY FOR GINA'S ITALY)
TOOLS | MACROMEDIA FREEHAND

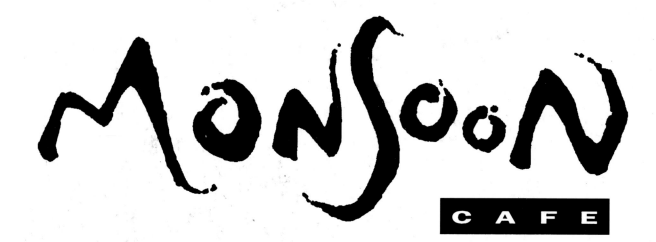

DESIGN FIRM | VRONTIKIS DESIGN OFFICE
ART DIRECTOR | PETRULA VRONTIKIS
DESIGNER | LISA CRITCHFIELD
CLIENT | HASEGAWA ENTERPRISES
TOOLS | QUARKXPRESS, ADOBE PHOTOSHOP

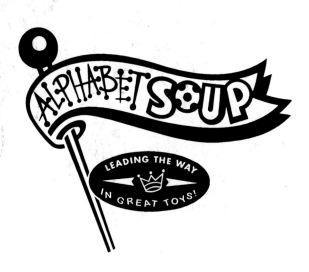

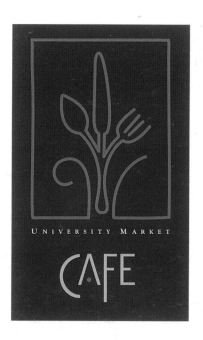

DESIGN FIRM | SAYLES GRAPHIC DESIGN
ALL DESIGN | JOHN SAYLES
CLIENT | ALPHABET SOUP

DESIGN FIRM | CORNOYER-HEDRICK, INC.
ART DIRECTOR | JIM BOLEK
DESIGNER/ILLUSTRATOR | LANIE GOTCHER
CLIENT | MOTOROLA
TOOLS | ADOBE ILLUSTRATOR

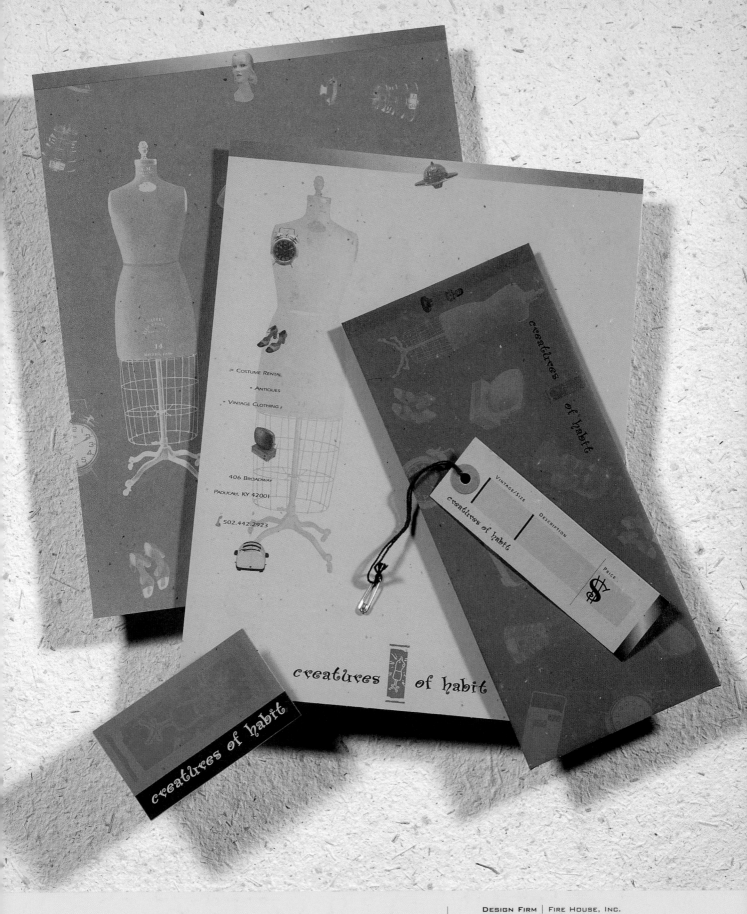

COSTUME RENTAL

ANTIQUES

VINTAGE CLOTHING

406 BROADWAY

PADUCAH, KY 42001

502.442.2923

creatures of habit

VINTAGE/SIZE

DESCRIPTION

PRICE

$

creatures of habit

DESIGN FIRM | FIRE HOUSE, INC.

ART DIRECTOR/DESIGNER | GREGORY R. FARMER

CLIENT | CREATURES OF HABIT

TOOLS | QUARKXPRESS, ADOBE PHOTOSHOP

PAPER/PRINTING | FOX RIVER CONFETTI, MOORE-LANGEN

PRINTING COMPANY, KENNY GRAPHICS

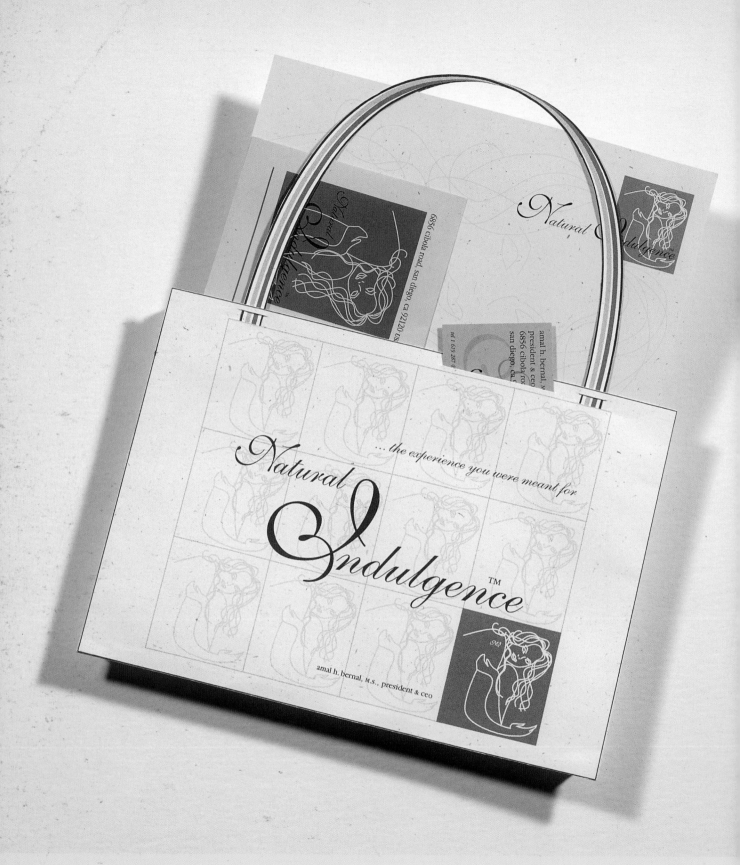

...the experience you were meant for

Natural Indulgence ™

amal h. bernal, M.S., president & ceo

DESIGN FIRM | THE PROVEN EDGE

ALL DESIGN | RITA GOLD

CLIENT | NATURAL INDULGENCE

TOOLS | ADOBE ILLUSTRATOR

PAPER/PRINTING | CROSS POINTE/FRASER AND HOPPER, PRIORITY
    PRINTERS AND EPSON STYLUS PRO WITH BINARY POWER RIP

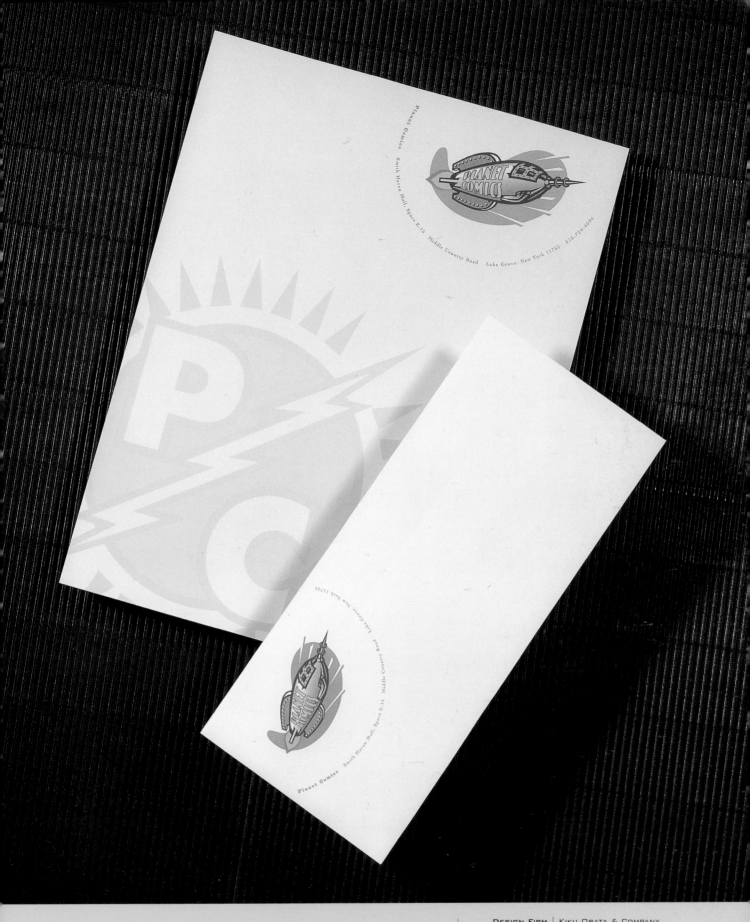

DESIGN FIRM | KIKU OBATA & COMPANY

ART DIRECTOR/DESIGNER | RICH NELSON

CLIENT | PLANET COMICS

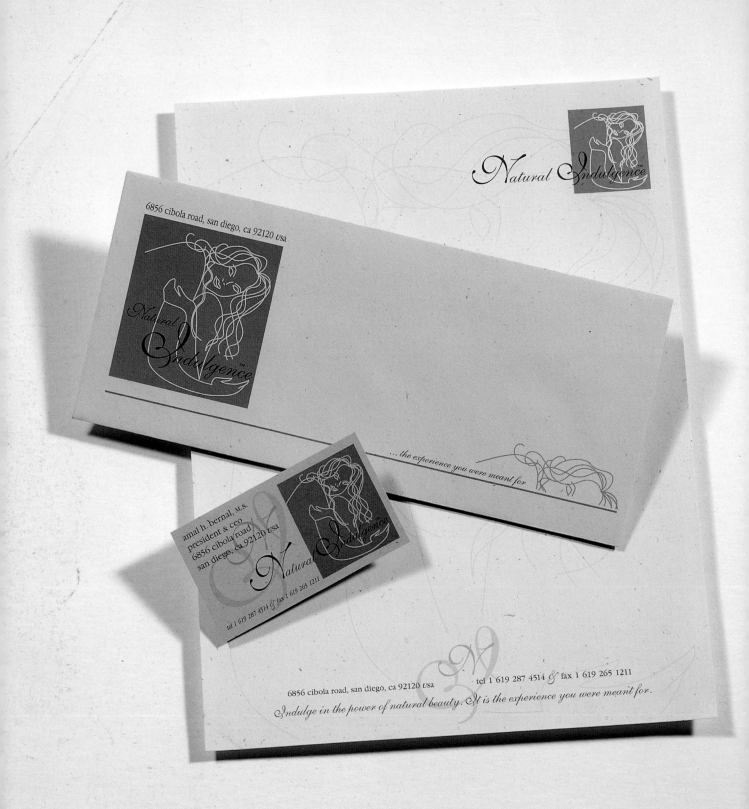

DESIGN FIRM | THE PROVEN EDGE

ALL DESIGN | RITA GOLD

CLIENT | NATURAL INDULGENCE

TOOLS | ADOBE ILLUSTRATOR

PAPER/PRINTING | CROSS POINTE/FRASER AND HOPPER, PRIORITY

PRINTERS AND EPSON STYLUS PRO WITH BINARY POWER RIP

DESIGN FIRM | ON THE EDGE
ART DIRECTOR | JEFF GASPER
DESIGNER | GINA MIMS
ILLUSTRATOR | RUSS MIMS
CLIENT | PLAYERS SPORTS GRILL
TOOLS | QUARKXPRESS, ADOBE ILLUSTRATOR,
ADOBE PHOTOSHOP
PAPER/PRINTING | EVERGREEN WHITE

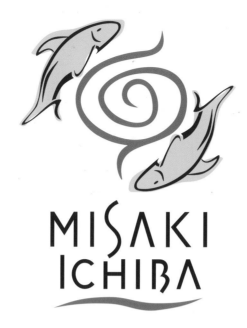

MISAKI ICHIBA

DESIGN FIRM | KIKU OBATA & COMPANY •
ART DIRECTOR | JOE FLORESCA
DESIGNERS | JOE FLORESCA, JEFF RIFKIN, ELEANOR SAFE
CLIENT | R.I.C. DESIGN

dog lips

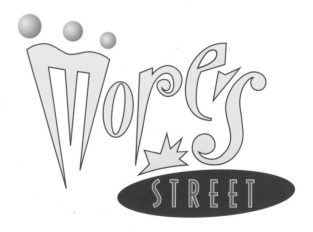

DESIGN FIRM | JUICE DESIGN
ART DIRECTOR/DESIGNER | BRETT M. CRITCHCHLOW
CLIENT | DOGLIPS

DESIGN FIRM | KIKU OBATA & COMPANY
ART DIRECTOR/DESIGNER | RICH NELSON
CLIENT | R.I.C. DESIGN

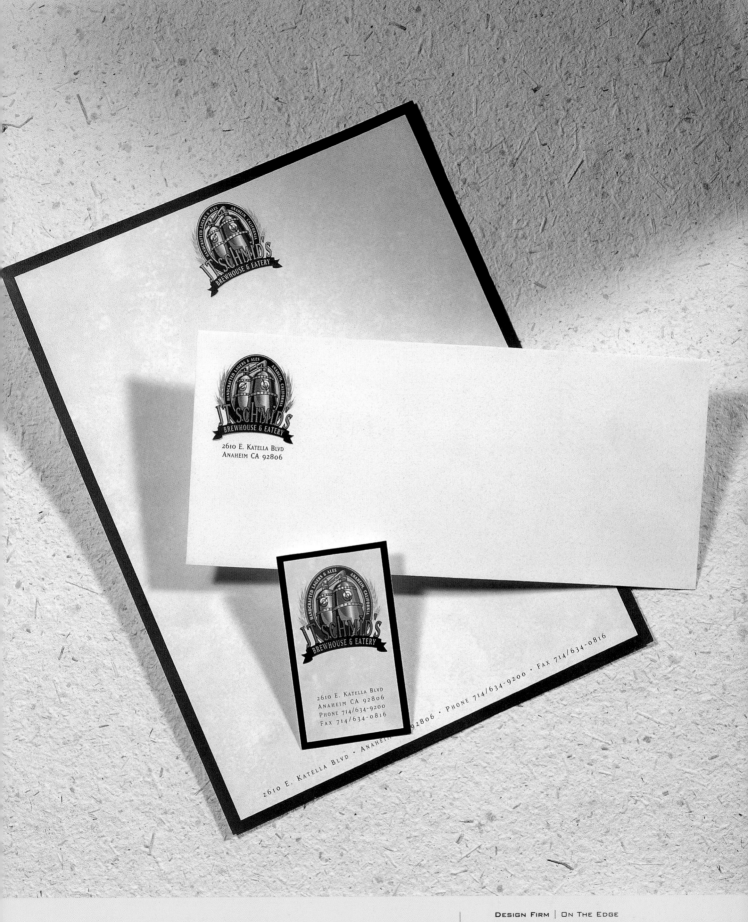

DESIGN FIRM | ON THE EDGE

ART DIRECTOR | JEFF GASPER

DESIGNER | GINA MIMS

ILLUSTRATOR | ERIC PETERSON

CLIENT | JT SCHMID'S BREWHOUSE & EATERY

TOOLS | ADOBE ILLUSTRATOR, QUARKXPRESS

PAPER/PRINTING | CLASSIC CREST IVORY CARD,

LUNA WHITE COVER/FIVE COLOR

La Bodega
Company Store & Deli

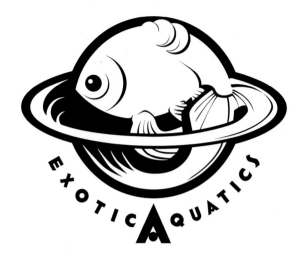

DESIGN FIRM | FLAHERTY ART & DESIGN
ALL DESIGN | MARIE FLAHERTY
CLIENT | LA BODEGA OF EATING UP THE COAST
TOOLS | ADOBE ILLUSTRATOR

DESIGN FIRM | S&N DESIGN
ALL DESIGN | CRAIG GOODMAN
CLIENT | EXOTIC AQUATICS
TOOLS | ADOBE ILLUSTRATOR

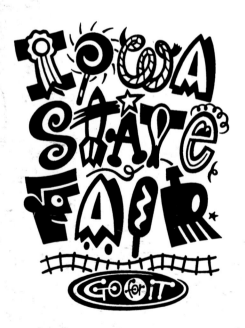

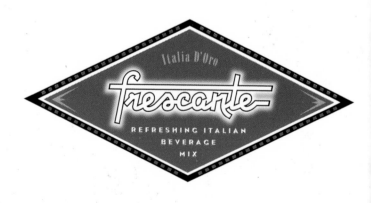

DESIGN FIRM | SAYLES GRAPHIC DESIGN
ART DIRECTOR/ILLUSTRATOR | JOHN SAYLES
DESIGNER | JOHN SAYLES, JENNIFER ELLIOTT
CLIENT | IOWA STATE FAIR

DESIGN FIRM | MIRES DESIGN
ART DIRECTORS | SCOTT MIRES, MIKE BROWER
DESIGNERS | MIKE BROWER, SCOTT MIRES
ILLUSTRATOR | TRACY SABIN
COPYWRITER | JOHN KURAOKA
CLIENT | FOOD GROUP/BOYDS COFFEE

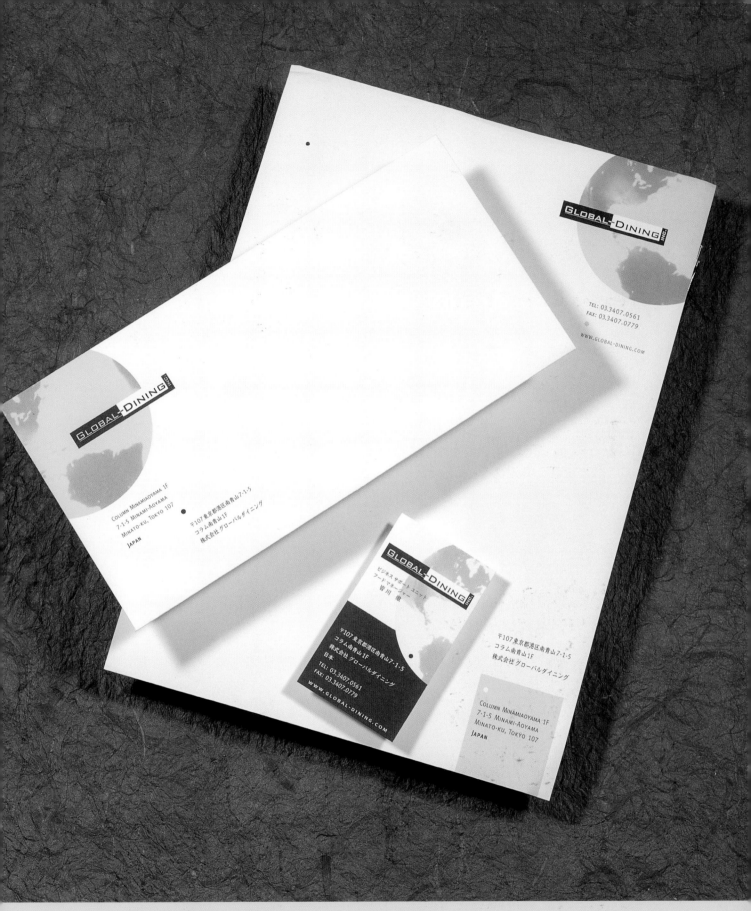

DESIGN FIRM | VRONTIKIS DESIGN OFFICE

ART DIRECTOR/DESIGNER | PETRULA VRONTIKIS

CLIENT | GLOBAL-DINING, INC.

TOOLS | QUARKXPRESS, ADOBE PHOTOSHOP

PAPER/PRINTING | NEENAH CLASSIC

CREST/DONAHUE PRINTING

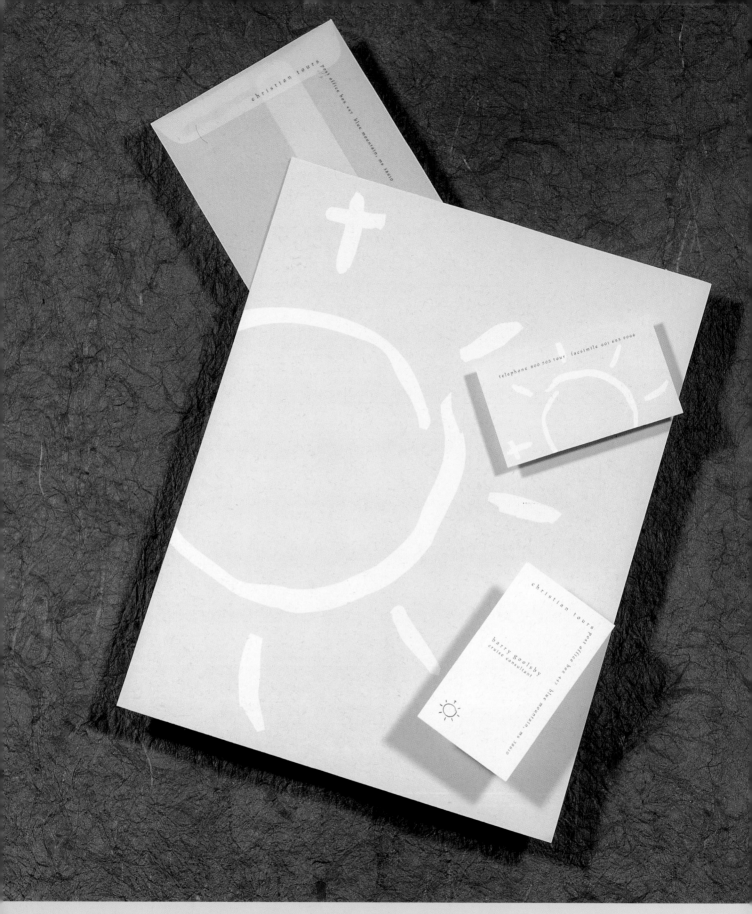

christian tours post office box 447 blue mountain, ms 38610

telephone 800 505 tour facsimile 601 693 9066

christian tours

barry goolsby
cruise consultant

post office box 447 blue mountain, ms 38610

DESIGN FIRM | DAVID CARTER DESIGN

ART DIRECTOR | LORI B. WILSON, GARY LOBUE, JR.

DESIGNER/ILLUSTRATOR | TRACY HUCK

CLIENT | CHRISTIAN TOURS

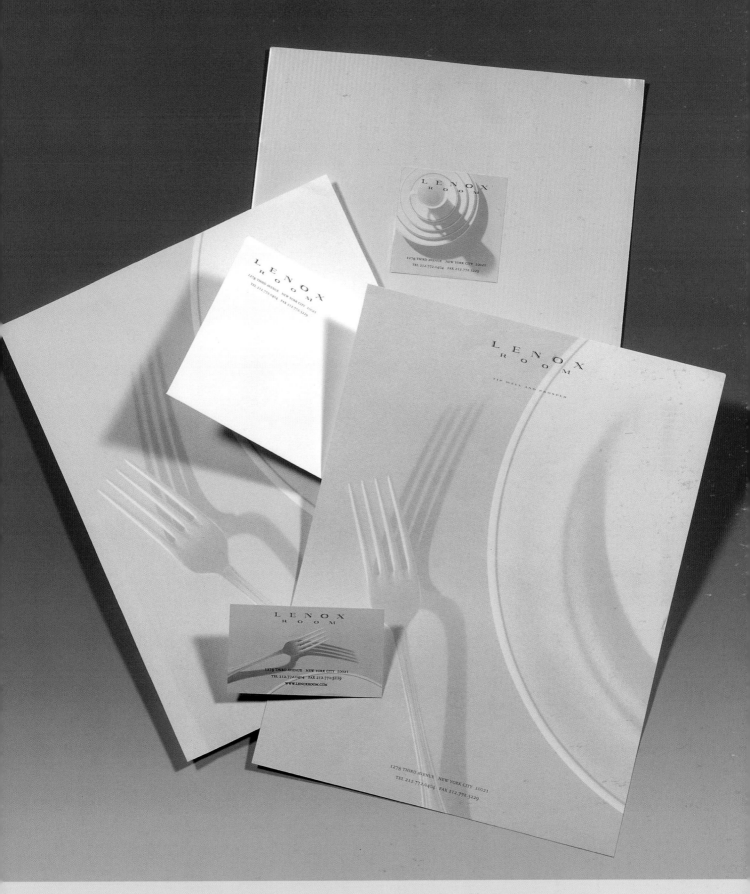

DESIGN FIRM | AERIAL

ART DIRECTOR/DESIGNER | TRACY MOON

PHOTOGRAPHY | R. J. MUNA

CLIENT | LENOX ROOM RESTAURANT

TOOLS | ADOBE PHOTOSHOP, QUARKXPRESS

PAPER/PRINTING | 24 LB. EVERGREEN IVORY

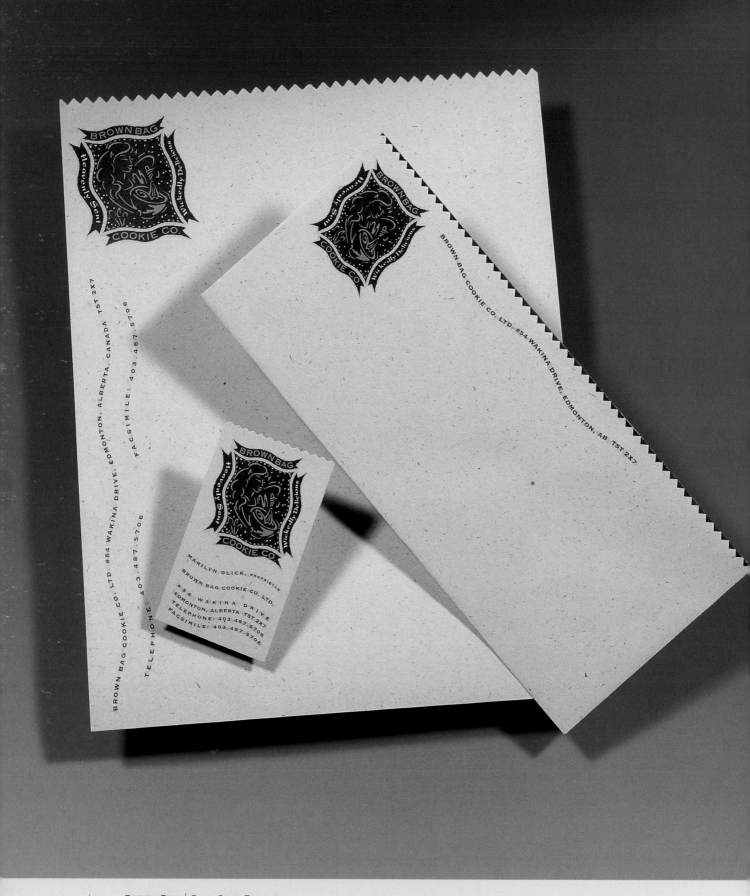

DESIGN FIRM | DUCK SOUP GRAPHICS

ALL DESIGN | WILLIAM DOUCETTE

CLIENT | BROWN BAG COOKIE COMPANY

TOOLS | ADOBE ILLUSTRATOR, QUARKXPRESS

PAPER/PRINTING | FRENCH SPECKLETONE/2 MATCH COLORS

La CACHETTE

Liza Utter & Jean Francois Meteigner
co-owners

Jean Francois
Meteigner
co-owner

La CACHETTE

10506 Santa Monica Blvd. Los Angeles, CA 90025
Phone 310•470•4992 Fax 310•470•7451

10506 Santa Monica Blvd.
Los Angeles, CA 90025

10506 Sar

ngeles, CA 90

La CACHETTE

La CACHETTE

DESIGN FIRM | ON THE EDGE
ART DIRECTOR | JEFF GASPER
DESIGNER | GINA MIMS
ILLUSTRATOR | JEFF GASPER
CLIENT | LA CACHETTE
TOOLS | QUARKXPRESS, ADOBE ILLUSTRATOR,
ADOBE PHOTOSHOP

GLOBAL-DINING INC.

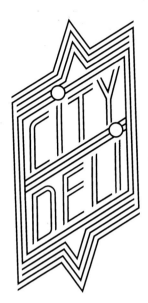

DESIGN FIRM | VRONTIKIS DESIGN OFFICE

ART DIRECTOR/DESIGNER | PETRULA VRONTIKIS

CLIENT | GLOBAL-DINING, INC.

TOOLS | QUARKXPRESS, ADOBE PHOTOSHOP

PAPER/PRINTING | NEENAH CLASSIC CREST/DONAHUE PRINTING

DESIGN FIRM | SOMMESE DESIGN

ART DIRECTOR/ILLUSTRATOR | LANNY SOMMESE

DESIGNER | LANNY SOMMESE, DEVIN PEDSWATER

CLIENT | PENNSYLVANIA STATE UNIVERSITY

TOOLS | ADOBE ILLUSTRATOR

Beach House

DESIGN FIRM | AERIAL

ART DIRECTOR/DESIGNER | TRACY MOON

CLIENT | BEACH HOUSE HOTEL

TOOLS | ADOBE ILLUSTRATOR

PAPER/PRINTING | LEEWOOD PRESS/SF

REBECCA'S
MIGHTY
MUFFINS

REBECCA'S
MIGHTY
MUFFINS

BAKERY • DELI CAFE
ESPRESSO BAR
514-A FRONT STREET
SANTA CRUZ, CA 95060
PHONE: 408-429-1940

DESIGN FIRM | FAIA DESIGN

ALL DESIGN | DON FAIA

CLIENT | REBECCA'S MIGHTY MUFFINS

TOOLS | ADOBE ILLUSTRATOR

PAPER/PRINTING | PROTOCOL WRITING/OFFSET

1212 3rd Street Promenade   Santa Monica, CA 90401

phone (310) 576-9996   (fax) (310) 576-9998   www.global-dining.com

DESIGN FIRM | VRONTIKIS DESIGN OFFICE
ART DIRECTOR | PETRULA VRONTIKIS
DESIGNER | LISA CRITCHFIELD
CLIENT | HASEGAWA ENTERPRISES
TOOLS | QUARKXPRESS, ADOBE PHOTOSHOP
PAPER/PRINTING | CROSSPOINTE SYNERGY/LOGIN PRINTING

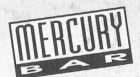

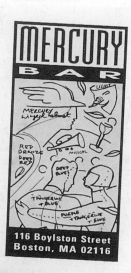

116 Boylston Street
Boston, MA 02116

MERCURY
BAR
BETHANY VAN DELFT
Manager
116 Boylston St. • Boston • (617) 482-7799

116 Boylston Street • Boston, MA, 02116 • (617) 482-7799 • FAX (617) 350-6603

DESIGN FIRM | ON THE EDGE
ART DIRECTOR | JEFF GASPER
DESIGNER | GINA MIMS
ILLUSTRATOR | ANN FIELD
CLIENT | MERCURY BAR
TOOLS | ADOBE PHOTOSHOP, QUARKXPRESS, ADOBE ILLUSTRATOR
PAPER/PRINTING | CLASSIC CREST WHITE, LUNA WHITE COVER/FOUR COLOR

PLaZaGRand

MANGGA DUA

DESIGN FIRM | THAT'S CADIZ! ORIGINALS
ART DIRECTOR/DESIGNER | MINELEO CADIZ
CLIENT | PT MANGGA DUA TOWER
TOOLS | MACROMEDIA FREEHAND

MAGICAL TOWER

DESIGN FIRM | KIKU OBATA & COMPANY
ART DIRECTOR | JOE FLORESCA
DESIGNERS | JOE FLORESCA, JEFF RIFKIN
CLIENT | R.I.C. DESIGN

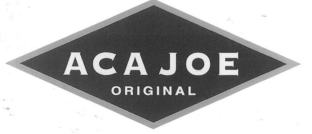

ACA JOE
ORIGINAL

DESIGN FIRM | FRCH DESIGN WORLD WIDE
ART DIRECTOR | JOAN DONNELLY
DESIGNER | TIM A. FRAME
CLIENT | ACA JOE
TOOLS | ADOBE ILLUSTRATOR

WOMEN CHEFS & RESTAURATEURS

DESIGN FIRM | TONI SCHOWALTER DESIGN
ALL DESIGN | TONI SCHOWALTER
CLIENT | WOMEN CHEFS & RESTAURATEURS
TOOLS | QUARKXPRESS, ADOBE ILLUSTRATOR

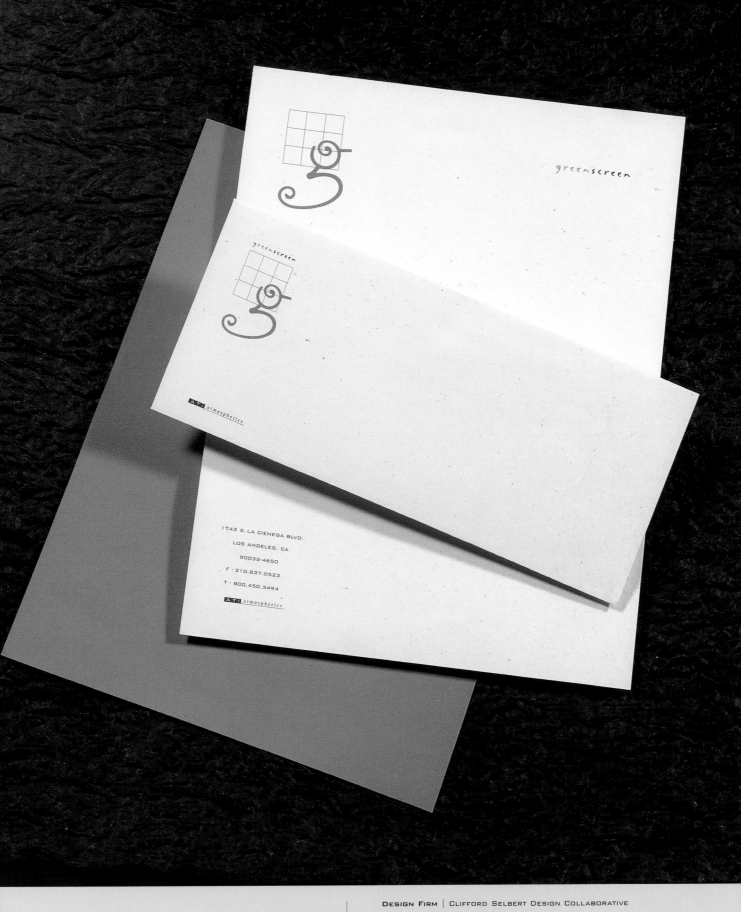

greenscreen

greenscreen

ATI atmospherics

1743 S. LA CIENEGA BLVD.

LOS ANGELES, CA

90035-4650

F - 310.837.0523

T - 800.450.3494

ATI atmospherics

DESIGN FIRM | CLIFFORD SELBERT DESIGN COLLABORATIVE

ART DIRECTOR | ROBIN PERKINS

DESIGNER | ROBIN PERKINS, HEATHER WATSON

CLIENT | ATMOSPHERICS

TOOLS | ADOBE ILLUSTRATOR

PAPER/PRINTING | GENESIS CROSS POINT 80 LB. TEXT/CHALLENGE GRAPHICS

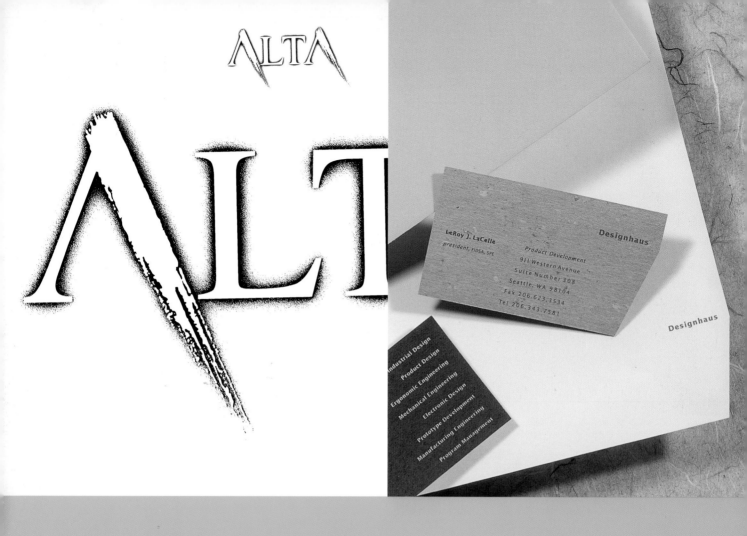

FUSION

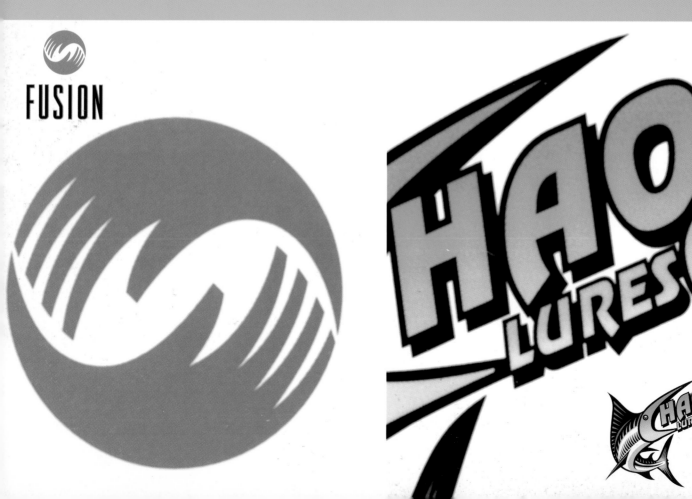

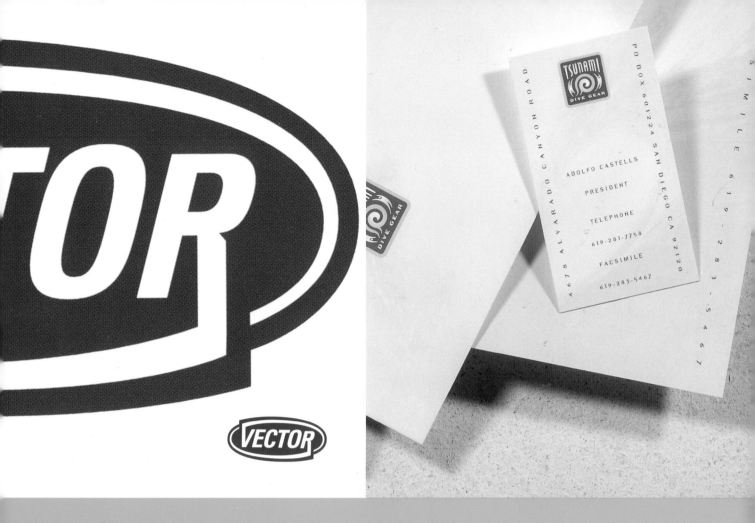

INDUSTRY AND MANUFACTURE

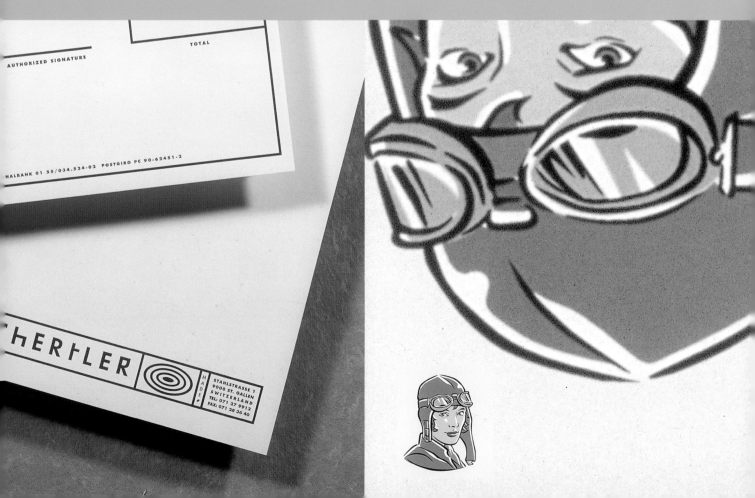

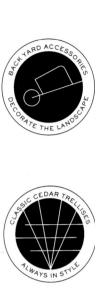

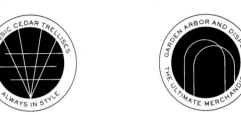

BACK YARD ACCESSORIES / DECORATE THE LANDSCAPE

DECORATIVE CEDAR / FOR THE BIRDS

IRON ACCESSORIES / LONG LASTING FINISH

CLASSIC CEDAR TRELLISES / ALWAYS IN STYLE

GARDEN ARBOR AND DISPLAY / THE ULTIMATE MERCHANDISER

DECORATIVE CRATES / ALWAYS IN STYLE

INDOOR OUTDOOR GARDENS / WITH CEDAR CRATE

IRON PLANT STANDS / LONG LASTING FINISH

SCROLL SHEPHERD HOOKS / LONG LASTING FINISH

CLASSIC SHEPHERD HOOKS / LONG LASTING FINISH

IRON TRELLISES / LONG LASTING FINISH

DECORATIVE BIRD HOUSES / LONG LASTING CEDAR

CEDAR FOR THE HOME / WEATHER RESISTANT

TRADITIONAL CEDAR BARRELS / ALWAYS IN STYLE

FLOWER BOXES & CRATES / WEATHER RESISTANT CEDAR

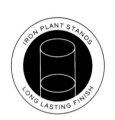
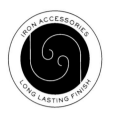
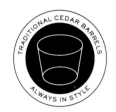
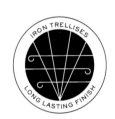
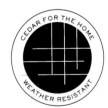
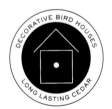
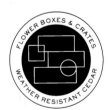
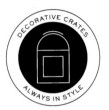
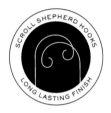

DESIGN FIRM | INSIGHT DESIGN COMMUNICATIONS

ALL DESIGN | SHERRIE AND TRACY HOLDEMAN

CLIENT | THE HAYES COMPANY

TOOLS | POWER MACINTOSH, MACROMEDIA FREEHAND

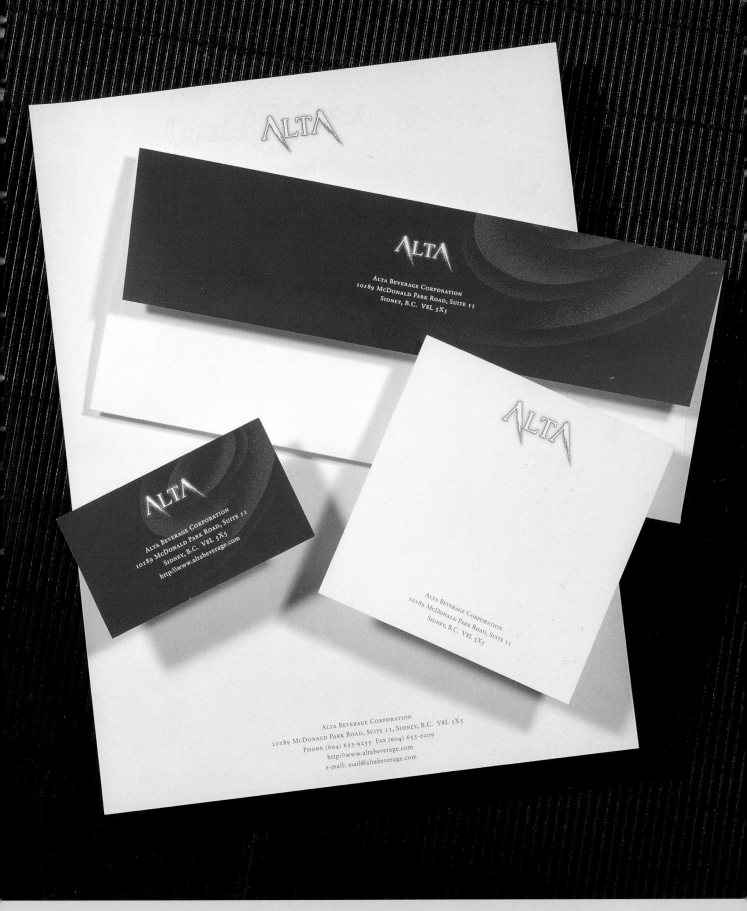

ALTA

ALTA

Alta Beverage Corporation
10189 McDonald Park Road, Suite 11
Sidney, B.C. V8L 5X5

ALTA

ALTA

Alta Beverage Corporation
10189 McDonald Park Road, Suite 11
Sidney, B.C. V8L 5X5
http:\\www.altabeverage.com

Alta Beverage Corporation
10189 McDonald Park Road, Suite 11
Sidney, B.C. V8L 5X5

Alta Beverage Corporation
10189 McDonald Park Road, Suite 11, Sidney, B.C. V8L 5X5
Phone (604) 655-9235 Fax (604) 655-0209
http:\\www.altabeverage.com
e-mail: mail@altabeverage.com

DESIGN FIRM | HORNALL ANDERSON DESIGN WORKS, INC.
ART DIRECTOR | JACK ANDERSON
DESIGNERS | JACK ANDERSON, LARRY ANDERSON,
JULIE KEENAN
CLIENT | ALTA BEVERAGE COMPANY

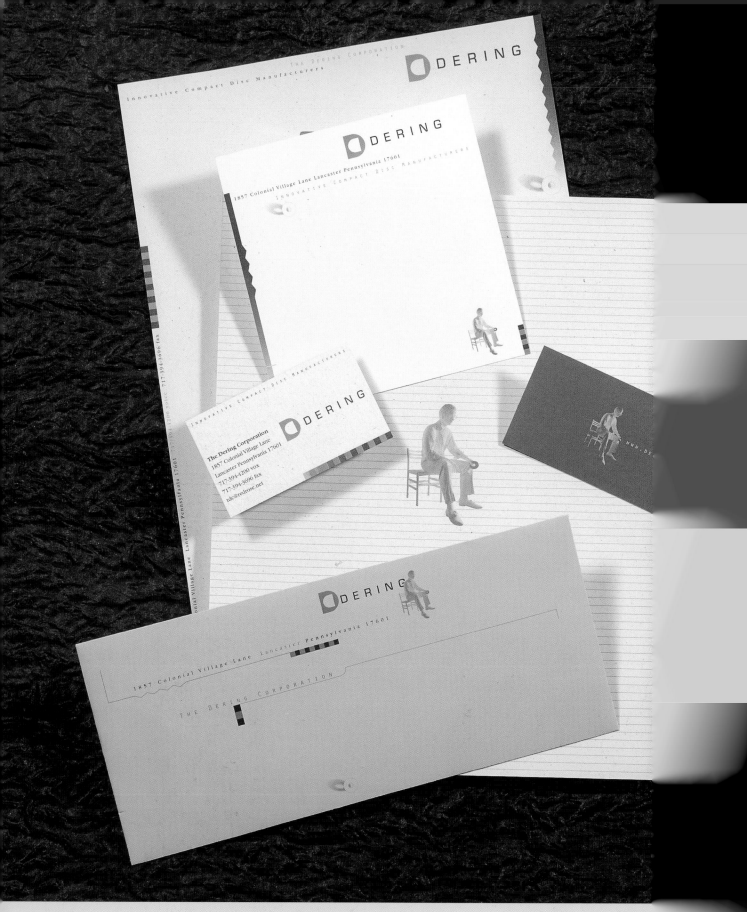

DESIGN FIRM | MUSSER DESIGN

ART DIRECTOR/DESIGNER | JERRY KING MUSSER

CLIENT | THE DERING CORPORATION

TOOLS | MACINTOSH, ADOBE ILLUSTRATOR

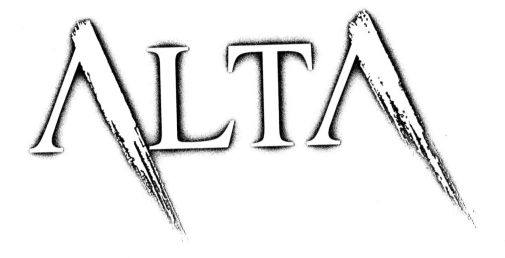

DESIGN FIRM | HORNALL ANDERSON DESIGN WORKS, INC.
ART DIRECTOR | JACK ANDERSON
DESIGNERS | JACK ANDERSON, LARRY ANDERSON, JULIE KEENAN
CLIENT | ALTA BEVERAGE COMPANY

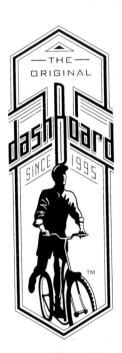

Virtual Garden

http://vg.com

DESIGN FIRM | THARP DID IT
ART DIRECTOR | RICK THARP
DESIGNERS | RICK THARP, NICOLE COLEMAN
CLIENT | TIME WARNER
TOOLS | MACINTOSH

DESIGN FIRM | THARP DID IT
ART DIRECTORS | RICK THARP, CHARLES DRUMMOND
DESIGNER | RICK THARP
ILLUSTRATOR | NICOLE COLEMAN
CLIENT | THE DASHBOARD COMPANY
TOOLS | INK, MACINTOSH

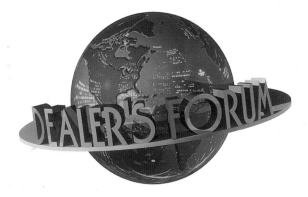

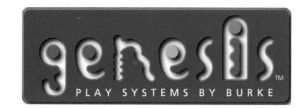

DESIGN FIRM | TRACY SABIN GRAPHIC DESIGN

ART DIRECTOR | RITA HOFFMAN

ILLUSTRATOR | TRACY SABIN

CLIENT | TAYLOR GUITARS

TOOLS | STRATA STUDIO PRO

PAPER/PRINTING | NEWSLETTER MEAD

DESIGN FIRM | HANSON/DODGE DESIGN

ART DIRECTOR | KEN HANSON

DESIGNER/ILLUSTRATOR | JACK HARGREAVES

CLIENT | BCI BURKE COMPANY

TOOLS | ADOBE ILLUSTRATOR, ADOBE PHOTOSHOP

PAPER/PRINTING | 60 LB. COATED TEXT/FOUR PROCESS COLORS

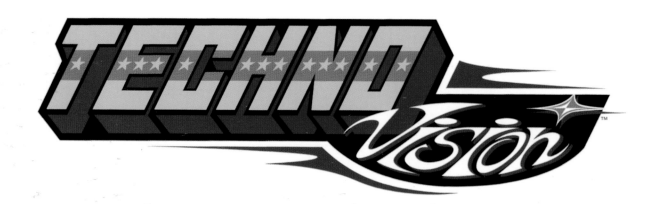

DESIGN FIRM | HANSON/DODGE DESIGN

ART DIRECTOR | LAURA SAMUELS

DESIGNER/ILLUSTRATOR | JACK HARGREAVES

CLIENT | TREK BICYCLE CORPORATION

TOOLS | ADOBE ILLUSTRATOR

PAPER/PRINTING | FOUR PROCESS COLORS PLUS GLOSS VARNISH, TEN POINT CIS

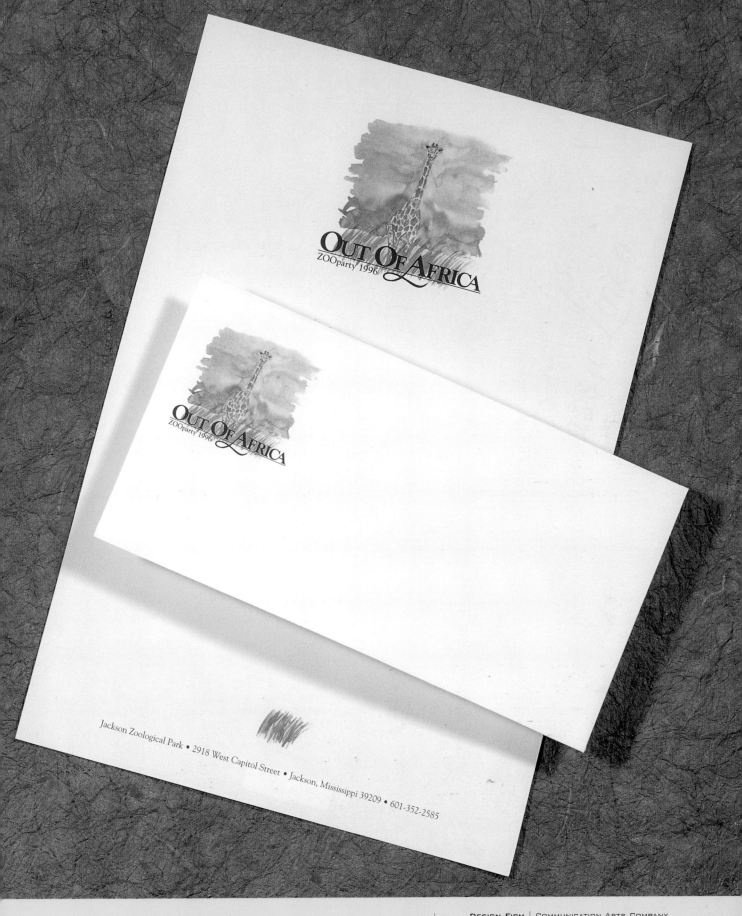

DESIGN FIRM | COMMUNICATION ARTS COMPANY

ART DIRECTOR | HAP OWEN

DESIGNER/ILLUSTRATOR | ANNE-MARIE OTVOS

CLIENT | JACKSON ZOOLOGICAL PARK

TOOLS | WATERCOLOR

PAPER/PRINTING | CLASSIC LINEN/OFFSET LITHOGRAPHY

Virtual Garden
221 Main Street
Suite 480
San Francisco, CA 94105
P 415.908.2000
F 415.908.2010

Virtual Garden
221 Main Street
Suite 480
San Francisco, CA 94105
P 415.908.4969
F 415.908.2010
E israelc@tpv.com
http://vg.com

Claire Israel
sales manager

http://vg.com

A Time Warner Company

DESIGN FIRM | THARP DID IT
ART DIRECTOR | RICK THARP
DESIGNERS | RICK THARP, NICOLE COLEMAN
ILLUSTRATOR | RIK OLSON
CLIENT | TIME WARNER
TOOLS | INK, MACINTOSH
PAPER/PRINTING | SIMPSON EVERGREEN/SIMON PRINTING

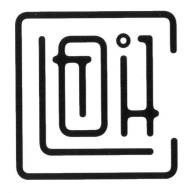

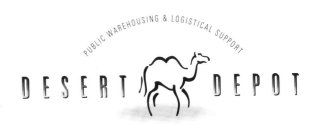

DESIGN FIRM | INSIGHT DESIGN COMMUNICATIONS

ALL DESIGN | SHERRIE AND TRACY HOLDEMAN

CLIENT | CLOTIA WOOD + METAL WORKS

TOOLS | POWER MACINTOSH, MACROMEDIA FREEHAND, ADOBE PHOTOSHOP

DESIGN FIRM | LORENZ ADVERTISING & DESIGN

ART DIRECTORS | BRIAN LORENZ, ARNE RATERMANIS

DESIGNERS | ARNE RATERMANIS, BRIAN LORENZ

ILLUSTRATOR | ARNE RATERMANIS

CLIENT | DESERT DEPOT

TOOLS | MACINTOSH, ADOBE ILLUSTRATOR

PAPER/PRINTING | CLASSIC CREST/THREE COLOR OFFSET

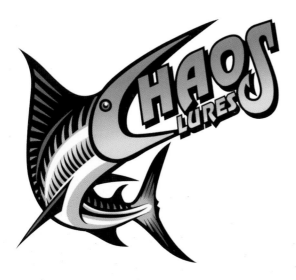

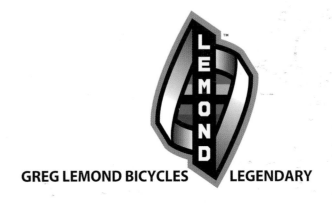

DESIGN FIRM | MIRES DESIGN

ART DIRECTOR/DESIGNER | JOSÉ A. SERRANO

ILLUSTRATOR | TRACY SABIN

CLIENT | CHAOS LURES

DESIGN FIRM | HANSON/DODGE DESIGN

ART DIRECTOR | JOE SUTTER

DESIGNER | SHAWN DOYLE

ILLUSTRATOR | JACK HARGREAVES

CLIENT | TREK BICYCLE CORPORATION

TOOLS | ADOBE ILLUSTRATOR

DESIGN FIRM | SAGMEISTER, INC.

ART DIRECTOR | STEFAN SAGMEISTER

DESIGNERS | STEFAN SAGMEISTER, PATRICK DAILY

ILLUSTRATOR | PATRICK DAILY

CLIENT | SCHERTLER AUDIO TRANSDUCERS

TOOLS | MACINTOSH

PAPER/PRINTING | STRATHMORE WRITING 25% COTTON

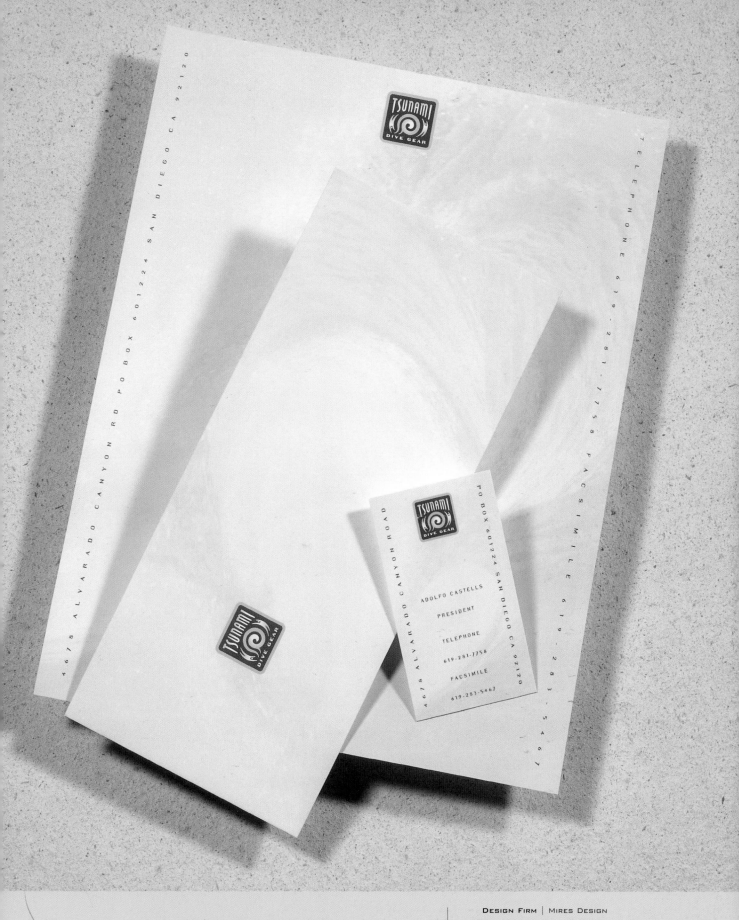

DESIGN FIRM | MIRES DESIGN
ART DIRECTOR | JOHN BALL
DESIGNERS | JOHN BALL, DEBORAH HORN
PHOTOGRAPHER | AARON CHANG
CLIENT | TSUNAMI DIVE GEAR
PAPER/PRINTING | STARWHITE VICKSBURG

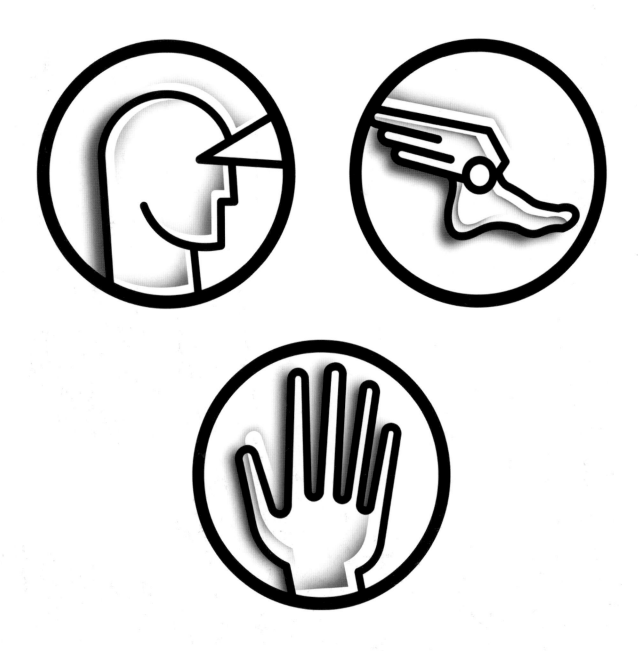

DESIGN FIRM | LOVE PACKAGING GROUP

ALL DESIGN | BRIAN MILLER

CLIENT | HOC INDUSTRIES

TOOLS | MACROMEDIA FREEHAND, ADOBE PHOTOSHOP

PAPER/PRINTING | CHAMPION

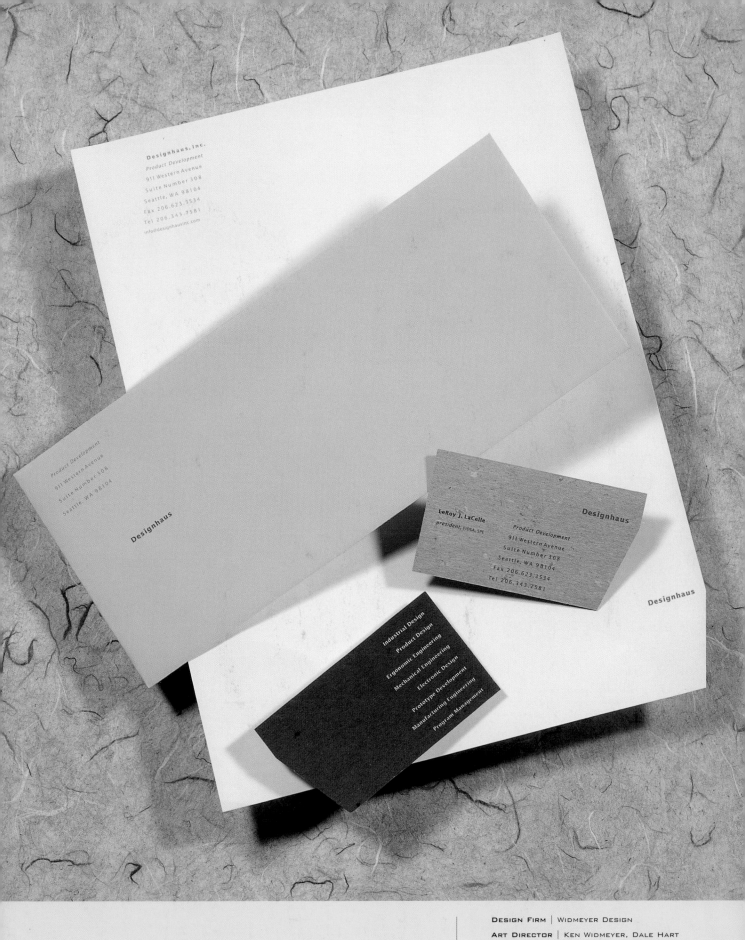

Designhaus, Inc.

Product Development

911 Western Avenue

Suite Number 308

Seattle, WA 98104

Fax 206.623.3534

Tel 206.343.7581

info@designhausinc.com

Product Development

911 Western Avenue

Suite Number 308

Seattle, WA 98104

Designhaus

Designhaus

LeRoy J. LaCelle
president, FIDSA, SPE

Product Development

911 Western Avenue

Suite Number 308

Seattle, WA 98104

Fax 206.623.3534

Tel 206.343.7581

Designhaus

Industrial Design

Product Design

Ergonomic Engineering

Mechanical Engineering

Electronic Design

Prototype Development

Manufacturing Engineering

Program Management

DESIGN FIRM | WIDMEYER DESIGN

ART DIRECTOR | KEN WIDMEYER, DALE HART

DESIGNER | DALE HART

CLIENT | DESIGNHAUS

TOOLS | POWER MACINTOSH, MACROMEDIA FREEHAND

PAPER/PRINTING | FRENCH PAPER/OFFSET

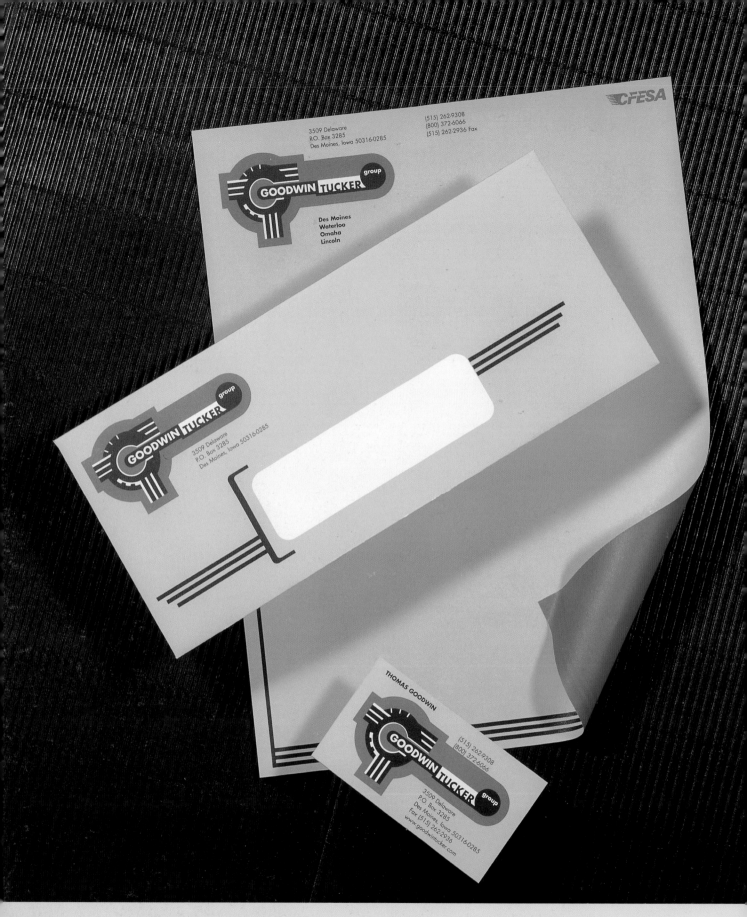

DESIGN FIRM | SAYLES GRAPHIC DESIGN

ART DIRECTOR/ILLUSTRATOR | JOHN SAYLES

DESIGNERS | JOHN SAYLES, JENNIFER ELLIOTT

CLIENT | GOODWIN TUCKER GROUP

PAPER/PRINTING | NEENAH ENVIRONMENT WHITE/OFFSET

DESIGN FIRM | GRETEMAN GROUP

ART DIRECTORS/DESIGNERS | SONIA GRETEMAN, JAMES STRANGE

ILLUSTRATOR | JAMES STRANGE

CLIENT | GRANT TELEGRAPH CENTRE

TOOLS | MACROMEDIA FREEHAND

PAPER/PRINTING | ASTRO PARCHMENT, SAND +

CONFETTI SABLE BLACK/OFFSET

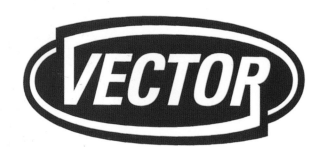

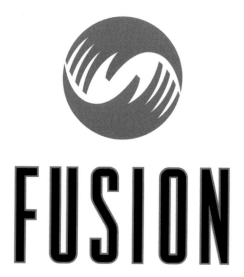

DESIGN FIRM | HANSON/DODGE DESIGN

ART DIRECTOR/DESIGNER | ANIA WASILEWSKA

ILLUSTRATOR | JACK HARGREAVES

CLIENT | VECTOR TECHNOLOGIES, INC.

TOOLS | ADOBE ILLUSTRATOR

DESIGN FIRM | MIRES DESIGN

ART DIRECTOR/DESIGNER | JOSÉ A. SERRANO

PHOTOGRAPHER | CARL VANDERSCHUIT

CLIENT | AGASSI ENTERPRISES

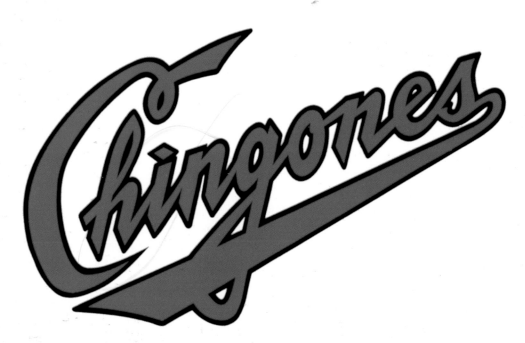

DESIGN FIRM | MIRES DESIGN

ART DIRECTOR/DESIGNER | JOSÉ A. SERRANO

ILLUSTRATOR | TRACY SABIN

CLIENT | CHINGONES

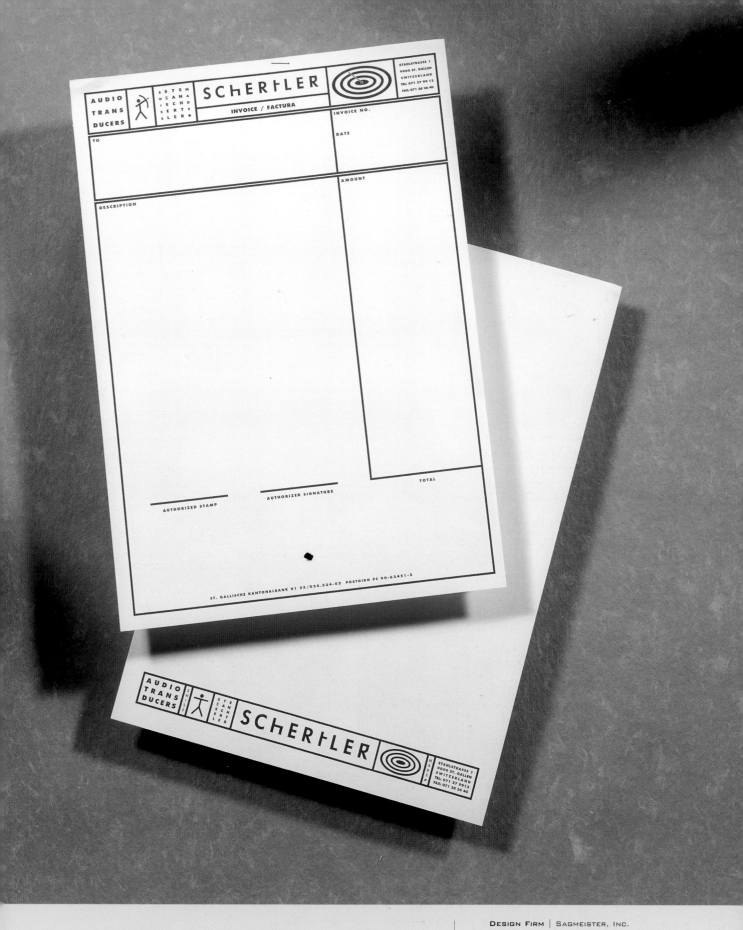

DESIGN FIRM | SAGMEISTER, INC.

ART DIRECTOR | STEFAN SAGMEISTER

DESIGNERS | STEFAN SAGMEISTER, VERONICA OH

PHOTOGRAPHY | MICHAEL GRIMM, STOCK

CLIENT | TOTO

TOOLS | MACINTOSH, 2 1/4 CAMERA

PAPER/PRINTING | STRATHMORE WRITING 25% COTTON

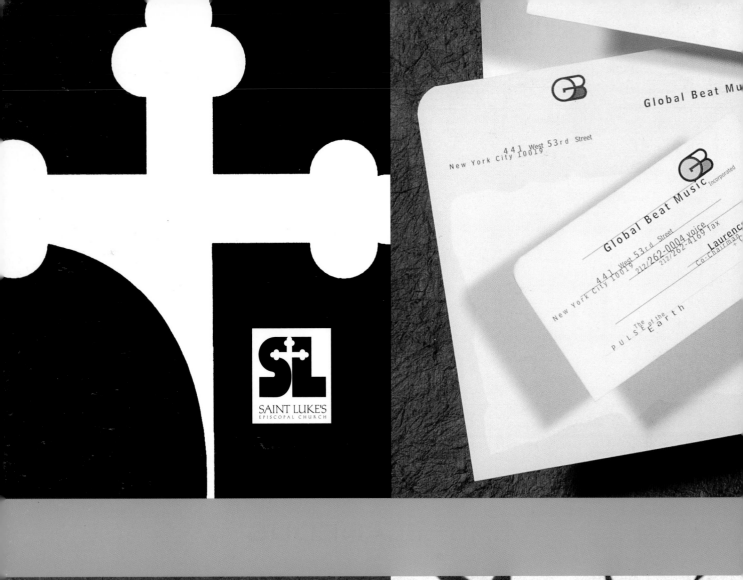

SAINT LUKE'S
EPISCOPAL CHURCH

Global Beat Music

441 West 53rd Street
New York City 10019

Global Beat Music Incorporated

441 West 53rd Street
New York City 10019   212/262-0004 voice
                       212/262-4169 fax   Laurence
                                           Co-Chairman

The
PULSE of the
              Earth

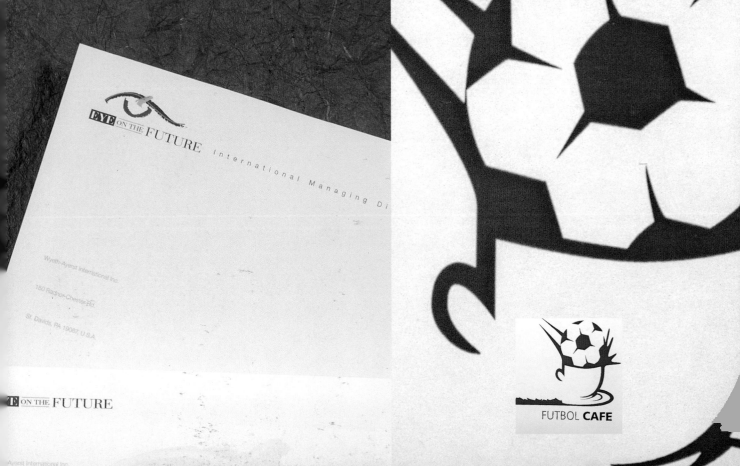

EYE ON THE FUTURE International Managing Di

Wyeth-Ayerst International Inc.

150 Radnor-Chester Rd.

St. Davids, PA 19087 U.S.A.

E ON THE FUTURE

FUTBOL CAFE

Wyeth-Ayerst International Inc.

UCLA *Multimedia*

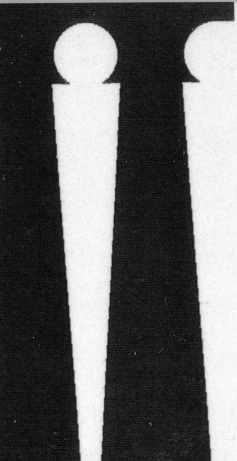

VICTORIAN REGION

585 BURWOOD ROAD

HAWTHORN VIC. 3122

PHONE (03) 819 6144

FAX (03) 819 6292

TELEX AA23760

POSTAL ADDRESS

18-20 QUEENS AVENUE

HAWTHORN VIC. 3122

MISCELLANEOUS

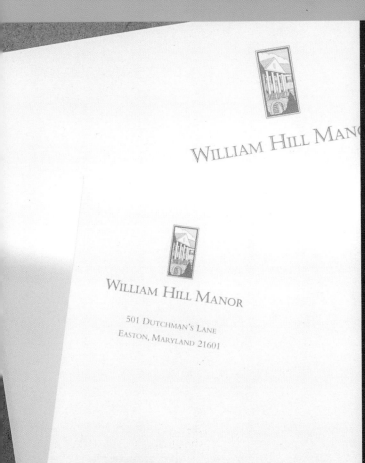

WILLIAM HILL MANOR

WILLIAM HILL MANOR

501 DUTCHMAN'S LANE

EASTON, MARYLAND 21601

JOSEPH & EDNA

JOSEPHSON

INSTITUTE

OF ETHICS

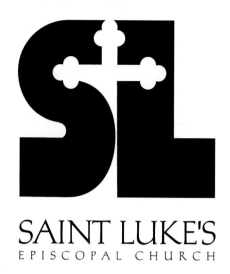

SAINT LUKE'S
EPISCOPAL CHURCH

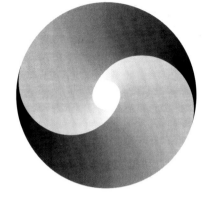

DESIGN FIRM | THE WELLER INSTITUTE
ALL DESIGN | DON WELLER
CLIENT | SAINT LUKE'S EPISCOPAL CHURCH
TOOLS | ADOBE ILLUSTRATOR, QUARKXPRESS

DESIGN FIRM | WITHERSPOON ADVERTISING
CREATIVE DIRECTOR | DEBRA MORROW
ART DIRECTOR/DESIGNER | RANDY PADORR-BLACK
ILLUSTRATOR | JAMES MELLARD
CLIENT | WOUND HEALING & HYPERBARIC MEDICINE CENTER

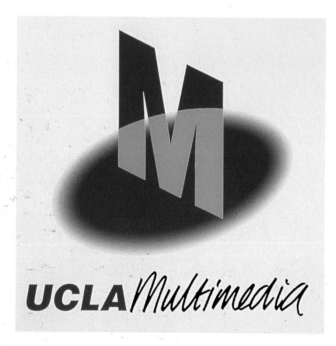

DESIGN FIRM | SHIMOKOCHI/REEVES
ART DIRECTOR | MAMORU SHIMOKOCHI, ANNE REEVES
CLIENT | UCLA MULTIMEDIA
TOOLS | ADOBE ILLUSTRATOR

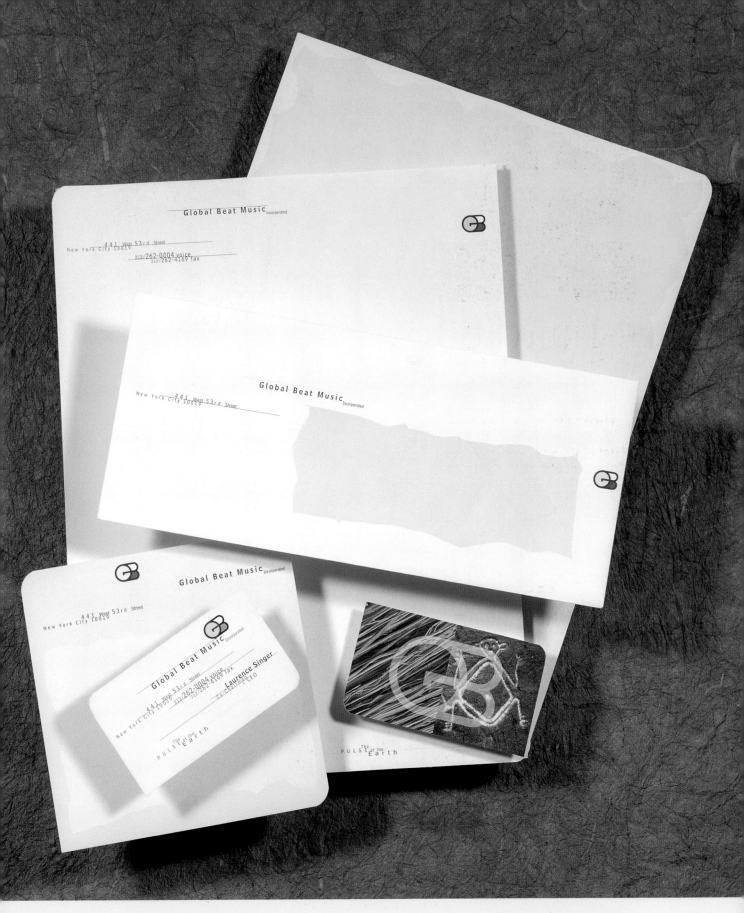

DESIGN FIRM | MUSSER DESIGN

ART DIRECTOR/DESIGNER | JERRY KING MUSSER

CLIENT | GLOBAL BEAT MEDIA

TOOLS | ADOBE ILLUSTRATOR

culinary arts & entertainment

culinary arts & entertainment
7610 e. mcdonald dr. suite h
scottsdale, az 85250

culinary arts & entertainment
7610 e. mcdonald dr. suite h
scottsdale, az 85250
tel: 602 998 5810
tel: 800 211 5844
fax: 602 998 9064

7610 e. mcdonald dr. suite h, scottsdale, az 85250   tel: 602 998 5810   tel: 800 211 5844 fax: 602 998 9064

DESIGN FIRM | AFTER HOURS CREATIVE
ART DIRECTOR/DESIGNER | AFTER HOURS CREATIVE
PHOTOGRAPHER | ART HOLEMAN
CLIENT | CULINARY ARTS & ENTERTAINMENT

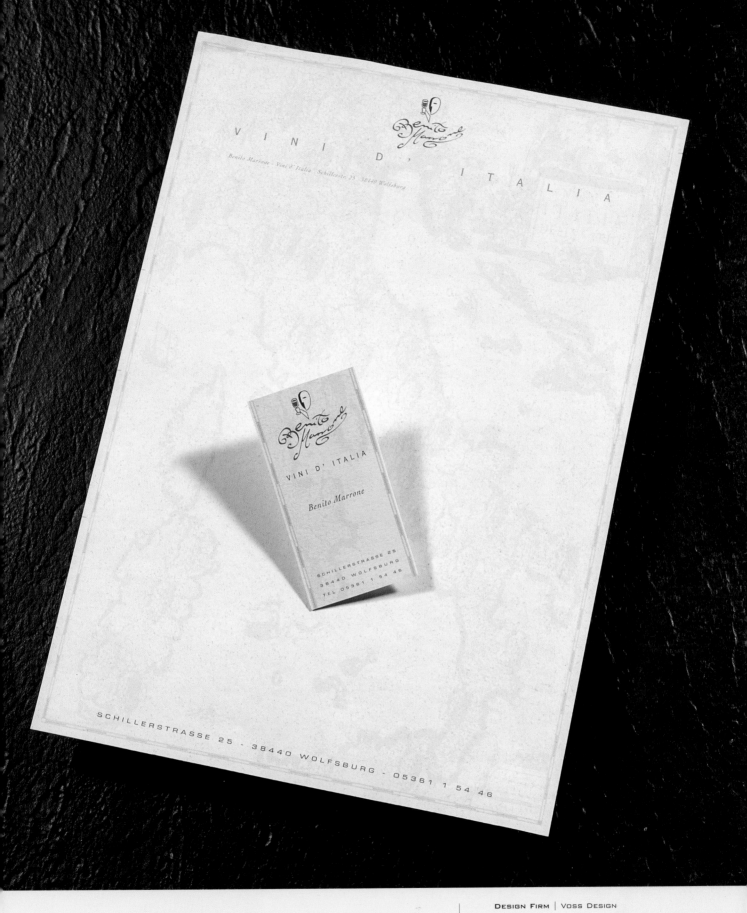

DESIGN FIRM | VOSS DESIGN
ART DIRECTOR/DESIGNER | AXEL VOSS
CLIENT | BENITO MARRONE
PAPER/PRINTING | COUNTRYSIDE

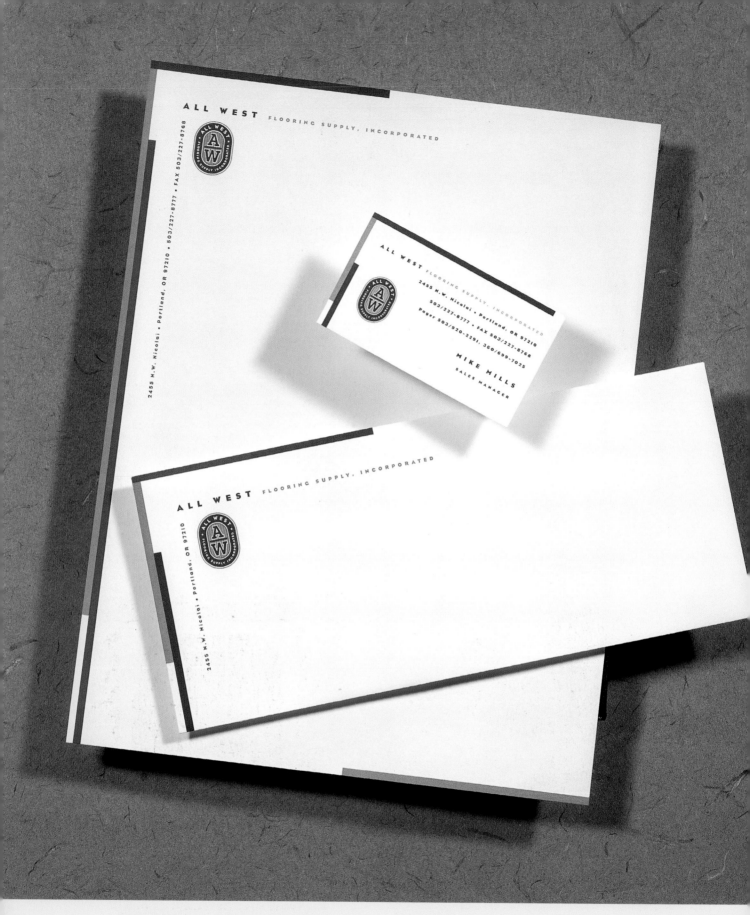

DESIGN FIRM | ROBERT BAILEY INCORPORATED

ART DIRECTOR | CONNIE LIGHTNER

DESIGNERS | CONNIE LIGHTNER, DAN FRANKLIN

CLIENT | ALL WEST FLOORING SUPPLY, INC.

TOOLS | MACROMEDIA FREEHAND, QUARKXPRESS

PAPER/PRINTING | PROTOCOL RECYCLED BRIGHT
WHITE/CNS GRAPHICS

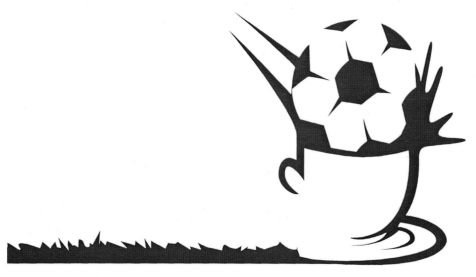

FUTBOL **CAFE**

DESIGN FIRM | CATO BERRO DISEÑO
ART DIRECTOR | GONZALO BERRO
DESIGNER | GONZALO BERRO/ESTEBAN SERRANO
ILLUSTRATOR | ESTEBAN SERRANO
CLIENT | FUTBOL CAFE/BAR
TOOLS | ADOBE ILLUSTRATOR

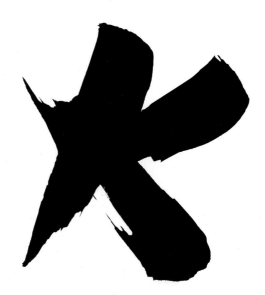

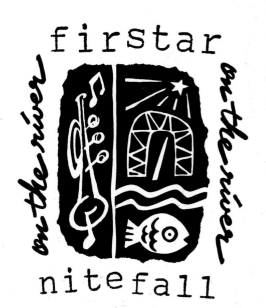

DESIGN FIRM | MICHAEL STANARD DESIGN, INC.
ART DIRECTOR | MICHAEL STANARD
DESIGNER/ILLUSTRATOR | MICHAEL STANARD, DEV HOMSI
CLIENT | NORTHWESTERN UNIVERSITY

DESIGN FIRM | SAYLES GRAPHIC DESIGN
ALL DESIGN | JOHN SAYLES
CLIENT | DES MOINES PARK & RECREATION DEPT.

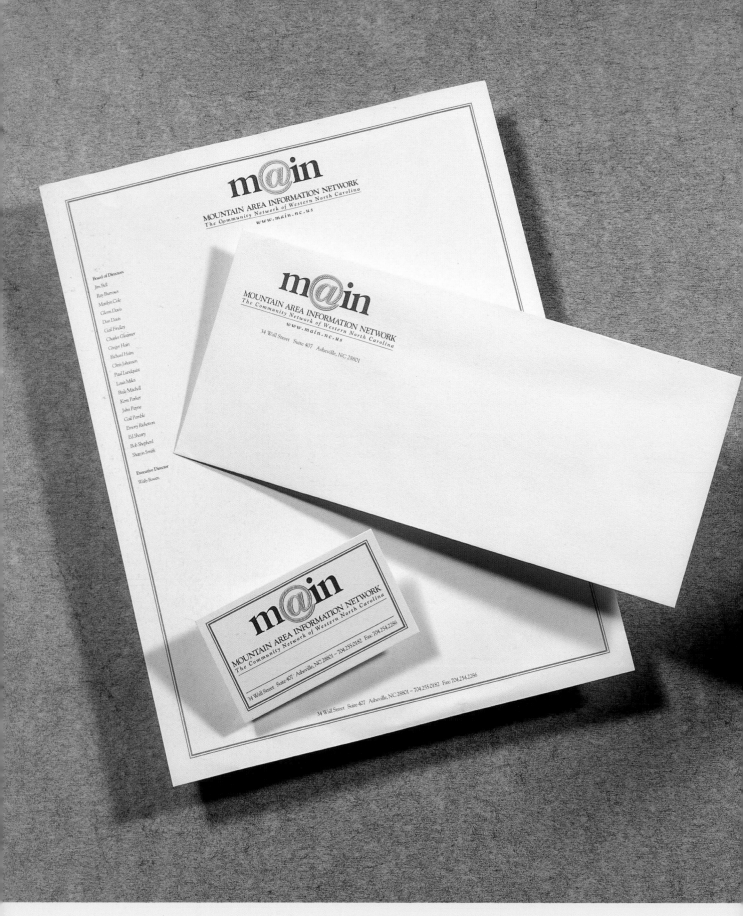

DESIGN FIRM | DESIGN ONE
DESIGNER | LYN FRANKLIN
CLIENT | MAIN

AUSTRALIAN TRANSPORT MANAGEMENT

ATM logistic solutions

AUSTRALIAN TRANSPORT MANAGEMENT PTY LTD • ACN 069 426 884
48 Elizabeth Street West Meadows Victoria Australia 3049
POSTAL ADDRESS: PO Box 745 Tullamarine Victoria 3043
TELEPHONE: 0419 334 563 • FACSIMILE: 03 9338 4894

DESIGN FIRM | MAMMOLITI CHAN DESIGN

ART DIRECTOR | TONY MAMMOLITI

DESIGNERS | CHWEE KUAN CHAN, TONY MAMMOLITI

ILLUSTRATOR | CHWEE KUAN CHAN

CLIENT | AUSTRALIAN TRANSPORT MANAGEMENT

PAPER/PRINTING | ONE PMS ON PARCHMENT STOCK

SPRING
HOLLOW

2750 S. 875 E ● Zionsville, IN ● 46077.9526 ● 317.769.6839

DESIGN FIRM | HELD DIEDRICH
ART DIRECTOR | DOUG DIEDRICH
DESIGNER/ILLUSTRATOR | MEGAN SNOW
CLIENT | SPRING HOLLOW
TOOLS | QUARKXPRESS, ADOBE ILLUSTRATOR
PAPER/PRINTING | NEENAH, CLASSIC LAID,
     NATURAL WHITE, LASER FINISH/OFFSET

PATEFA · GOLFING · SOCIETY

VICTORIAN REGION
585 BURWOOD ROAD
HAWTHORN VIC. 3122
~
PHONE (03) 819 6144
FAX (03) 819 6292
TELEX AA23760
~
POSTAL ADDRESS
18-20 QUEENS AVENUE
HAWTHORN VIC. 3122

DESIGN FIRM | WATTS GRAPHIC DESIGN
ART DIRECTORS/DESIGNERS | HELEN AND PETER WATTS
CLIENT | PATEFA GOLFING SOCIETY

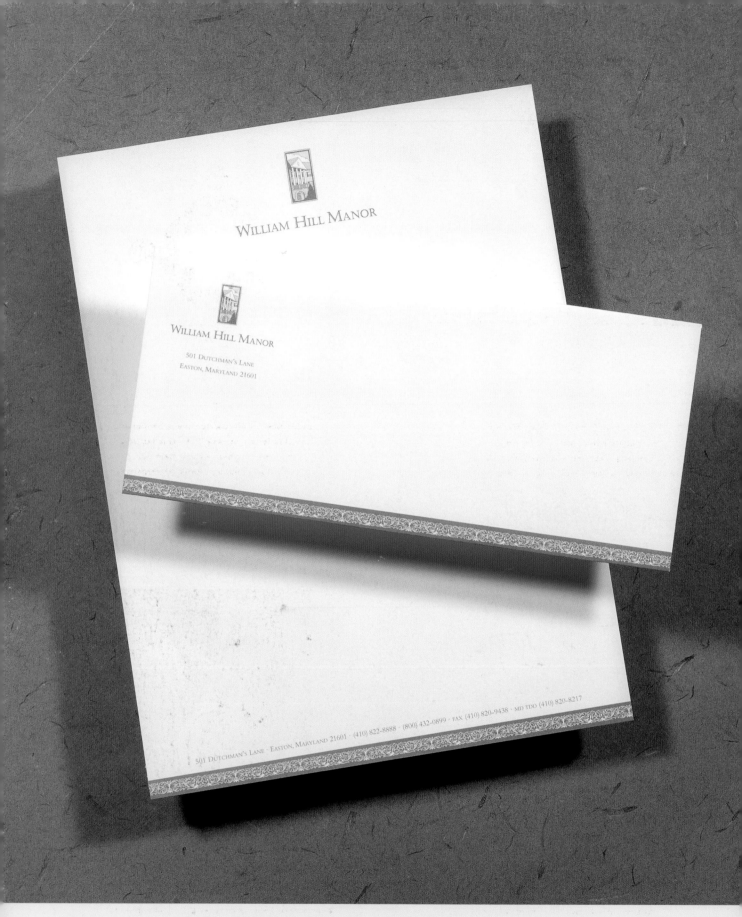

WILLIAM HILL MANOR

WILLIAM HILL MANOR

501 DUTCHMAN'S LANE
EASTON, MARYLAND 21601

501 DUTCHMAN'S LANE · EASTON, MARYLAND 21601 · (410) 822-8888 · (800) 432-0899 · FAX (410) 820-9438 · MD TDD (410) 820-8217

DESIGN FIRM | WHITNEY EDWARDS DESIGN

ALL DESIGN | CHARLENE WHITNEY EDWARDS

CLIENT | WILLIAM HILL MANOR

TOOLS | ADOBE PHOTOSHOP, ADOBE ILLUSTRATOR,
    QUARKXPRESS

PAPER/PRINTING | CRANES/ONE COLOR

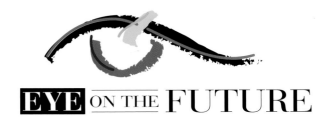

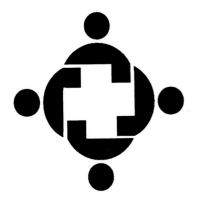

DESIGN FIRM | MUELLER & WISTER, INC.
ALL DESIGN | JOSEPH M. DELICH
CLIENT | WYETH-AYERST INTERNATIONAL
TOOLS | ADOBE PHOTOSHOP, STREAMLINE, MACROMEDIA FREEHAND

DESIGN FIRM | ARMINDA HOPKINS & ASSOCIATES
ART DIRECTOR/DESIGNER | MELANIE MATSON
CLIENT | FREDONIA HEALTH SYSTEMS
TOOLS | QUARKXPRESS, ADOBE ILLUSTRATOR

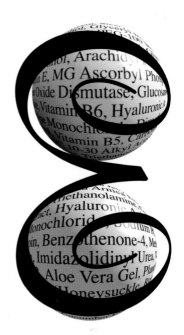

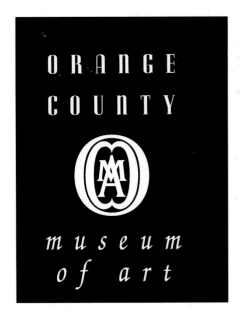

DESIGN FIRM | LOVE PACKAGING GROUP
ALL DESIGN | BRIAN MILLER
CLIENT | ELOGEN, INC.
TOOLS | MACROMEDIA FREEHAND, ADOBE PHOTOSHOP

DESIGN FIRM | MIKE SALISBURY COMMUNICATIONS, INC.
ART DIRECTOR | MIKE SALISBURY
DESIGNER | MARY EVELYN MCGOUGH
ILLUSTRATOR | BOB MAILE
CLIENT | ORANGE COUNTY MUSEUM OF ART

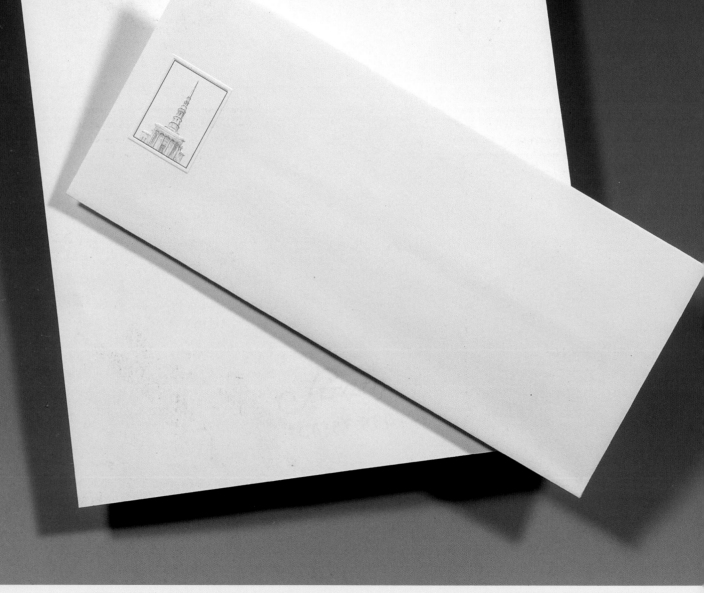

CATHEDRAL OF ST. PETER IN CHAINS

325 West Eighth Street / Cincinnati, Ohio 45202 - 1977 / Phone: 513 - 421 - 5354 / Fax: 513 - 241 - 9517

DESIGN FIRM | WOOD/BROD DESIGN
ART DIRECTOR/DESIGNER | STAN BROD
CLIENT | CATHEDRAL OF ST. PETER IN CHAINS
TOOLS | ADOBE ILLUSTRATOR
PAPER/PRINTING | STRATHMORE/HENNEGAN COMPANY

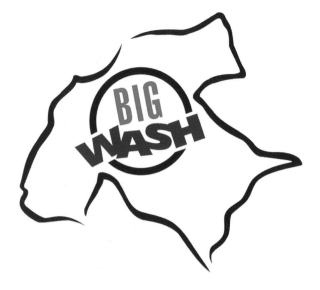

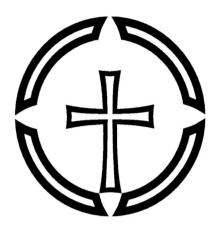

DESIGN FIRM | CLARK DESIGN
ART DIRECTOR | ANNEMARIE CLARK
DESIGNER | CRAIG STOUT
CLIENT | HOPE HOUSING/BIG WASH
TOOLS | ADOBE ILLUSTRATOR

DESIGN FIRM | RICK EIBER DESIGN (RED)
ART DIRECTOR/DESIGNER | RICK EIBER
CLIENT | COLUMBIA BAPTIST CONFERENCE
TOOLS | ADOBE ILLUSTRATOR

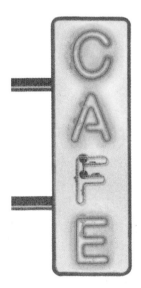

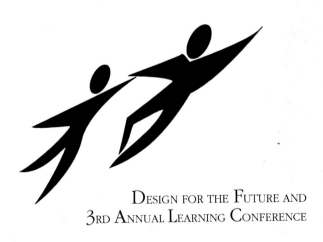

DESIGN FOR THE FUTURE AND
3RD ANNUAL LEARNING CONFERENCE

DESIGN FIRM | AFTER HOURS CREATIVE
ART DIRECTOR/DESIGNER | AFTER HOURS CREATIVE
PHOTOGRAPHER | ART HOLEMAN
CLIENT | CULINARY ARTS & ENTERTAINMENT

DESIGN FIRM | CECILY ROBERTS DESIGN
ALL DESIGN | CECILY ROBERTS
CLIENT | KAISER PERMANENTE/DESIGN FOR THE FUTURE CONFERENCE
TOOLS | MACROMEDIA FREEHAND, QUARKXPRESS

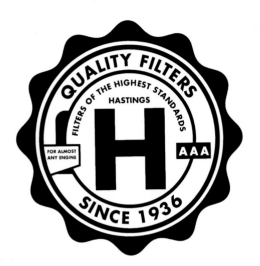

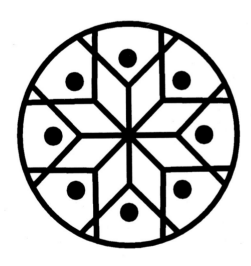

DESIGN FIRM | INSIGHT DESIGN COMMUNICATIONS

ALL DESIGN | SHERRIE AND TRACY HOLDEMAN

CLIENT | WORLD FITNESS, INC.

TOOLS | MACROMEDIA FREEHAND

DESIGN FIRM | CHRIS ST. CYR GRAPHIC DESIGN

ART DIRECTOR/DESIGNER | CHRIS ST. CYR

CLIENT | STREET PROJECT BOSTON

TOOLS | ADOBE PHOTOSHOP, QUARKXPRESS

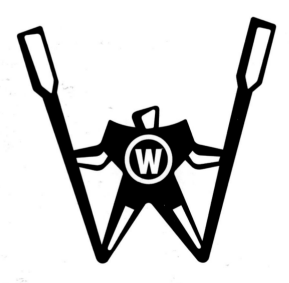

DESIGN FIRM | LOVE PACKAGING GROUP

ALL DESIGN | BRIAN MILLER

CLIENT | WICHITA STATE UNIVERSITY, MEN'S CREW TEAM

TOOLS | MACROMEDIA FREEHAND

DESIGN FIRM | RICK EIBER DESIGN (RED)

ART DIRECTOR/DESIGNER | RICK EIBER

CLIENT | COLUMBIA BAPTIST CONFERENCE

TOOLS | ADOBE ILLUSTRATOR

PAPER/PRINTING | CURTIS BRIGHTWATER/TWO COLOR OVER TWO COLOR

EYE ON THE FUTURE   International Managing Directors' Meeting

Wyeth-Ayerst International Inc.

150 Radnor-Chester Rd.

St. Davids, PA 19087, U.S.A.

EYE ON THE FUTURE

Wyeth-Ayerst International Inc.

150 Radnor-Chester Rd.

St. Davids, PA 19087, U.S.A.

DESIGN FIRM | MUELLER & WISTER, INC.

ALL DESIGN | JOSEPH DELICH

CLIENT | WYETH-AYERST INTERNATIONAL, INC.

TOOLS | ADOBE ILLUSTRATOR

DESIGN FIRM | PARHAM SANTANA, INC.

ART DIRECTOR/DESIGNER | RICK TESORO

CLIENT | PROJECT FOR PUBLIC SPACES

PAPER/PRINTING | LETTERHEAD & ENVELOPE: STARWHITE

VICKSBURG TIARA 70 LB., BUSINESS CARD: STARWHITE

VICKSBURG TIARA 130 LB. DOUBLE COVER, LABEL:

BROWNBRIDGE WHITE ULTRA-MATTE CRACK N PEEL

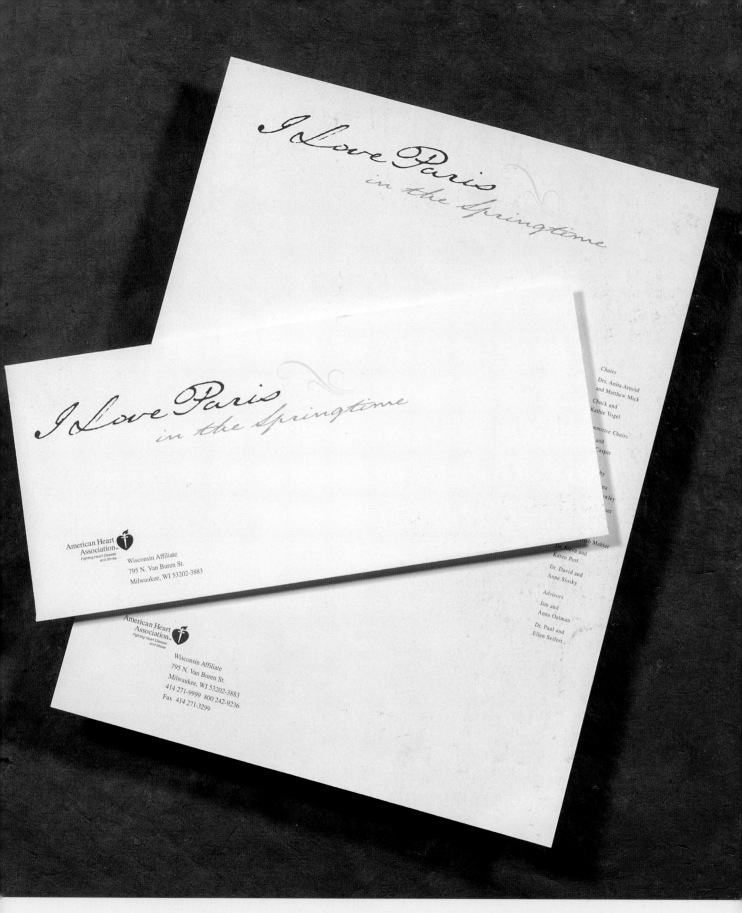

I Love Paris in the Springtime

I Love Paris in the Springtime

American Heart Association
Fighting Heart Disease and Stroke

Wisconsin Affiliate
795 N. Van Buren St.
Milwaukee, WI 53202-3883

American Heart Association
Fighting Heart Disease and Stroke

Wisconsin Affiliate
795 N. Van Buren St.
Milwaukee, WI 53202-3883
414 271-9999 800 242-9236
Fax 414 271-3299

Chairs

Drs. Anita Arnold
and Matthew Mick

Chuck and
Kathie Vogel

Committee Chairs

Dr. Steve and
Karen Port

Dr. David and
Anne Slosky

Advisors

Jim and
Anna Oatman

Dr. Paul and
Ellen Seifert

DESIGN FIRM | BECKER DESIGN

ART DIRECTOR/DESIGNER | NEIL BECKER

CLIENT | AMERICAN HEART ASSOCIATION

TOOLS | QUARKXPRESS, ADOBE ILLUSTRATOR

PAPER/PRINTING | NEENAH CLASSIC CREST RECYCLED

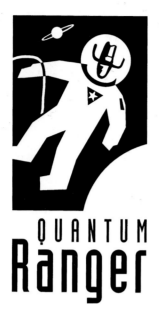

QUANTUM
Ranger

DESIGN FIRM | DESIGN CENTER
ART DIRECTOR | JOHN REGER
DESIGNER | CORY DOCKEN
CLIENT | SCIMED

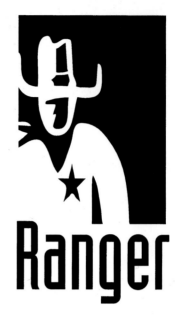

Ranger

DESIGN FIRM | DESIGN CENTER
ART DIRECTOR | JOHN REGER
DESIGNER | CORY DOCKEN
CLIENT | SCIMED

Universität Kaiserslautern

DESIGN FIRM | GEFFERT DESIGN
DESIGNER | GERALD GEFFERT
CLIENT | UNIVERSITÄT KAISERSLAUTERN

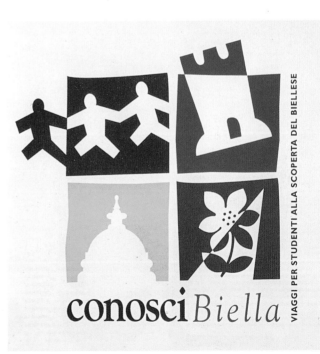

conosci Biella

VIAGGI PER STUDENTI ALLA SCOPERTA DEL BIELLESE

DESIGN FIRM | IMPRESS SAS
CLIENT | PROVINCIA DI BIELLA

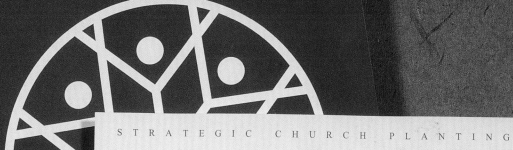

STRATEGIC CHURCH PLANTING

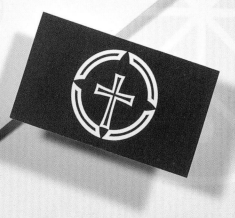

MATT HANNAN, DIRECTOR OF CHURCH PLANTING, COLUMBIA BAPTIST CONFERENCE
7913 N.E. 58TH AVENUE, VANCOUVER, WA 98665   360.694.4985   FAX 360.694.0219

DESIGN FIRM | RICK EIBER DESIGN (RED)
ART DIRECTOR/DESIGNER | RICK EIBER
CLIENT | COLUMBIA BAPTIST CONFERENCE
TOOLS | ADOBE ILLUSTRATOR
PAPER/PRINTING | CURTIS BRIGHTWATER/TWO
    COLOR OVER TWO COLOR

INDEX AND DIRECTORY